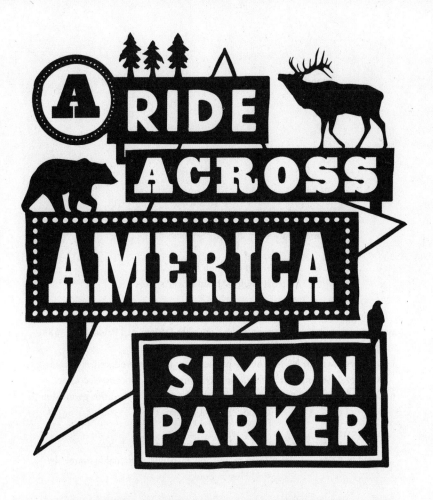

A RIDE ACROSS AMERICA

SIMON PARKER

A 4,000-MILE ADVENTURE THROUGH THE
SMALL TOWNS & BIG ISSUES OF THE USA

1 3 5 7 9 10 8 6 4 2

First published in 2024 by September Publishing

Copyright © Simon Parker 2024
Map copyright © Liam Roberts 2024

Typeset by RefineCatch Limited, www.refinecatch.com
Printed in Poland on paper from responsibly managed, sustainable sources by
Hussar Books

ISBN 9781914613593
Ebook ISBN 9781914613609

September Publishing
www.septemberpublishing.org

To my daughter.
Whose imminent arrival made this deadline even tighter.

CONTENTS

AUTHOR'S NOTE

Everything you are about to read is true. Every encounter, every saddle sore, every burger and fries. Every conversation in this book happened with a real, living, breathing human being (and the occasional angry dog). I have, however, abridged some long and rambling conversations in the interests of brevity.

I have also changed a few names to protect identities. People were extremely honest and generous with their time and opinions. That demands my respect and, in some cases, their anonymity. While in a handful of other cases, conversations were so brief that I didn't catch a name.

Before I go any further, I also feel it's necessary to state that throughout the following text, I naturally offer my own musings and opinions on America, its people, foods and habits. These ramblings are not intended to offend. This journey and book came from a place of intrigue, love and admiration. If you're American and I do touch the occasional nerve, I apologise and welcome you to visit Britain, to poke fun at our bad teeth, incessant rain and warm beer.

But for those of you who stick with me: I doff my cycling cap to you. Saddle up, apply a generous splodge of chamois cream, stay hydrated and don't forget to pack an extra inner tube or two.

PROLOGUE

The curtains reeked of crack cocaine – a sour, acrid stench, something like burnt plastic or creosote. Where the carpet wasn't curling back from rotting floorboards, it contained islands of grime and detritus. Soiled napkins. Used cutlery. Splintered cocktail sticks. A Petri dish-like dinner plate, turquoise with mould. A crucifix hung from the wall beside a large American flag. On a table at shin level, two dozen empty beer cans, exclusively Bud Lite and Rolling Rock, had been coated in an avalanche of grey cigarette ash. At one corner, I spotted the sun-bleached pages of a firearms magazine titled, unequivocally: *GUNS*. 'Resurrecting an UZI', read one subtitle. 'Colt's 1911. More than a mere legend', stated another.

Less than an hour before, I'd been alone and – now with the power of hindsight – splendidly carefree, cycling solo and unsupported across the United States, along a desolate potholed highway with only the occasional swirling dust devil for company. In the thick heat of late afternoon, I'd spotted refuge for the night: a small town on the eastern horizon, a bulbous water tower hovering over its inhabitants like a UFO.

As I raced closer, across asphalt sticky with a day's solar energy, I passed a shuttered-up drive-in movie theatre, a spooky-looking scrapyard, then a baseball field coated in fine golden sand. After ten hours on the road, and 100-odd miles on the clock, I found a convenience store, grabbed a beer from the fridge and stumbled, thirstily, towards the teenage checkout clerk.

'You got ID?'

'I'm 28.'

'No ID, no sale.'

'Look at me,' I said, pointing to crow's feet at the corners of my eyes, a scraggly beard and chapped lips. 'I look 48. At best.'

'Sorry, Sir. No ID, no sale.'

I stared contemptuously at the boy's acne for a few seconds, then marched outside to my bike's crammed panniers and set about searching for my passport, which I'd hidden somewhere deep in their muddled bowels. Out came dirty pants, sweat-stained T-shirts, odd socks, half-eaten cereal bars, hydration tablets, bars of motel soap, ketchup sachets, sun cream, spare inner tubes, roll-on deodorant, a foul-smelling towel, a multitool, a Swiss Army knife, a sleeping bag, approximately 60 loose pages of Bill Bryson's *The Lost Continent: Travels in Small-Town America*, seven AA batteries of unknown charge, eight spare spokes, a small bottle of chain oil, then – finally – my passport.

As I began throwing the contents back in, a cool shadow was cast across my shoulders. 'Beer?' said a stocky, shaven-headed man with a tribal neck tattoo, a farmer's tan and an oily black goatee, as he handed me a 12-ounce can, dripping with delicious condensation.

'Wow, thank you,' I replied. And without thinking, I ripped the ring pull clean off and began glugging at the rasping liquid. Within five transformative seconds, my elbows dropped and my toes tingled with glorious booze.

'British?'

'Sure am.'

'You got some place to crash?'

'Umm, no. Thought I'd camp.'

'I got a couch.'

'Wow. OK.'

'And beer.'

'Great. Thanks.'

'I'll drive. You follow.'

Thousands of miles from the familiar streets of New York, Los Angeles and the theme parks of Florida, I was traversing a land where foreign tourists seldom venture. I've no idea of the town's name. I don't even recall which state I was in. All I can say with confidence is that it was somewhere within a 1,500-mile tract between South Dakota and Ohio, in the northern reaches of the mostly pancake-flat American

Midwest, celebrated for its agriculture, industry and empty landscapes.

My fleeting exchange with a man I'd only just met could be described as foolhardy or blasé. Is a 30-second meeting enough time to judge a person's motives or character? Let alone agree to an overnight stay in their home? Almost certainly not. But travel, especially on one's own, has the peculiar power to cloud normal standards of human discourse. Alcohol certainly helps, too.

I had found myself in this situation umpteen times before. By opening myself up to the kindness, generosity and hospitality of strangers, and by throwing all normal cautions to the wind, good things only ever happened.

A film degree, majoring in American New Wave Cinema (1967–1982), had fostered a love of the USA, its landscapes and arts. But I'd also gorged on hundreds of horror movies, from Hitchcock to Carpenter, via Craven and Roth. As I followed the man's beaten-up Ford pickup, faded blue with a broken taillight and rusted towbar, travelling further and further from the town's centre, I began to catastrophise. Had I fully thought this through? Absolutely not. Was I about to be violently dismembered and dissolved in an oil drum filled with hydrofluoric acid? Maybe.

We passed a neon-lit diner, then turned left down a residential side street, pulling up to a weathered clapboard house, with wine bottle windchimes hanging from its cobwebbed eaves and torn net curtains chock-full with sundried flies. The mile or so between me and civilisation felt like a galaxy. Tentatively, I parked my bike next to a broken motorcycle, its wires dribbling into the dirt like the entrails of a large, disembowelled mammal, and entered through a porch strewn with unread mail, used pizza boxes and soggy cat litter.

I'd never smoked crack cocaine personally but I recognised its lingering, acerbic stench from assignments in the favelas of South America. Regular users can display volatile mood swings and set off on haphazard, ranting tangents.

'So!' shouted the man, as he clinked around his fridge and I looked for somewhere cleanish to sit in the adjacent living room, 'what do you think about Brexit? You're going to finally sling those fuckin' immigrants out! I fuckin' hope so! Hey, can I fix you up something to eat?'

With assorted gun periodicals draped across the arms of chairs, the setting was so alien it was hard to comprehend. I felt like Louis Theroux without a camera crew.

For the next half an hour, the man set out on a chaotic diatribe aimed at everyone and everything, from the *Washington Post* to avocados, via 3G phone masts and *Saturday Night Live*, stopping to take swipes at all the 'Latinos', 'Japs', 'Gays' and 'Blacks' in between. It was hard to conclude if the man had any discernible political affiliations or if he simply hated everyone. Fifty per cent captivating, 50 per cent terrifying, he spoke in explosive soundbites. All 'bullshit' this and 'cocksucker' that. Caught in his orbit, I only took my eyes off him for a few split seconds at a time, to survey for rodents in my direct vicinity and to determine if the cockroach on the wall was getting any closer. I could hear a dog barking in the yard and spotted occult-like doodles on a notepad peeking out from beneath the couch.

What made this encounter even more confusing, though, was how – when he wasn't being overtly racist, discriminatory or inciting violence of some sort – oddly *affable* he was. A volatile character, sure, but nonetheless desperate to make me feel comfortable and at home. A sheep in wolf's clothing, with hot-blooded political opinions, who delivered them with a warm smile and a side order of Pringles.

If I'd read this man's rants in an illicit dark web chat room, my mind's eye wouldn't have conjured up this living, breathing human, plumping pillows on the sofa. By the time I'd drunk half my beer he was already rooting around in the fridge, looking for another. This pattern played out for over an hour until I was half cut and dozy.

'They've got us just where they want us!' he whispered, as a thick blue vein bulged across his sweaty brow and he fiddled with a piece of smoke-stained tin foil.

'They? Who is they?' I enquired.

'Them. The elite. The Deep State.'

'To be honest, I'm not too ...'

'Hey, can I make you a sandwich?'

'Umm, I think I should ...'

'Who's your team? Chelsea? Manchester United?'

'Well, actually ...'

'Hey, have you ever shot a Beretta before?'

My journalist brain was urging me to stay, to sit it out and hear his point of view. My heart, too, wanted to be polite. On a one-to-one level, this man wasn't a bad host. I just don't think he'd spoken to another human for a while. But with the adrenaline levels in my body beginning to fall, my words slurring and eyes drooping, my gut was telling me to run. Around 40 per cent of US households contain guns, and I got a hunch that this one had more than its fair share.

'You want to watch YouTube videos?' he asked enthusiastically, as I disguised a yawn with my grubby fist. 'There's hidden messages in them, if you watch closely.'

I didn't respond.

'Hey, man. Have you ever fired a crossbow?'

When he started slugging bourbon directly from the bottle and pontificating about the crooked, cabal-like nature of the mainstream media I knew it was time to leave. It was surely only a matter of time before he asked me what I did for a living, or at the very least challenged me to a round of bare-chested Russian roulette.

When he got up to grab another beer from the kitchen, I began nervously mumbling about how I'd promised to call my parents from a nearby phone box. I then made a handful of pathetic apologies and edged past him, through the front door and back out to my bike.

'I'm sorry,' I said, as I jumped into the saddle and began pedalling away. 'It was ... lovely to meet you.'

1

AMERICAN DREAMS

A couple of months earlier, in the winter of 2015/16, I had finally landed one of the meaty mega-assignments that I'd daydreamed about for so long. A project, rather than just a shift. It was goodbye to the windowless studios of central London, the glitching autocues and egotistical editors, and hello to adventure, with its fresh air and unknowns.

I'd been commissioned by the BBC World Service to make a radio documentary about 'human endurance', to investigate what possessed people to leave the comfort of their so-called 'normal lives' and pit themselves against huge physical endeavours. However, rather than simply interview a handful of ultra-marathon runners, mountaineers and polar explorers, I'd dreamt up an idea for an expedition of my own. To sail and cycle halfway around the world, racing on land and sea with and alongside the 2015–16 Clipper Round the World Yacht Race – a 40,000 mile circumnavigation of the planet aimed at serious amateur sailors.

A journey within a journey. I would travel 15,000 miles from China to London, west to east, entirely wind and muscle powered. I'd be sailing in a team across the Pacific from Qingdao to Seattle and cycling solo across the USA to New York. Then I'd return to the yacht to sail the Atlantic to Northern Ireland and then cycle alone again for the final few hundred miles to London.

Straightforward, on paper, kind of. But having blagged myself a place as a journalist across the North Pacific, I quickly discovered that I categorically and indisputably despised a life at sea. Some adventures sound better in your head than they turn out to be in the flesh.

Claustrophobic and constantly moving, the 70-foot fibreglass yacht stank of burnt porridge and the viscous fluorescent urine of dehydrated bladders, which sloshed out of the toilet and ran through a channel beneath our bunkbeds. Heeling at 45 degrees to harness the wind as efficiently as possible and cut through the ocean like the sharp edge of a snowboard, we slammed relentlessly eastwards, jostling with 11 blinking dots on our navigation system.

Human endurance? This went way beyond what I'd had in mind. Sleep deprived and malnourished, factory-farmed chickens are kept in better conditions than ocean racing sailors. In a fleet of identical yachts, marginal gains are achieved by sailing close to, but not quite into, powerful storms, and by pushing the vessel and its components to (and often beyond) their limits. On a good, albeit uncomfortable day, we'd cover 300 miles, tacking and jibing in a zigzag motion on a northeasterly bearing. On a bad one, we'd race so close to breaking point that the inch-thick ropes holding our sails in place would snap under the immense tension and send us into violent, dizzying spins. This was not a pleasure cruise but a sprint from one side of the planet to the other, as every blunt object onboard attempted to maim or decapitate. Each morning, someone would be nursing a new sprain, cut or bruise.

I have never felt so lonely, so vulnerable and so starved of stimulation as I did on that Pacific voyage. I grew furious with myself for allowing my thirst for adventure to reach such a preposterous level. 'I'm going to die out here. I'm going to fucking die out here,' I said to myself, hundreds of times, as I retreated deeper and deeper into my shell.

To make my predicament worse, I was not blessed with sea legs, and for 30 days I was rendered mostly useless by incapacitating bouts of seasickness. With my eyes and inner ear thrown out of sync, I spent most of my time spraying partially digested noodles across the boots of a crew who considered me a superfluous dead weight. To this day, the mere whiff of sweet chilli sauce makes me retch. For 7,000 miles, it was the only thing we had to flavour our pasta, rice and porridge. Combined with stomach acid and bile, it was enough to leave my throat and mouth covered in angry sores. I just about managed to secure the handful of interviews I needed for the start of my documentary. However, unsurprisingly, I didn't particularly endear myself to a group of sailors who were trying to race from one side of the planet to the other as quickly (and as cleanly) as possible.

When we finally reached Seattle, I'd lost roughly eight kilograms in bodyweight. Burning 6,000 calories a day, while ingesting almost none, will do that to a person. Worse still, my lungs rattled with a chunky green phlegm. The ocean had rusted me from the inside out. I was in the worst possible shape of my life, scrawny and emaciated. But waiting for me at the marina was a plywood box with a few chastening words seared into its splintered flanks: AIR FREIGHT. PROPERTY OF MR SIMON PARKER. 1 BICYCLE. 1 TRAILER. ASSORTED BAGGAGE. CUSTOMS CHECKED.

Now I had to cycle across America.

If I'd have visited a doctor, they would have almost certainly told me to throw in the towel and fly home. But naively, I'd promised the BBC that I was not just *sailing* but also *cycling* halfway around the world. As it stood, I only had a third of the content required for my assignment, and through fear of reneging on the biggest commission of my career, I set off less than a week later on the £500 aluminium bike I used to cycle around London, pulling a second-hand trailer sourced from eBay filled with all manner of unnecessary clobber.

Until then, I'd only cycled 1,000 miles in one go, across France and Italy, with a support vehicle carrying my luggage. But now, here I was, staring down a solo 4,000-mile bike ride from Seattle to New York. I needed to average 600 miles a week for the next month and a half if I was to stand any chance of reaching the Big Apple in time for the Clipper Round the World Yacht Race's final leg across the Atlantic: my ride back to Britain. In fact, there was no backup plan, or plane ticket booked, just in case. This half-baked idea was an all or nothing – fake it till you make it – endeavour.

Having been unable to coax any significant expenses out of the BBC, I had just $1,000 to my name, about £700 in crumpled cash hidden in and around my bike. For the first few days, I either slept in laybys or pitched my tent in national parks. Only later would I discover that spring is a notoriously dangerous season for bear attacks, who emerge cranky and hungry from their hibernations.

Anyone who has travelled on a shoestring, however, will

know that this penniless curse can become a blessing. Because without a financial nest egg to rely upon, I was forced to embrace a style of happy-go-lucky living that opened me up to a world of incomprehensible generosity. A brand of kindness and hospitality that I would come to regard as being profoundly and unambiguously 'American'.

When I wasn't camping, I was taken in by complete strangers, for no other reason but pure and unadulterated altruism. An English accent certainly helped. Just asking politely for 'water' with a hard T in my best received pronunciation, rather than 'waaaarder' like most North Americans and Australians do, would turn heads in gas stations, diners and convenience stores. People would hear my voice, then queue up to tell me about a long-lost relative back in Blighty, their adoration of the British monarchy or an obsession with the long-running TV series *Midsomer Murders*. On one occasion, a bespectacled woman with tears streaming down her cheeks flagged me into a layby and forced a crisp $20 bill into my hands 'to get something decent to eat. You look terrible, and your mother must be worried sick!'

My bicycle became an esteemed wingman, a curiosity people could spot a mile away through swirling heat mirage or torrential rain. With its bulging panniers, chaotically packed trailer and fluttering Nepalese prayer flags – given to me by a lady in her seventies 'to ward off bad vibes' – it served as a conversation starter like none other.

'Where you headed?' said a few dozen people a day, as they surveyed my cumbersome, intriguing steed. It had a clown horn fastened to the handlebars and a bouquet of plastic flowers protruding from beneath the saddle.

'New York. I hope.'

Most were rendered speechless. One woman dropped her coffee. Another ran to the car and called her mother, who was dying of a terminal illness in a nearby hospital. 'Mom, you have got to talk to this crazy British guy I just met at the 7-Eleven ... Hey, do you know Prince Charles?'

After the routine and claustrophobia of the racing yacht, the risk of death and the lingering scent of vomit, my bike unleashed a sense of overwhelming freedom within me. Exposed to the changing elements, without protection from a window, a roll bar or airbag, I felt connected with the land and its people in a way I'd seldom experienced before. Most liberating of all, however, was the way I could pause for rest when I needed it. To stop and contemplate a landscape when I wanted to: the sleet-dusted Rockies, the grassy Great Plains, the forested Appalachians. When things got too tough, or too wet, or too cold, I could simply take refuge somewhere and wait for the next chapter of the adventure to unfold. Unlike the unrelenting monotone of the Pacific, and the mind-numbing routine of being stuck in a fibre-glass box, America was a kaleidoscope of infinite colour and variation.

That's not to say the cycling wasn't gruelling. Especially in my frail state. But at least the hard graft came with the payoff of pretty pictures: blistering sunsets, stacks of fluffy pancakes, straight roads gobbled up by the horizon. The sort of empty highways that Hollywood protagonists disappear on, at the appropriate moment in their blockbusters, to infer a sense of freedom, or sometimes a feeling of immense loneliness. Think *Easy Rider* (1969), *Midnight Cowboy* (1969), *Thelma & Louise* (1991). With these strands of hot tarmac almost entirely to myself, I could ride and ride, from before dusk to beyond dawn, often in a blissful, trance-like state.

Fascinatingly, many of the small towns I found along the way seemed to be stuck in a time warp. I cycled past rusted 1940s Studebakers and big red fire hydrants that bore the scars of long, hot summers. I found derelict train stations, boarded-up art deco theatres, struggling local newspapers and stainless steel diners that served Coke floats, home fries and big slabs of blueberry pie. Even more intriguing, though, was that this otherworld was filled with millions of American citizens that I'd barely seen portrayed on the silver screen, let alone on the BBC, Fox News or CNN. Forty per cent (128 million) of the American population lives in its coastal counties, crammed into cities such as Los Angeles, New York and Miami. The rest, however, reside in the immense, and often ignored, expanse between.

When I wasn't cycling, I chatted to Middle America's farmhands, fishermen, musicians, checkout clerks, carpenters, truckers, barmaids and bike mechanics. I slept in the pool house of a millionaire soya bean farmer and in a hammock on the porch of a Lutheran pastor. I stayed in the mice-infested hayloft of an evangelical rancher and camped in the backyard of a halfway house occupied by recovering heroin addicts. These people felt like forgotten Americans, living in the geographical and cultural hinterlands of mainstream society.

It's true that I did meet some extraordinarily intense people. Not least the hospitable skinhead conspiracy theorist with the neck tattoos and erratic mannerisms. Any long-distance trip has them. Heck, we're all weird in one way or another. But overall, I found kind and cordial people who wanted to do what kind and cordial people do best: chew the fat. Boy, do Americans love to chat.

It was just a shame that I felt in such a rush. Averaging more than 600 miles a week, I was moving faster than you would on most driving holidays. By turning this journey into a time trial, a race to sail home, it felt like I'd missed the point entirely.

After 3,707 miles in the saddle, I rolled wearily into New York. Above me, Manhattan's skyscrapers blinked and twinkled in the hazy twilight. Epic, no doubt. And a huge sense of accomplishment – I'd cycled across the USA. But if I'm totally honest, I felt deflated, underwhelmed. The city stank of rotting garbage and throbbed with noisy sirens. I yearned for Middle America and the people I'd met there.

All of us will look back on the moments that have shaped us: enlightening periods of our education, a particularly carefree summer, a formative teenage relationship. Often, it takes years or decades for us to fully appreciate their significance in creating who we are. But I knew – right there and then – that this journey had changed the course of my career. By practising journalism at the gentle(ish) pace of a bicycle, sometimes just five or six miles per hour, I'd experienced a professional epiphany. Without a camera crew, bright lights and scary microphones, people opened up to me – a grubby British bloke in shorts and a T-shirt – in a way I'd never experienced before. Most nationalities require a bit of warming up, a few minutes of foreplay. Not Americans. Most cut right to the chase. They say it how it is. Candid hot takes.

No-holds-barred opinions. Freedom of speech is so enshrined into the US Constitution it can sometimes be hard to get a word in edgeways.

As I continued my half-circumnavigation, this time sailing across the Atlantic on another 70-foot racing yacht, and once again spraying the contents of my stomach across anyone who dared get too close, I grew haunted by the thought of that tattooed Midwestern man and a missed opportunity.

'I should have seen it through,' I grumbled to myself. 'I should have stayed the night and heard him out.' My documentary about 'human endurance' was wishy-washy flimflam in contrast to all the meat I'd gnawed off America's bones along the way. 'He was the *real* story. Not this.'

On 8 November 2016, 100 days after I returned to Britain, the United States elected its forty-fifth president. Hillary Clinton won the popular vote with 48 per cent but lost the White House to Donald Trump's 46 per cent, due to the quirks of the American electoral college system.

Returning to the daily trudge of freelance journalism, I remember the period, perhaps not fondly, but well. The world's cameras focused on the USA. What might President Trump say or do next? America was box office, albeit often freakishly so.

Simultaneously, our newsgathering seemed to enter a cynical, toxic age. In the biz, perhaps more than ever, our interviewees needed to clearly represent one thing or another. If there had ever been an age of nuance, it was unequivocally now over. In a four-minute news segment, you could watch a mouthy newspaper columnist argue about primary school syllabuses with a shouty Mumsnet blogger, often for no other editorial justification than to ignite televisual dynamite.

The Twitter algorithm, too, pitted A versus B. With just 140 characters to make a point, users were forced to shout, rather than discuss. From President Trump to Z-list celebrities, via all the loonies with smartphones in between, online social and political discourse became a contest of who could say the most extreme thing in the quickest and pithiest fashion.

Fascinatingly, but somewhat irksomely, I saw a disconnect between the country I'd just experienced at ground level and the one I was now seeing portrayed on page and screen. Yes, most of the Americans I'd met were highly politicised and rarely shy about it. But the way the media and politicians lazily lumped people into camps – right, left, liberal, conservative, red, blue – felt like an erroneous over-simplification of a country that was considerably more complex. Rather than searching out America's softly spoken middle ground – its farmers, fishermen, drug users and teachers – journalists amplified the people screaming loudest. The pseudo-intellectuals, the think-tank clones, the fame-hungry legislators. All this did, however, was create an angry caricature. A parody of America.

In October 2018, halfway through Donald Trump's first (and, at time of writing, only) term, I decided that I needed to get back, to see America again for myself. To practise the 'slow journalism' I craved so much. President Trump had promised to reduce illegal immigration. Therefore, I cooked up another hairbrained idea – to cycle 2,500 miles beside the US–Mexico border. The journey would allow me to ask border officials, Mexican migrants, Texan ranchers, young people, old people, rich and poor, what life was really like at this geopolitical flashpoint. Rather than collect a handful of snappy vox pops, my plan was to conduct hundreds of long-form interviews with the people at the centre of the story. In theory, my plan made sense. So, I flew to Austin, took a bus to the Gulf of Mexico, and started my cycle west, following the border as closely as possible.

I'd studied long-range weather forecasts and average temperatures for the past two decades and concluded that I'd spend six weeks travelling in a very agreeable 22 degrees centigrade. Well, that was the idea. In 2018, Texas's autumn had other plans.

I got 300 miles in before I almost died of heat stroke in the Chihuahuan Desert, where temperatures exceeded 40 degrees centigrade. Dangerously exposed and overheated, I limped into a partly bulldozed house and collapsed in the shade of a garage. Some minutes or hours later, I woke up covered in ice, with a middle-aged man with shoulder-length silver hair and a crucifix dangling from his neck encouraging me to take small sips of Gatorade. There is still a little part of me that wonders if this man was, in fact, an apparition, a hallucination in my over-heated imagination. But as a blood-red sun simmered into the horizon, he convinced me that my journey, for now at least, was a fool's errand. 'You'll die out there, dude,' he insisted. 'America isn't going anywhere. And it's definitely not going to get any less fucked up.'

The man was on to something. Because since Donald Trump was elected president in 2016, followed by the 2020 administration of Joe Biden and the storming of the Capitol Building on 6 January 2021, the United States of America has – from a distance, at least – appeared anything but united. Between 2016 and 2023, the country's federal debt grew from circa $20 trillion to more than $30 trillion. All while the economies of China and India snapped at its Converse-clad heels. In December 2021, the final US troops withdrew from Afghanistan, where 2,448 American servicemen and women had lost their lives, alongside 3,848 US contractors, 66,000 Afghan national military and police, and 47,245 Afghan civilians. A success?

I grew up in the 1990s seeing the USA as the Big Daddy of geopolitics, the World Police. But seven years after my first ride across America, I looked across the pond and saw a nation that I didn't fully recognise. Had the country finally lost its swagger? Was its star finally fading?

Memories of my cross-country journey in 2016 were seared to the back of my mind's eye as halcyon days. But were they clouded in an unhelpful rose tint? A case of travellers' Stockholm syndrome, perhaps?

By late 2022, when the idea for this book developed from a few random daydreams into a full-blown obsession, I started to wonder if, psychologically, I'd somehow misremembered my time there. Had I been so focused on the physicality of the bike ride that I'd failed to scrutinise the country with the journalistic rigour it deserved? With its omnipresence in global popular culture, it can be easy to look at the United States and feel like you've worked it out. I have friends who would scoff at the mere suggestion of a holiday in the 'brash, samey' USA. Perhaps that's the greatest – albeit somewhat paradoxical – success of 'brand USA'. Its landscapes, products and accents are so instantly recognisable and ubiquitous within popular culture. You could show a photo of a cheeseburger, a baseball or a Cadillac to an Amazonian tribesman and he'd probably be able to point to the country on a map.

Nevertheless, even I now questioned how much of the American cultural landscape I genuinely, fully understood. And by 'cultural' I don't mean its films, books and TV shows. I could hold my own in a pub quiz. I know my Steinbeck from my Spielberg. But more so the big topics and so-called 'culture wars' that hogged most of its news coverage. Evergreen subjects we instantly associate with America: gun ownership, abortion rights, Christianity, private healthcare, big pharma, the military and freedom. But also emerging contemporary topics that have entered the lexicon in just the past few decades: election fraud, climate change, the alt-right, critical race theory, trans rights, the opioid crisis, Fentanyl, Covid-19, QAnon, and the Deep State. It was easy to hear these words and phrases on the news, day after day, and grow hardened to their meaning, without fully engaging with or understanding exactly what each issue entailed.

I believe, evangelically, however, that travel is the greatest form of education. I have learned more about people and place from week-long trips than I have from a dozen books. I am the archetypal kinaesthetic learner. I need to touch and taste to fully understand.

By spring 2023 I was hatching a plan: to ride across America. Again. A year before the 2024 presidential election. Only this time, to go slower, to look up rather than down and record hundreds of conversations along the way. To immerse myself in its beguiling yet fragile landscapes, while striving to better understand the country, its politics and problems. Notably, with the help of *real* people, met mostly on the roadside, rather than the same old talking heads on TV. How much had the country changed in seven years and nearly three elections? Would I find optimism and hope? Or discover division, doom and gloom?

I wanted to cycle coast to coast again, with a clearly defined A to B. An end-to-end journey would have the power to keep me enthralled and pushing forwards, even at the most challenging moments. I liked the idea of returning to the Northwest again, to catch up with a few of the people I'd met on my first journey. Seattle is the most northwesterly point of the contiguous (the lower 48) United States, right?

Wrong. When I zoomed in on Google Maps, I was struck by just how far away it is from the Pacific Ocean. In fact, Seattle sits 160 miles east of the vast, pixilated blue of the planet's biggest body of water. To the west of the city, I saw a forested green peninsula, and at the furthest point north, a place called Cape Flattery, the northwestern-most point of the contiguous United States.

It was love at first sight. I'd been skewered by one of Cupid's golden arrows. I had my starting point, a place that made my eyes bulge with intrigue. But where to? Naturally, my next Google search was 'extreme points of the USA' and BOOM, up popped Key West, Florida, the southeastern-most point of the contiguous USA, and a place I knew very little about. All I could picture was palm trees and piña coladas.

Cape Flattery and Key West were a whopping 4,000 miles apart. Surpassing my first cycle across the USA (3,707 miles), it would be my biggest ever bike ride. The journey would take me through roughly a dozen geographically and culturally diverse states, through great swathes of agriculture, over lofty mountain ranges, across vast plains and into hundreds of small towns. Better still, the route was unlike anything I'd seen before. The popular cross-country itineraries followed either a northern, central or southern path, on a mostly horizontal trajectory. In contrast, mine wiggled diagonally, from top left to bottom right.

For the first time in my life, I actually trained for this journey. Albeit, somewhat under duress. My normal approach to these big bike rides was to use the first week or two as 'training', to ease myself in gently. However, since 2016, my life had changed considerably. I was no longer a single man, wandering around the world from one hotel room to the next. I was happily married.

I'd met Alana through work, while setting up a story for the BBC in Arctic Finland. And within a few love-pained weeks, she made me realise there was more to life than filling a passport with stamps. My thirst for adventure would need to be balanced with my responsibilities and vows as a husband. She was adamant that I not only prepared for the ride beforehand but then looked after myself adequately while on it.

I therefore agreed to a few sessions with a personal trainer, to build up my quadriceps, calves, hamstrings and shoulders. I also had my bike's saddle and handlebars professionally fitted to my exact shape and size and settled on a handful of health supplements that – ever the sceptic hack – I'd previously dismissed as baloney. Namely:

- Branch chain amino acids. To help reduce muscle breakdown.
- Glutamine. To remove excess ammonia and assist with immune system function.
- Magnesium. To maintain healthy muscles, nerves, bones and blood sugar levels.
- Zinc. To help recover from strenuous exercise and clear free radicals.
- Electrolytes. To stay hydrated before, during and after exercise.
- Whey protein. To repair and rebuild weary muscles.

All these extra powders and pills had to be counted, weighed and measured. Even just a few weeks' worth squished tightly into a transparent freezer bag took up half a pannier. It looked as though I was preparing to traffic a 2kg brick of uncut Afghan heroin.

Our spare bedroom became a hectic mission control. Cycling jerseys hung from bookshelves, spare tyres looped over the back of my office chair, a freshly waterproofed cagoule was sun drying in the window. I packed a spare bicycle chain and half a dozen drybags filled with socks, insurance documents, tyre levers, puncture patches and emergency $100 bills.

And then the tech. Essential for my job as a journalist but a lot of extra weight:

- MacBook Pro laptop (2.14kg)
- Sony RX100 video camera (240g)

- Rode Go 11 microphones and transmitter (96g)
- Zoom H4n Pro Handy Recorder and Tascam omnidirectional microphone (650g)
- DJI Mini 3 Pro drone, remote control and spare batteries (884g)
- Assorted memory cards, power cables, microphone windshields, travel plug adapters, spare batteries, camera lenses, neutral density filters and protective cases (3kg)

Before I'd even packed a single set of 'civvies' – the non-cycling clothes I'd wear in the evenings and on rest days – or a morsel of food, I had over 13kg of stuff, just to get started.

As summer waned, my commandeering of the spare room became a bone of marital contention. Occasionally, this manifested as tears. Sometimes we argued about chain oil on the carpets. But mostly about how distracted I was by the trip, when I should have been making the most of every precious moment left at home. Growing increasingly aware of each other's physical presence, Alana and I touched, held hands and cuddled as much as we could. Nevertheless, the slow packing of my bags became a stark and obvious reminder of my imminent exodus.

In many of these books about brave adventurer types pitting themselves against the elements, not enough is said about the people left at home. The spouses that made a commitment to spend their life with someone, only for that itchy-footed partner to disappear for weeks and months at a time, often causing great emotional, logistical and financial strain. In Alana, I had a wife who, within reason, supported me and my crazy ideas. Travel writing has afforded us some mind-boggling holidays: five-star hotels, helicopter rides, safaris. Albeit, with barely a pension between us. Travel is in our bones. But this trip felt different. Risky.

Life also has a funny habit of sneaking up on you when you least expect it. The morning she drove me to Heathrow, lugging a bike in a cardboard box, we finally got to the bottom of the 'food poisoning' she'd been suffering. Alana was a month pregnant.

As we stood at Terminal 3, vomit smeared across Alana's cuff and tears streaming down both our cheeks, our life was about to change forever. It was hard to conclude if this was a brilliant or terrible time for us to have a baby. I had a 4,000-mile bike ride and a book to write in the interim. Nevertheless, the bun was in the oven. And by hook or by crook, I was determined to ride across America.

2

SLEEPLESS IN SEATTLE

Seattle's downtown wheezed with haze. The Air Quality Index, which ranks pollutants in the atmosphere worldwide, gave it the worst score of any city on the planet that day. 'Wildfires in Canada,' said a man in a grubby tie-dye T-shirt holding a cereal box inscribed with the words 'NEED TO EAT', as I dragged my bike into the refuge of my hotel. 'Worst I've ever seen.'

By the time I made it to my room on the fifth floor, I was hawking phlegm into the bathroom sink. Thank goodness for a roof over my head and the windows around me. On the streets beneath, a dozen souls were not so lucky. Heavy backpacks slung across withered shoulders. Tents bundled behind the prison-like bars of basement carparks. Two bearded, spindly figures huddled in a glass-sided bus stop across the street. Seattle has one of the highest rates of homelessness in the United States. Myriad and complex factors are to blame. The cost of living, for example, is one of the highest in the country. Amazon, Microsoft, Boeing and Starbucks all have their headquarters in or around the city.

As a late summer sun struggled to penetrate the nicotine-coloured smog, I set about reassembling my bike. Not the £500 aluminium off-the-shelf steed I'd wobbled across America on seven years before, but a custom-made titanium touring bike, generously donated by Van Nicholas, based in the Netherlands. Their bikes aren't cheap – this one retailed at around 6,000 euros – but are largely indestructible. Nevertheless, the process of packaging and flying the bike to Seattle had created more stress than the thought of cycling from one side of the country to the other. With a solo, self-supported journey between two places 4,000 miles apart, I couldn't exactly transport it in an expensive hard case, only to discard it at the start line.

Instead, I'd blagged an E-bike cardboard box from my local bike shop and had done my best to protect the frame, headset and forks with bubble wrap and clothing. Thankfully, it emerged in one piece. Albeit, in a twisted, yogic state, with handlebars, mudguards, bottle cages, wheels and kickstands contorted in one way or another.

Over the course of two chaotic hours, hundreds of items – from fingernail-sized screws to spare socks – found their place, either in or on the bike. Finally finished, I leant its sleek slate-grey frame against the windowpane and stood back to admire my handiwork.

'Shit!' I screamed, as I looked past the bike and out to the city streets. At the bus stop beneath me, where I'd seen the two men huddled, one of them was now ... dead. Sprawled out on his back, he had a syringe hanging from his upper right arm. I watched his friend attempt to resuscitate his jaundiced, unresponsive body, punching his chest violently, presumably breaking ribs in the process. The deceased had so much movement forced through his limp diaphragm that his shoes were thrown from his feet.

I was frozen, with no idea how to react. Should I stay put or run down and assist somehow? Most pedestrians simply walked on by. One, thank goodness, stopped to call an ambulance and took turns giving CPR. What made the scene even more tragic, though, was that as the man lay dying, several similarly bedraggled figures emerged from the background and robbed his possessions. His sleeping bag, his rucksack, his shoes. They even rifled through his jeans and pulled out small wraps of tissue paper and half-smoked cigarettes. All while his ribs were being cracked in a desperate attempt to stir motion into his lifeless heart.

After a few torturous minutes, I ran from my room to see if I could help. 'There's someone fucking dying down there!' I yelled at a startled old lady in the elevator. But as I reached the street and sprinted towards the bus stop, a miraculous thing happened. The man opened his eyes and sat up, just as an ambulance and police car pulled up beside him.

His first act on rebirth? To spark up a cigarette. He then refused any medical care from the paramedics and the ambulance was gone within 90 seconds. The attending police officers didn't even get out of their vehicle. I sat on a wall across the street and watched the characters scatter as fast as they had assembled. The man gathered any loose change that hadn't been pilfered and drifted off down the gloomy street, barefooted.

I had reported from the murder capital of Mexico, migrant camps in Greece, countless sketchy borders. I thought I was hardened to the harsh brutality of human life. Nevertheless, for those first few hours in Seattle, I experienced a culture shock unlike anything I had before. My nerves were jangled but I was also hopelessly jetlagged. This was the furthest I'd flown east or west for almost a decade. It was no accident that most of my work took place in the Arctic, western Europe or southern Africa, allowing for a smooth transition through degrees of longitude, north or south, rather than the circadian rhythm-glitching nature of travel from east to west.

Back home it was midnight but on the west coast of the United States it was only 4pm. I was flagging but also famished, so in a desperate attempt to stay awake I wandered a few blocks down a steep street to Seattle's harbour, a main drag busy with tourists and more homeless locals.

Everything seemed expensive. Sure, I was at a touristy hotspot of seafood kiosks and burger joints, but this wasn't fine dining by any stretch of the imagination. Just fried food served in paper cartons. A small portion of chips and three fish fingers cost $17, plus a 10.25 per cent sales tax. And then, when I tapped my phone at the reader, a tip: 18 per cent. 20 per cent. 25 per cent. No tip. As I looked at the screen in a state of penny-pinching British disbelief, I could feel the server's eyes on me and settled on 18 per cent.

To be clear, this wasn't for exceptional service in a sit-down restaurant. There was no friendly small talk, no 'how are you?', no preamble about the weather. I paid an extra $3.40 for someone to hand me a paper plate from behind a counter, without as much as a strained cheek muscle. The whole thing cost almost £20.

I wasn't broke. I had just enough money to do this trip. But as I sat on a nearby bench, savouring each underwhelming bite as though it was my last, the sight of Seattle's homeless population grew bleaker. Men and women, with all their worldly possessions packed into duffel bags or shopping trolleys, relying on handouts from passers-by. There was a navy veteran with an amputated leg in a wheelchair asking tourists for loose change. A young woman, probably about 18, with just a few threadbare clothes to protect her modesty, held out a Burger King cup.

An African American man with a limp and a shopping bag filled with fizzy drinks took a shine to me. Perhaps because he'd been ignored by everyone else on the street. He sat next to me with a Bluetooth speaker blaring out Rage Against the Machine's 1993 anthem 'Killing in the Name', a song inspired by police brutality aimed at the African American man Rodney King and the subsequent 1992 Los Angeles riots. Coincidentally, it happens to be one of my favourite songs. Its famous outro repeats the lyrics: 'Fuck you, I won't do what you tell me!'

We sat for a few awkward moments and mouthed the words of the song aloud before he turned the speaker down and spoke.

'He sprayed stuff in my face!'

'Who did?'

'The dude where I live.'

'Yeah?'

'I went to the hospital but I was cut, man. From Medicare.'

Originally from Miami, the man had lived in Seattle for two decades. In his late forties, I guessed, he was polite and talkative, and ended every other sentence with 'You know what I'm sayin'?'

It was hard to decipher exactly what had happened – not only that afternoon but in the preceding years. He was, nevertheless, angered by the hands he had been dealt in life. He told me that he had been sent to jail for a crime he didn't commit, that he'd been the victim of multiple physical assaults and that his daughter had been sexually abused.

'I lost my house. I lost my job. My councillor. She set me up, man. They all called me nigger, man. It was bad. They spit on me.'

It was hard to keep up. He jumped from one tangent to the next. One thing was certain, though. He had endured a troubled and unsettled existence. He kept repeating that he was the son of the American Baptist minister and civil rights campaigner Martin

Luther King Jr. The greatest struggle of his life, however, had been convincing people. He was, he told me, at the centre of a conspiracy.

'Did you see that dude with a gun?' he asked me.

'No, which one?'

'He was over there, man. He had a pistol on his hip. Caucasians, man. They scare me.'

I was wary of asking the man too many probing, and potentially triggering, questions. As a journalist, sometimes you must recognise when to stop talking. Instead, we sat for a few minutes more, this time with the Seattle band Pearl Jam blaring out from his speaker. Tourists walked past us with popcorn and burgers. We watched the navy veteran rattle loose change in his cap.

'Hey, Simon. Can you buy me some food?' the man asked, sheepishly.

I thought for a few seconds. Had I been played? Maybe. Either way, the right thing to do was to buy the man dinner. He ordered a small fish and chips, a bowl of clam chowder and a soda. With tax and a tip, it came to almost $30 (£24).

My first few hours had been a baptism of fire. Nevertheless, I returned to my hotel and fell asleep almost immediately, at 8.05pm. Six hours later, I awoke feeling fresh and ready for the day ahead. It was midmorning back home. In Seattle, however, it was just after 2am.

In the past, I'd have been desperate to get my trip started as quickly as possible. But as you grow older, you learn to respect the ebb and flow of your body's finite energy reserves. So, instead of departing the city in a state of delirious jetlag, I had decided to give myself two more nights in the city to adapt to the time zone.

By 7am, I was in the saddle for the first time and cruising between wide city blocks. Like a bicycle courier, running errands. The morning was cool, with the first hint of autumn. Plumes of white steam swirled up from gaps in the sidewalk. Commuters wearing thick jumpers emerged from subway stations and stopped for bagels and coffee on their way to work.

For the sheer quantity and scale of the city's skyscrapers, I had never cycled anywhere quite like it. The smoky haze had cleared a little, and where clouds blew gently over their faraway roofs, it created a sense of vertigo in reverse. Looking up, with my head pushed back between my shoulder blades, made me feel queasy.

I started with my most important job: taking out a three-month phone contract, giving me unlimited coverage across the United States. For $60 per month, I'd get all the maps, social media, calls and emails I could ever need. It also included hotspot data, which would allow me to upload weekly YouTube films directly from my laptop. Part of me longed to just head off on an adventure without as much as a phone, but this was work as well as a jolly.

Breakfast was a stack of buttermilk pancakes and a side of crispy bacon, drowned in half a litre of sticky maple syrup. A rite of passage. And to my taste buds, nothing said 'Welcome to America' quite like this sweet and smoky combination, as perfect a food pairing as cheese and onion or beer and crisps.

Equally, though, I had my first taste of the 'coffee', in name only, by global standards. While most Italians consume their brain fuel in short, robust espresso shots, and Norwegians enjoy their midnight oil in chunky ceramic mugs, so strong you can practically stand a spoon in it, in America, you're more likely to find people adding sweetener and cream to pint-sized cups of dirty water. My first breakfast was therefore spent in a fitting, albeit underwhelming fashion, grimacing through three helpings of refillable drip 'coffee', clucking for just a small flutter of caffeine-induced titillation.

Seattle is, however, the coffee capital of the United States. Seattleites consume more of the black stuff, per capita, than any other city in the country. The brew's popularity is believed to be linked to the often damp and drizzly climate. Locals have been hunkering down in cosy coffeehouses since the first bean roasters opened in 1887.

The global coffee giant Starbucks launched its first store there in 1971, beside the cobblestone streets of Seattle's historic Pike Place Market. Thankfully, it was just a couple of blocks away and, after a 30-minute queue, beside a hundred fellow caffeine-starved tourists, I restarted my day with a double espresso.

Pike Place Market attracts more than 10 million visitors a year and since the early twentieth century has served as the city's culinary hub. Inside, cruise ship passengers mooched toe-to-heel taking photos of pink-bellied salmon leaping from one fishmonger to another. Just outside, a teenage boy in a starched red shirt and a black dinner suit played the Bobby McFerrin tune 'Don't Worry Be Happy' on a screeching clarinet.

The most popular snacks were either corndogs – sausages on sticks covered in deep-fried cornmeal batter – or bright yellow corn on the cob, smothered in gloopy orange cheese. Brilliant food for the small hours. Perhaps after ten pints of beer. But I had just eaten about 2,000 calories worth of bacon and pancakes.

I had, however, been invited for an early lunch with Traci Calderon, owner and executive chef of the Atrium Kitchen. Her business caters for corporate and private clients in and around Seattle. Dressed in bright chef's whites and a jet-black apron, she welcomed me into a stainless steel kitchen used for cooking demonstrations.

'When I first came here from California in 2009, I found a city that was very accepting of a female chef,' she told me, as I grazed from a wooden board of cured meats, soft cheeses, pickled vegetables, soft madeleines and a focaccia sprinkled with rock salt and rosemary.

'This market is known as an incubator for small business. Sure, we have the oldest Starbucks, but it moved here in the 1970s. That was before the market created a charter saying that no big franchises were allowed in.'

Traci used the kitchen to host small groups looking for an interactive dining experience, but also lent the space to up-and-coming local chefs who were looking to hone their skills in a professional environment. 'There are few cities quite like it,' she told me, as we set off on a wander through the market, among bouquets of plump dahlias and beekeepers selling local honey. 'You can drive for ten minutes in any direction and you hit water. We've got the Olympic Peninsula to the west and the North Cascades to the east. Both offer world-class hiking.'

She did, however, concede that Seattle had changed considerably in the 14 years since she'd moved there. 'The shift I've seen is disheartening. I don't feel safe in certain parts of the city, where before I hadn't given it a second thought. I've seen teenagers shooting up on the streets.'

Traci had witnessed the biggest change since the Covid-19 pandemic. 'There is a rampant drug issue here, along with mental illness. That does create an element of ... dodginess. What I've heard, and I can't verify this, is that other large cities across the US were providing free bus tickets to Seattle during the pandemic because Seattle was known for taking care of its homeless folks.'

It is hard to corroborate this theory. However, according to a report commissioned by Seattle council member Andrew Lewis in 2021, the pandemic did put extra pressure on the city's already struggling shelter system, delaying funds for new housing and leading to an increase in homelessness.

With her restaurant closed to private clients, Traci changed the direction of her business. Between March 2020 and August 2022, her Nourished Neighbourhood food programme provided over 50,000 free meals to homebound seniors and people living with food insecurity.

'I don't know how to help people overcome serious drug addiction, that's not my area of expertise. My superpower, however, is feeding people, and that's how I decided I could help my community.'

I spent the afternoon exploring the city. Seattle boasts dozens of art galleries and museums, but I was more interested in a graffitied bench in Viretta Park. Scribbled with hundreds of messages, it serves as a memorial to the late Nirvana singer Kurt Cobain, who took his own life in his nearby home in 1994, aged just 27. I was only seven at the time of his death but, like many millions of disaffected teenagers around the world, turned to his music a few years later.

Nirvana's punky, rocky, gravelly tunes became the soundtrack to smoking joints in any remotely dry place my friends and I could find. When a few of us decided to start a band, the only song we came close to mastering was their 1992 hit 'Come As You Are', from their second album *Nevermind*. Many people will know it for the iconic cover alone: a naked baby boy swimming underwater beside a dollar bill on a fishhook. I sat down for a few contemplative minutes beside a posy of wilting roses, a bottle of beer and a half-smoked spliff. Offerings to the great man, but also nostalgic vestiges to my own life.

I continued across town, to the city's iconic Space Needle. At 605 feet high, it was once the tallest structure west of the Mississippi River. Film nerds will know it from the 1993 romantic comedy *Sleepless in Seattle* starring Tom Hanks and Meg Ryan. From a distance, it resembles a rocket about to be launched to the moon.

From the summit, I could see 20 miles in each direction. To the east, seaplanes with banana-like floats instead of wheels vroomed into land across Lake Union, a 580-acre abyss. To the north, I spotted cruise ships destined for Alaska and an MSC container ship navigating slowly out of Puget Sound towards the open ocean and, probably, Asia. To the south, I couldn't quite see Mount Rainier, the enormous stratovolcano some 90 miles away. But I could make out Lumen Field, the 69,000-seater home of the Seattle Seahawks, winners of the 2014 Superbowl.

It was, however, the northwestern horizon that intrigued me the most. Because in less than 36 hours I'd be starting my journey proper. With one eye closed and my finger pointed out ahead of me, I could trace a course around a low-lying coastline, pockmarked with expensive seaside homes. Somewhere, through the smoke, was the Olympic Peninsula and Cape Flattery.

When I unchained my bike from the railings at ground level, I enjoyed a brief interlude with a mother about my age, while she cajoled a toddler into a stroller.

'I'm about to cycle across America. I think. I hope,' I told them.

'Oh wow. That's amazing.'

'How long will that take, Mommy?' asked the boy, as they walked off towards the subway.

'Oh, about 20 days I guess.'

As I munched through all the leftover cheese, madeleines and slices of focaccia that I hadn't managed to eat at lunchtime, the woman's words – 'about 20 days, I guess' – whizzed around my mind on loop, reminding me of my first journey across the USA. Most Americans have no grasp of just how enormous their country really is, or just how slow bicycle travel is compared to a car.

By her reckoning, I'd be cycling 200 miles a day, for three weeks straight. To put that into context, when Scottish cyclist Mark Beaumont broke the Guinness World Record for the fastest 18,000-mile circumnavigation of the planet, he did it in 78 days, 14 hours and 40 minutes, averaging 230 miles a day. Not only did he achieve the feat on a svelte carbon-fibre bike, with barely a water bottle weighing him down, but he also had a support vehicle, masseur and crew.

Bedtime was a minor improvement on the night before: 8.45pm. But by 3.30am I was wide awake and staring out of my hotel window watching dumpsters throw trash cans into their trailers. I was itching to get moving, and Facebook threw me a lifeline.

SAILING TODAY? CAN WORK AROUND YOUR SCHEDULE

I'd picked up hundreds of American Facebook followers on my first journey across the USA and one of them, John Price, lived in Seattle. By early afternoon, I was travelling across town, over the Lake Washington Ship Canal and out to Shilshole Bay Marina, on the east coast of Puget Sound.

It felt like a blind date. Two strangers meeting in a public place, with almost zero knowledge of each other. But when I found John, tinkering around on the bright white deck of a 40-foot yacht, with Crosby, Stills, Nash & Young tittering out from his smartphone and a bucket of beers covered in ice, I could see we were kindred spirits.

Aged 50, dressed in blue jeans, a long-sleeved black T-shirt, a green baseball cap and wraparound shades, John had saltwater running through his veins. Working as a commercial fishing boat captain, he disappeared into the Pacific for weeks on end.

Feeling safe under his command, I had just one job: to slip the stern spring and jump on deck before the gap between me and the pontoon widened. It was a task I only just managed and panicked my limbs aboard. We then manoeuvred gently through the parking bays, taking extra care not to create a wake or startle fellow sailors on their floating homes. This was a courtesy that experienced mariners, like John, took seriously. Because when a chubby motor cruiser rushed towards us, helmed by a shirtless teenage boy with a gold chain dangled around his chest, John briefly lost his cool. 'Slow the fuck down! Jackass!' he screamed, as we rounded a breakwater and entered Puget Sound, Seattle's watery playground.

For a fair-weather sailor like me, the conditions were next to perfect. And by 'perfect' I mean barely a breath of wind. When we limped in from the Pacific in April 2016, our bowsprit had been snapped and hung forlornly from the foredeck. Our mainsail flaunted dinnerplate-sized wounds and resembled a giant motheaten bedsheet. Seven years on and I was back again, sipping cold beer under a crisp blue sky. It was easy to forget about the 4,000-mile bike ride that started the next morning.

John, however, was concerned for my wellbeing. 'I can't even begin to fathom how ridiculous things are going to get for you out there,' he said, as we switched off the motor and threw up a flaccid spinnaker sail. More out of routine than a genuine hope of catching the wind.

John had spent two years in the United States Marine Corps, before being discharged with a heart problem. The military was hardwired into his sense of self. 'I was never deployed,' he said, as a few fluffy cumulus clouds reflected in his mirrored shades. 'It's not uncommon for people who have never been deployed to feel a little guilty that they never had the chance to go and fight, and I'm one of those people.'

In the space of just a few hundred years, America had, in John's opinion, become 'the financial and military leader of the world' – an entity worth defending. This rise to superpower status had helped create the 'pull up your bootstraps and get it done' attitude that many Americans still live their lives by. He did, however, concede that times were changing. American supremacy had waned. Moreover, having chartered boats all over the world, he could view his country from a foreign perspective. 'People see America as arrogant, overstated,' said John. 'And increasingly confused about its role in the world.'

This contradicted the romanticised view instilled within him by his grandfather, who saw America as 'the greatest country on earth'. A nation that championed healthy debate on home soil but fought common enemies overseas.

'People who have grown up in the past 20 or 30 years haven't had a war to rally around like my grandfather did. All they've had is a lot of hyperbole and reasons to try to not get along with people. Back then, it was all about coming together and I think he would be disappointed that doesn't exist today.'

John and I enjoyed a couple of hours in deep conversation, simply pootling around on Puget Sound. We admired swanky seaside homes with swimming pools, solar panels and private moorings. We rescued a rubber ring that had escaped from a passing cruise ship and admired double-crested cormorants drying their outstretched wings atop barnacled crags.

We decided, however, to call it a day when we saw an ominous charcoal-coloured cloud gaining ground on us from the west. A weather front saturating the Olympic Peninsula. Exactly where I'd be heading the next morning.

Instead of dropping me off at my hotel, John gave me a lift to the University District, a bustling neighbourhood filled with fresh faces. Even at 36 I felt ancient, already twice the age of the freshmen around me. I was also feeling half cut and ready for bed, but I had one final meeting, with Professor Mark Smith, a political scientist from the University of Washington. I'd been drawn to his work on American domestic politics, religion and public policy while planning my trip, and he'd generously agreed to meet up for a beer at a local brewery. He was a svelte and casually dressed man in his early fifties, wearing jeans and a bright red Philadelphia Phillies T-shirt.

'There will be parts of this country where you're going to see lots of American flags,' Mark told me, as we surveyed the vast selection of porters, pilsners and pale ales. 'But then in others you'll hardly see any flags. That is a pretty strong indicator of the political leanings of that area.'

According to a 2018 Pew Research Center poll, 50 per cent of Republicans described public displays of the American flag as 'very important' to being a good citizen, compared with just 25 per cent of Democrats. 'You'll also see a lot of overt religious symbols. Billboards with things like: JESUS SAVES. And that will correlate with the number of flags.'

Washington State hadn't elected a Republican candidate since 1984. In 2020, Joe Biden defeated Donald Trump by a margin of 58 per cent to 39 per cent. Seattle remains a blue Democrat stronghold within a mostly red Republican state. Statistically, this mirrors a trend seen across the United States, and in Britain. Conservative voters are more likely to reside in rural areas.

'The same kind of places that supported Brexit will be the same kind of places that supported Trump,' said Mark, as we settled into a second beer. He was fascinated by what I might find on my journey and curious to understand what intimidated me the most. The huge distances? The weather?

'I think the thing I'm worried about most is meeting overtly religious people,' I replied. 'Christians especially. And not knowing what to say.'

'In regard to?'

'Well, I would consider myself a ... christened atheist? But I'm not Christian. I'm fascinated by religion, and how people choose to live their lives, but personally I don't believe in God.'

'I think if you describe yourself as a "christened atheist" then you'll confuse people. But if you explain what you really mean by that, and that you respect the Christian heritage, even though you don't accept the supernatural claims, then I don't think too many people will be surprised by that answer.'

In his lifetime, Mark had seen Christianity go from being the dominant religion in the United States to now 'feeling more like an embattled minority'. According to a poll conducted by Gallup in 1989, 82 per cent of Americans described themselves as Christian. In surveys conducted by the Pew Research Center in 2018 and 2019, that number had declined to 65 per cent.

With miles to ride, and academic papers to read, respectively, we decided that two beers were enough. But as I stumbled off to catch a cab, I asked Mark one final question.

'What words will I hear more than any other?'

'God. Guns. And Country.'

3

AN OLYMPIC FEAT

When I opened my eyes the next morning, the first thing I saw was my bike. Packed and poised at the end of my bed, as sobering as an ice-cold shower. So far, this cycle tour had been easy, with barely any cycling involved. But this was it. Time to hit the road.

Nursing a hangover, I downed two pints of water, a can of 'full fat' Coca-Cola and three paracetamols. And after a final check of my belongings: passport, laptop, camera, etc, I checked out and descended seven steep city blocks to Seattle's ferry terminal: my ticket to pastures new.

It was a sunglasses and gloves start to the day, and as the passenger ferry rumbled westward across Puget Sound, the city grew wider behind me, like a cinema screen swelling to 16:9. I was determined to at least start the trip with good eating habits, so refrained from the greasy breakfast sandwich – sausage, egg and cheese – and chose the oatmeal instead. Albeit, drizzled in a double helping of sticky maple syrup.

I was, of course, travelling in the wrong direction. Mostly out of gluttony for punishment, rather than any other rational explanation. I would need to spend the entire day on public transport, weaving my way northwest around the coast of the Olympic Peninsula, making changes at Bainbridge Island, Port Angeles and Neah Bay. All going to plan, I'd arrive at Cape Flattery at some point in late afternoon.

For the first few hours, I had the company of two fellow touring cyclists, a delightful couple in their mid-seventies named Dave and Julie. They were on their way to Vancouver Island for nine days' cycling and camping. The front of

Julie's T-shirt read: LIFE IS SIMPLE. EAT, SLEEP, EAT. RIDE MY BIKE.

With two hours to kill at Bainbridge, we huddled into a bus stop for protection from the bracing seaside wind. Dave and I shared a copy of the local newspaper, the *Bainbridge Island Review*. Top story: Bainbridge opens arms to distraught Maui pickleball players after devastating fires. Julie pulled out her knitting needles and started tip-tapping away.

'What are you making?' I asked.

'A dishcloth. They're my speciality.'

In their younger days, both had embarked upon much longer bicycle expeditions. Dave had gone to Britain, to ride John o' Groats to Land's End, but confessed to taking a train to Portsmouth when snow engulfed the Cairngorms. Julie, however, had cycled coast to coast across the USA in the summer of 2002. Less than a year after the 9/11 terrorist attacks on New York and the Pentagon.

'I went partly because of 9/11 and partly in spite of 9/11,' said Julie, as she looked up from her knitting needles and out to a pair of silky-black ravens, skipping like toddlers around the bus park. 'I wanted to feel a renewed sense of connection with America.'

Like many people on this planet, American or otherwise, I remember 11 September 2001 vividly. Returning home from school and flicking on the TV, I wasn't met with trashy kids' programming but live coverage of New York in turmoil. A catastrophic, historic event, playing out not in the pages of a textbook, but in real time.

In the months that followed, Julie felt unsafe in Seattle. She wanted to be as far away from major cities as possible. She yearned to explore the wild places at the centre of the country. So, travelling in a small group, she camped on farms and in national parks. She chatted to ranchers about drought and climate change. The trip opened her eyes to the epic scale and diversity of America. A nation grieving.

'We were all proud of the United States then,' said Julie. 'We felt more together. Now I think we are more divided than I've ever experienced, in a bitter way. When you get into politics, that's maybe ... painful.'

Politics, said Dave, had become a taboo subject within their family and friendship groups. His sister was a vociferous Trump supporter. 'It's best to not even go there anymore,' he told me, with a bounce of his bushy eyebrows.

He was adamant that I would find good people across the country, irrespective of their political affiliation. He did, however, raise an issue I'd not considered before.

'Your bike is likely to give people the impression that you're left-leaning. A liberal.'

'A bike? Are you serious?'

'A bicycle in the US is a political statement. It shows you're thinking about the planet by not using gas.'

Our conversation ended abruptly when the bus arrived. Frantically, we set about throwing our panniers into the storage hold and then secured our bicycles to a precarious-looking frame at the front, on the outside, beneath the driver's windscreen.

We didn't say much more after that. Instead, we took our seats and set off on a winding black road through a vast forest. Dense with Douglas firs, Sitka spruce and western red cedars, the tallest trees rose almost 300 feet. A hint of Canadian wildfire still lingered on the wind. When the noon sun broke through, it cast laser-like beams through the canopy.

I spent the first half hour of the journey fretting about how secure – or insecure – my bicycle looked at the front of the bus. It was hooked on only by a flimsy metal clip and I was convinced it would fall beneath the wheels and be crumpled like an aluminium can. I then spent the next hour mulling over what Dave had said, about a bicycle being a lefty political statement. Sure, my bicycle was an icebreaker, an object that attracted strangers. But I certainly didn't want to repel anyone, either. I didn't want my interviewees to think that I had an agenda or bias. I just wanted to meet strangers at random. To better understand America, at a gentle pace.

By the time I arrived in Port Angeles, a small seaside town on the Strait of Juan de Fuca, just 23 nautical miles south of the Canadian town of Victoria, I had made peace with the idea that some outcomes might be uncontrollable.

I scoffed a quick lunch with the local tourism officer, Marsha Massey, who kindly armed me with a bagful of snacks and a can of noxious capsicum spray, capable of stopping a bear from 40 feet away. Then I took two further buses westward to Neah Bay, the northwestern-most town in the contiguous United States, home of the Makah, a Native American tribe that have lived in the region for almost 4,000 years. A quiet seaside community of just 1,100 people, with a gas station, a couple of motels and a takeaway taco restaurant, the Makah refer to themselves as the *qʷidičča?aˑtx̌*, which translates, roughly, to 'the people who live by the rocks and seagulls'.

In 1855, a Makah council signed the Treaty of Neah Bay with the US federal government, ceding much of their historic lands. This restricted them to just 48 square miles but did preserve their right to hunt seals and whales, harpooned from cedar canoes. In 1936, the tribe signed the Makah Constitution, accepting the Indian Reorganization Act. This US federal legislation encouraged the preservation of Native American cultures and traditions. Originally, the Makah lived in longhouses. Now, however, their homes are made mostly from single-storey clapboard, with views north towards Canada. I found front yards filled with intricately carved, multicoloured totems depicting whales and eagles, but also scrap cars, lawnmowers and plastic children's toys. Much of the local economy depends on fishing and tourism. For many, Neah Bay is seen as a place of escape and pilgrimage, attracting fishermen, holidaymakers and waifs like me, desperate to reach the very edge of the map.

On the bus, I'd eavesdropped on a conversation between two men sharing a small bottle of bourbon. One of them, aged about 20, was 'just drifting about, seeing the country for a while'. He was wary of the 'suffocation of office jobs' and 'conforming to normality'. The other man, about 40, had refurbished a yacht and was about to begin a five-year circumnavigation of the planet.

At the bus stop, I met a male touring cyclist in his early thirties. He had spent 18 months cycling 3,000 miles from Alabama, in the southeast of the country. 'I go where the work takes me,' he said, while attaching panniers to his bike. 'Seasonal work, mostly. Picking grapes, apples, lobsters, oysters.'

Weather-beaten and visibly exhausted, he gave off a jaded vibe.

Disillusioned with adventure, he only answered questions when asked. It was an awkward and one-sided conversation. What made him even more curious was that he was doing it all with a chihuahua, sat in a small box on the back of his bike.

Neah Bay was just eight miles east of Cape Flattery, but with no more public transport for assistance, I would need to either cycle or hitch there. I was desperate to ride and finally get moving. The biggest issue, however, was the fading light. It was now four o'clock, and a cool, murky dusk had already descended.

Thankfully, Zaliyah – the helpful young lady at the tourist information centre – had a plan. For $20, her brother, Ou'axs, could give me a ride in his truck. So, with my bike and panniers lobbed into the cargo bed, we set off west, into a dingy green forest, screeching around tight corners and past big blue signposts warning of catastrophic Pacific Ocean tsunamis.

Zaliyah and Ou'axs, aged 20 and 19, respectively, felt caught at a cultural crossroads – members of an indigenous culture, while also living in an often hyper-modern country.

'We're not very … What's the word? Committed to America,' said Zaliyah.

'Is that a family thing?' I asked. 'Or a cultural thing? Were you taught that at school?'

'Going to a pretty much all-white school, pretty much all my classmates were racist,' said Ou'axs. 'Experiencing that made me feel … not a part of America. In my class, there were Black people, Asian people, white people and me. It made me feel separate from other people.'

According to the Native American Center for Excellence, 20.8 per cent of Native Americans aged 18 to 25 have experienced alcohol use disorders. Illegal drug use is higher than in any other ethnic minority. People from indigenous cultures are statistically more likely to take their own lives. They have the highest rate of death from hepatitis C.

Had centuries of racial, cultural, political and economic subjugation left them resenting America?

'I feel like that resentment is more in young people's minds, like mine,' said Zaliyah. 'If there was a resentment held by the majority of our community, then a lot of our community wouldn't be Christian, because Christians have an historic past of treating Native Americans horribly.'

As the road grew steeper and then steeper some more, I was glad I wasn't cycling. I'd never have made it before dark. I was in awe of Zaliyah and Ou'axs' honesty. Especially towards some random British bloke they'd only just met, asking increasingly awkward questions. I wasn't surprised they didn't feel particularly at one with the wider United States. Nevertheless, their gregarious and talkative manner was, to me, an unequivocally American trait. Unfiltered, honest, concise.

No more so was this evident than when we reached Cape Flattery. As a trans tribesperson, Ou'axs had struggled to make sense of their place within the Makah.

'No one wants to, like … modernise our culture, or let it expand at all. I'm a trans masculine person, and a couple of years ago I tried dancing the men's dance and I got in trouble with the elders. That made me not want to sing or dance or be part of the culture. When I asked people if we could have both feminine and masculine energies, I had people laugh in my face and tell me that there is only male or female.'

They dropped me off at the Cape Flattery trailhead and wished me good luck. It was almost 5pm but this still wasn't the start line. Instead, I had to hide my bike behind a tree and run. I hadn't come all this way not to see the Pacific Ocean.

A 4,000-mile cross-country bike ride therefore began with a two-mile jog, along a treacherous boardwalk covered in slippery moss and fallen branches. I passed day trippers tiptoeing slowly with Nordic poles. They only needed to get back to their cars by nightfall. In contrast, my 'slow journalism' journey was beginning in an almighty rush. Goodness knows what I must have looked like. This was high-speed tourism. But I somehow made it down to an observation deck without breaking an ankle and then finally clapped eyes on the ocean. I could see dumpy little islets browned by seaweed. Some were big enough to support trees. On others, I spotted dopey harbour seals, with dog-like faces and greasy pelts, speckled in creamy-beige spots. If I'd have spent a few hours appreciating the view, I might have seen killer, humpback or gray whales, all of which migrate through the Strait of Juan de Fuca. Instead, I took a couple of photos and was out of there in a flash. I sprinted back to my bike and hastily threw on some cycling clothes.

I'd twinged a hamstring before making a single rotation of the pedals. Nonetheless, this was finally it. Under starter's orders. And with night falling rapidly, I hit the road and grinned until my jaw ached. One car slowed down and tooted its horn. 'Yeaaahhhhhhhhhhh, dude!' screamed a man from the passenger-side window.

I have few hard and fast rules as a touring cyclist. It's best to try to go with the flow. But rule one is sacrosanct: do not cycle at night. Or worse: dusk. Visibility is often dreadful at the transition between day and night, and this evening was no different. An eerie fog blanketed the road like froth on a cappuccino. Cars raced up behind me, then suddenly dropped their revs when they saw my bright red panniers in the twilight.

I followed a winding road engulfed by trees. Spooky and impenetrable, the forest echoed with rustles, whistles and hoots. A few miles in, a large rat-like creature, most likely an Olympic marmot, scrambled across the asphalt. Bears scared me the most, though. Black ones. Smaller and darker than their grizzly cousins, but no less capable of inflicting serious harm, especially when spooked or with cubs. There was also the risk of bumping into a cougar; these cats can weigh up to 100 kilograms and run at 50mph. Less than a month before my arrival, an eight-year-old boy had been attacked by one near Port Angeles, miraculously escaping serious injury.

My sense of danger, however, was amplified by exhaustion. In wild places, especially at night, the human mind can play tricks on itself. It was easy to imagine eyes staring back at me from the undergrowth. This was Sasquatch territory, A.K.A. Big Foot, the hairy human-like creature purported to roam the forests of the Pacific Northwest. On the bus journey, I'd seen coffee shops, convenience stores and restaurants guarded by 10-foot-tall cedar carvings. Most resembled stocky nightclub bouncers in desperate need of an Immac.

It took me an hour to get back to Neah Bay. Feeling rushed but famished, I stopped for an 'Indian taco' at Pat's Place. The restaurant's owner, and namesake, welcomed me into the greasy warmth like an old friend.

'Some people come here because they think it's the end of the world,' said Pat, as she handed me a wedge of deep-fried bread covered in minced beef, iceberg lettuce, tomato salsa and grated cheese. 'But us locals prefer to see Neah Bay as the beginning of the world.'

Stuffed, I dragged myself back out into the cold and continued eastward into the night for a further 90 minutes, to a motel in Sekiu, a small village with a north-facing, granite-coloured beach scattered with sodden driftwood.

When I cycled across the USA in 2016, I camped pretty much every night. In national parks, on the roadside, on sports fields. I didn't have much choice. I was flat broke but determined to get across the country by any means. On this trip, however, I'd decided to use cheap motels – partly out of safety, for myself and my possessions. My bicycle and tech had a combined value of roughly £10,000. And partly out of necessity. To do my job as a journalist my gadgets needed to be dry and fully charged. I had interviews to record and log for this book, and videos to film and edit for my YouTube channel and theatre tour.

If I'm also totally honest, as I've grown older, I've become less evangelical about wild camping, especially where bears roam. At the end of a long day getting beaten by the elements, I prefer to close a door and feel safe. I am not one of those people who can simply curl up on a park bench and get eight hours' restful sleep. The physicality of the trip ahead of me demanded proper rest. Without it, I'd risk making silly decisions on the road and almost certainly fall ill. Go a few days without proper sleep and your immune system takes a nosedive.

My motel that night gave off a Hitchcockian *Psycho* vibe. Many cheap motels do. Nevertheless, for $50 I got a double bed, a microwave, refrigerator and all the electricity a journalist could ever need. The elderly man at reception also kindly gifted me a cold beer, to celebrate the start of my journey.

'Quite the trip. Quite the trip,' he repeated about half a dozen times.

'Do you think I really need this bear spray?' I asked, showing him the can I'd been lugging around all day.

'You might not need it for anything with four legs. But I'd definitely keep hold of it for those with two.'

I rolled out early the next morning on to Highway 112, eager to establish a sense of routine. Overnight, my phone had received a text message welcoming me to Canada. Across the Strait of Juan de Fuca, I could just make out mountains on Vancouver Island, partially cloaked in a silvery haze.

On American soil, it was a cold, bright dawn, lulled by the hum of gently lapping waves. The road was lumpy but enjoyable. Up and down. Up and down. Like a rollercoaster, fringed with pastel-hued lupins, their bell-like petals heavy with a sequined dew.

Out of nowhere, I felt a swoosh of energy just a few feet above my head. A bald eagle – the national bird of the United States – with seven-foot-wide russet wings. It had a bright white head and a hook-like, mustardy beak. As I let out an involuntary squeal of both fear and excitement, I watched it glide off down the road, its talons dangling limply.

The forest canopy paraded the first signs of a golden-red autumn. This was a wild and calming place. Apart from the huge trucks. They zoomed up behind me, pulling 30-tonne trailers chock-full of spruce and fir trunks already stripped of their bark, resembling giant unsharpened pencils. In some places, the shoulder narrowed to just a few inches and I winced as they roared towards me. All I could do was hope that I'd been seen and that the burly truckers behind their wheels hadn't missed their early morning brews.

The local tourism office had warned against cycling the narrow Highway 112, instead championing the Olympic Discovery Trail (ODT), one of America's newest long-distance biking routes. It was billed as a much safer and even prettier alternative. First, though, I'd need to stock up on supplies. If the map was to be believed, then I was committing to a greatly protracted route, with no reliable pitstops.

At the gas station in Clallam Bay, I bought a coffee, four bagels, 250 grams of peanut butter, a litre of Gatorade, two bananas, a few sachets of peanuts and a small sandwich. It all came to a surprisingly expensive $30.

On the road south, I saw just three cars in two hours, but I did pass sprawling forested properties with cabins hidden deep within their shadows. Some flew flags from their roadside fences. Mostly of a left-leaning persuasion. Outside one home a billboard read: 'IN THIS HOUSE WE BELIEVE ... LOVE IS LOVE. BLACK LIVES MATTER. SCIENCE IS REAL. FEMINISM IS FOR EVERYONE. NO HUMAN IS ILLEGAL. KINDNESS IS EVERYTHING.'

A couple of miles further down the road, though, another property conformed to the rural, Republican-supporting tropes that political scientist Mark Smith had told me to expect. I spotted four dinner-table-sized flags: a star-spangled banner, one with a coiled snake and the words 'DON'T TREAD ON ME.' Another read 'TRUMP 2024: FUCK YOUR FEELINGS.' And a final one: 'FUCK BIDEN.'

In Britain, you might see the occasional A4-sized glossy placard in a kitchen window expressing support for the Liberal Democrats. Here, in a remote corner of the Pacific Northwest, American citizens aired their views across square footages bigger than my two-bedroom flat.

The ODT certainly didn't disappoint. A mostly sealed or gravel bicycle route, at times it was heavily forested and hemmed in by ferns, at others it opened out into 50-acre bowls of savannah-like grassland. Thank goodness it was cool, just 11 or 12 degrees centigrade, because there was barely a flat section to speak of. When I stopped at the top of a 500-foot climb to finally remove my waterproof trousers and jacket, my body gave off swirling plumes of steam. It was as though I'd just emerged from a Turkish hammam.

About 50 miles east of Neah Bay, I bumped into the first people I'd seen all day. Four middle-aged men on expensive mountain bikes, stopping for lunch. Proud Northwesterners, they enjoyed spending time in the great outdoors and wouldn't dream of living anywhere else in the country.

'I have never seen this country more fucked up,' said one, as he fiddled with a front brake pad. 'I won't step foot in Florida ever again. I won't give them a fucking dime.'

He was enraged by the state's governor, Ron DeSantis, and his so-called 'War on Woke'.

'Do you think I'm stupid to cycle across the country?' I asked.

The men paused for a moment's thought.

'You'll find good people, that's for sure. But I hope you're ready to see guns, son. Because you're going to see shitloads of guns! You be really fucking careful out there, buddy.'

I left them to their packed lunches and continued east, around the north coast of Lake Crescent, a bright blue body of water spread across more than 5,000 shimmering acres. Low levels of nitrogen have inhibited the growth of algae, making for exceptional clarity. As I followed the trail, at stages almost overhanging the lake, I could see huge sunken logs. Some must have been 40 or 50 feet beneath the surface.

Twisting and turning, up and down, the trail was beautiful but indirect. Feeling heavy, I daydreamed about throwing all my weighty possessions into the nearest trashcan. The irony, however, was that I was probably travelling lighter than I ever had before.

Most cycle routes are designed for local people on slow-moving day rides, not for touring cyclists attempting to get from one side of the country to the other. The ODT is spectacular, easily one of the best trails in America, and I'd love to get back there for a week-long holiday. But I needed to be wary of taking route advice from people who clearly didn't cycle. It is an innocent flaw of the non-cyclist, to fail to fully grasp how challenging a ride may be. By taking the ODT, I turned a 50-mile day into 90 miles and climbed around 3,000 unnecessary feet.

On the flipside, however, a sparsely inhabited route is excellent for meeting people. Because when you do eventually encounter another soul, it feels like a mini event. It would feel rude to just cycle on by.

Somewhere around the northeast corner of the lake, I was passed by two recumbent cyclists in their seventies. They saw my panniers and turned back. We started with the formalities but then quickly got into the meaty stuff.

'Hey, let me ask you a question,' said the man, as he handed me an apple. 'You're a millennial, right?'

'Yeah, pretty much.'

'Well, supposedly you guys and us, the baby boomers, we hate each other, yeah? That's just hype. It's not true. It just sells papers. That stereotype is not right.'

The couple had moved from Seattle to the forest during the pandemic. Country life, they told me, was a much friendlier, calmer existence. Most of their friends were half their age. America, however, had changed considerably in their lifetimes.

'The flames are being fanned by the mainstream media,' the man went on. 'It's good for the election, put it that way. But it's just not real.'

The couple were worried about the southern border with Mexico, the struggling economy and rising homelessness. Before retiring, the lady had worked as a healthcare professional 'taking care of the poor'. Since then, however, she had lost faith in America's approach to supporting those in need.

'It's a failure,' said the woman. 'There are people down on their luck but I don't think our [Democrat] policies are helping at all. It's getting worse.'

'Can you really pin that on a Democrat administration?' I asked.

'The people in my field are generally very liberal. But we have a liberal government now and the homeless population has never been like this. So, is it a correlation? Or is it a cause and effect?'

By the time I reached Port Angeles, almost 12 hours after leaving Sekiu, every muscle burned. It had been nowhere near the gentle first day I'd planned. I checked into a cheap motel, downed a can of lager and dined on a crab sandwich with fries, slathered in lashings of creamy mayonnaise.

With a perfect half-moon glistening high in the sky, I spent the evening lying prone, lactic acid filling my legs and stomach acid singeing my oesophagus. A case of savage indigestion. Unsurprising, really, considering the random smorgasbord of food I'd consumed that day:

- Two bagels smothered in peanut butter
- One packet of cookies
- Two bananas
- Three packets of peanuts
- A bag of Haribo
- Two litres of Gatorade
- A litre of Cherry Coke
- A turkey and cheese sandwich
- Four apples
- Ten litres of water with electrolyte, glutamine and BCAA powder
- A can of beer
- A crab sandwich with fries
- Three Gaviscon Double Action

4

OLD-NEW FRIENDS

I set off at 6.30 the next morning, deciding to ignore Google's cycle route and follow the busier but more direct Highway 101 instead. I'd woken to a stream of messages on my social media feeds from people all over the world. Most were posts of support, wishing me fair winds and good luck for the days and weeks ahead. One, however, left me feeling peeved: 'IT LOOKS LIKE YOU'RE CARRYING TOO MUCH WEIGHT.'

In the subculture of bicycle touring this is the ultimate passive aggression, almost always dished out by a middle-aged keyboard warrior – self-anointed experts who believe they ride bicycles better than any other adult, or toddler, on planet earth. I wrote out a narky reply but deleted it. It wasn't worth the stress. Instead, I left a few people to quarrel among themselves and opted to savour the ephemeral beauty around me. This was my real life journey, after all.

The morning was grey, dry and windless, optimum conditions for covering ground. My saddle, however, felt harder than the one I'd stepped off the night before. The next few days would be plagued with aches and pains.

On the edge of town, beneath the golden arches of a McDonald's, eight deer skipped through the parking lot and down the centre of the four-lane highway. I stopped to get my first 'Maccers' of the trip. Calories, but of little nutritional value. As I munched through two breakfast muffins and a pot of plaster of Paris-like oatmeal, I reminded myself that some food was better than none.

The highway was lined with vape stores, adult toy emporiums, delivery depots and tennis-court-sized billboards inscribed with slogans like 'CHRIST IS LORD'. I passed a warehouse selling healing crystals. It had a car-sized image of glistening quartz on its corrugated iron roof. There were also half a dozen cannabis dispensaries – recreational use is legal in Washington – selling pipes, bongs and fresh donuts. One shop proudly offered a 'discount' of '30 per cent off every day', which struck me as business logic dreamed up after a particularly big day on the high grade.

The shoulder was as wide as a British country lane but, unlike on the pristine ODT, cars rushed beside me. It was hard to determine if I was getting healthier from the cycling or sicker from the fumes. It was therefore a relief to reach the wild edge of Sequim Bay State Park and join a smaller, quieter road, Highway 101, oddly dedicated to the Sequim Picklers, the local pickleball club.

Since the mid-1980s, America's Adopt-a-Highway programme has encouraged local volunteers to not just name but be responsible for clearing litter from a particular section of highway. When I cycled across the USA in 2016, it became a source of uplifting, albeit wry humour. I travelled on roads dedicated to local politicians, florists, high school quarterbacks and dog groomers. In principle, the scheme is open to all and sundry; however, it did become a point of controversy when the Ku Klux Klan adopted a portion of Interstate 55 just south of St Louis, Missouri.

I spent the next hour amusing myself with a few British alternatives. The Frank Skinner Highway, connecting West Bromwich with Birmingham. The Diane Abbott Byway, between Hackney and Leyton. The Mr Blobby Ring Road, linking Crinkley Bottom with … itself.

East of Sequim, Highway 101 became a hellish road. Just a single lane running in either direction with a narrow sliver of black tarmac serving as a meagre, trash-filled shoulder. I swerved around used syringes and smashed tequila bottles, flipflops, bungee straps, nappies. Two-litre soda bottles filled with fluorescent orange urine: the unmistakable calling card of a trucker in a hurry.

There was also an abattoir's quantity of roadkill, all in various states of decomposition. Black-tailed deer, their stomachs bloated with gas. A beautiful boreal owl, its fluffy plumage trembling in the breeze. With one eye wide open and the other one closed, it had been frozen in a comical yet spooky wink. A few miles further down the road, I bumped over the feather-duster-like tail of a racoon. Occupying the full width of the shoulder with its arms and legs outstretched, it resembled a cricketer diving for a catch at gully.

I was desperate to get to the other side of Seattle, where I knew Washington's highways cut through sprawling fields of wheat. The trade-off, however, would be the heat. The state's agricultural heartland had been experiencing a searing, summer-long heatwave. But for now, I had cool temperatures and a gentle tailwind. Enough to feel like I was making progress. The main problem that day was getting used to the bike again. Nothing, apart from riding, can adequately prepare you for spending long periods in the saddle. For the entire afternoon, I wriggled from one arse cheek to the other, desperately searching for a sense of oneness between my perineum and the flexible rubber beneath.

At the end of a slightly easier day than the previous one, I reached Poulsbo, 73 miles southeast of Port Angeles. I'd been invited to stay at the Ground Zero Center for Nonviolent Action, a 2.5-acre property that backs on to the US Navy's Bangor Trident Base, the highest concentration of nuclear weapons on earth.

I left the road and entered through a tunnel of spruce trees. Sunflowers and conifers surrounded a Buddhist peace pagoda and a conference hall. For more than 50 years, the centre has served as a hub for America's Campaign for Nuclear Disarmament. Oddly, I'd mentioned my visit to about a dozen people in the previous days but no one had heard of it – or the arsenal. There was enough uranium housed there to blow our earth to smithereens, yet the place went under the radar. In Britain, you can barely erect a garden shed without the parish council getting involved. Yet here stood the world's biggest collection of nuclear weapons and people living a few miles away didn't know it existed.

'This place was bought in the 1970s as a way of bringing people together, to work against the nuclear weapons that are based right on the other side of the fence,' said Kathryn Railsback, the centre's resident activist, who welcomed me with a big smile and a glass of iced water. 'We just had nine people arrested for blocking the gates during part of our Hiroshima-Nagasaki remembrance event.'

Kathryn lived with her Chinese-American husband, Bill,

and their 15-year-old deaf and blind terrier, Buddy. After a quick shower, she took me on a tour of the property and to see the fence that separated their land from the naval base. Harshly juxtaposed with the tranquillity of their flower gardens, the wire barrier stood roughly 12 feet tall. One sign read: 'WARNING. RESTRICTED AREA. KEEP OUT. AUTHORIZED PERSONNEL ONLY.' Another read: 'WARNING. PATROLLED BY MILITARY WORKING DOGS.'

It took less than five minutes for a white pickup filled with armed men to drive slowly past us on the other side. I had been tempted to fly my drone over the pagoda but decided that the US Navy was an enemy I didn't need. At least not this early in the trip.

'We have always tried to maintain good relations with the base,' said Kathryn. 'To let them know that this is not about them personally, it's more about protesting against the weapons themselves, which we feel are horrific and shouldn't exist. It's also a waste of resources, to be designing them, maintaining them and storing them.'

The Unites States owns 5,240 nuclear warheads, second only to Russia, with more than 6,000. Less than 15 miles from where we stood, around 1,200 bombs were stored, either on land or within the US Navy's Pacific fleet of Trident submarines. In 2023, the United States dedicated $817 billion to its military, more than any other country on earth.

In an act of peaceful protest, Kathryn and her fellow activists had hung multicoloured paper garlands from the fence. Mother Nature was also doing her bit. Fifty sunflowers with bright yellow petals pointed defiantly towards the base. Buddy played his part, too. He ambled over and cocked his right hind leg.

Inside the centre, bookshelves burst with tomes dedicated to peaceful protest, beside sketches of Mahatma Gandhi and Martin Luther King Jr. A rainbow peace flag dangled from a staircase. Dozens of posters were inscribed with messages like: 'SEEKING ASYLUM IS A HUMAN RIGHT' and 'BELIEVE THERE IS GOOD IN THE WORLD'.

Bill was a superb cook and whizzed up a delicious dinner of sweet and sour shrimp, roast chicken, brown rice and foo young

(Chinese omelette). When their two adult children left home, Kathryn convinced him they should move to Poulsbo from Minneapolis to look after the centre. It was an unpaid position but provided them with a free place to live. Their work involved hosting academics, campaigners and the occasional journalist, while also helping to arrange peaceful blockades on nearby roads. Fascinatingly, Kathryn told me that the US Navy had taught a team of dolphins to assist with underwater surveillance. Trained in the warm waters off San Diego before then being relocated to the frigid Northwest, one of the centre's light-hearted campaigns had been to offer them woolly jumpers.

'My understanding is that they're trained to attack possible intruders and defend the nuclear weapons, I guess due to their superior diving skills. And I think it's a terrible use of these animals that are so impressive.'

Not long after we'd finished eating, a few fellow activists arrived clutching cheesecakes, cookies and tubs of ice cream, and I spent the next hour hearing stories of arrests and run-ins with the law. One of the activists, 82-year-old Sue Ablao, had served as a previous caretaker. She had been arrested 'five or six times', most recently just a few weeks before.

'This time there was a group of us that blocked the road and did a little flash mob dance,' said Sue. 'And then the State Patrol gave us about five minutes in the road. Then they said that anyone left in the road after that will be arrested.'

Sue stayed and was given a citation by the police 'for being a person in the road illegally' followed by a court summons. Instead of pleading guilty, many of the protesters choose to 'mitigate' their sentencing. This gives them the right to voice their opinions publicly in court. Sometimes the fine is as little as $5 or the charge is thrown out by the judge entirely. The naval base is, however, ringed by a painted blue line. Step over it and the misdemeanour is escalated to a federal court. 'All you have to do is cross the line, then it's six months in prison and a $5,000 fine,' said Sue.

Some protesters had gone the whole hog, just to prove their point. Sue, however, believed she was of more use outside a jail cell. Albeit, in the face of powerful political forces.

'I think people are more aware now, both financially and existentially, of the cost of nuclear weapons. But I haven't seen a whole lot of change in policy. For that to happen, we would have to have a huge change in the system as a whole. Our government is run and financed by big corporations. As long as that is happening, things aren't going to change much. Sometimes it feels like you're beating your head against a brick wall, but sometimes that's what it takes to make a change.'

I was given the guest room, which also doubled up as a store cupboard for rolled-up banners and placards on sticks. I'd only been on the road for a few days but already my panniers were in a state of chaos, so I emptied everything out, then put everything back in. I then attempted to fall asleep, knowing that just outside my bedroom window were enough nuclear warheads to vaporise me and the entire western hemisphere in seconds. Not exactly 'Twinkle, Twinkle, Little Star'.

After filling me with strong black coffee, scrambled eggs and toast, Katherine, Bill and Buddy waved me off at dawn, down the spruce-lined road and into a morning of quiet contemplation. Their efforts, while admirable, seemed somewhat futile. What would it take for America, and its fellow superpowers, to reassess the 'nuclear deterrent'? The bizarre human falsehood of Mutual Assured Destruction (MAD). How long until a mishap or terrorist attack? A planet-sized burden rests in the hands of a tiny – sometimes unhinged and despotic – minority.

Just south of Poulsbo, I passed the naval base and its thick blue line, then continued through sprawling lavender farms turning enormous patches of scorched summer earth a vivid lilac. When the plants' perfume hit the acrid gasoline of the highway, it created an artificial scent, reminiscent of toilet bleach.

I had to get around Seattle in the easiest and safest way possible, so I decided to venture south before then heading east. In theory, it was meant to be an easy morning. In reality, I spent most of it hugging the side of a narrow single-lane road. I became stuck in a bottleneck on a busy road with few options for cyclists. Such was the peril of inventing an idea in my mind without giving too much thought to its realities in the flesh. On screens, my route had seemed simple: cycle between the northwestern and southeastern extremities of the country. I had pictured empty prairies and open roads, but hadn't given enough thought to the densely populated beginning and end. Thankfully, most motorists were reasonably courteous and slowed down as they approached from behind. A few, however, had zero regard for my wellbeing and raced past at 60mph.

About 20 miles into the day, a Winnebago grazed past me pulling a 4×4. I'd only been on the road for a few days but this was becoming a familiar sight. Vehicles pulling other vehicles. Pickup trucks hauling speedboats. RVs dragging family saloons.

I was taken aback by the sheer size of vehicles. By European standards, the cars were garishly and unfathomably enormous. I stopped at a gas station for supplies and watched a woman, probably in her nineties, use a ladder to climb out of a Hummer the size of an elephant. No one, apart from me and my twee British sensibilities, batted an eyelid. Almost every car was inappropriately huge for the driver behind the wheel. A few minutes later, a teenage girl pulled up in a 450-horsepower V8 Ford Raptor and pumped it full of 110 litres of gasoline. For the rest of the morning, I played a silly game with myself to see if the backs of the colossal pickup trucks were actually being used. The results: probably about two in ten. The others were as clean as the day they were born.

I cycled through leafy neighbourhoods on the outskirts of Seattle featuring large clapboard houses surrounded by white picket fences, each with two or three SUVs on their driveways. I was now seeing Stars and Stripes. Lots of them. Fluttering in the same Pacific breeze that blew in from the northwest and pushed me southeast.

On a patch of scrubby wasteland, I stumbled across a boy, probably about nine or ten, shooting beer bottles off a tree stump with an arm-pumped pellet rifle, the first gun I'd seen on my journey so far. Ironically, in the hands of a child.

It was a relatively short and lazy day's cycling, around 50 miles, because I'd been offered a place to stay in Tacoma with Dianne and Tony Steffanko, a couple I'd met in 2016 and had stayed in touch with via Facebook. Somewhere east of the Rocky Mountains, they'd seen me struggling along an empty road and decided to stop in a layby to give me snacks and sports drinks. They then found me places to stay with their friends and family further east and had been keen supporters of my adventures ever since. It would have been remiss of me to cycle through the region and not pay them a visit.

Such was their commitment to the cause that they rode out to meet me about ten miles north of Tacoma and gave me an escort across the Tacoma Narrows Bridge. The 1.3-mile suspension bridge replaced the original 'Galloping Gertie' structure in 1950, after the original one collapsed just four months after opening. Thankfully, this one remains steady as a rock. From the centre of its 188-foot-high roadway we could see men in small boats, fishing for salmon on the glossy surface of Puget Sound.

At their house in Tacoma's southern suburbs, Dianne and Tony began by showing me around my room for the night, a bright white RV with electric blue stripes down its sides. Inside, it had every imaginable modern convenience. Leather seats, double bed, coffee machine, kitchen sink, two-burner hob and an ensuite bathroom. A palace on wheels. It was also wonderfully air conditioned, so we closed the door and pulled a round of ice-cold beers from the refrigerator.

'This is our third RV,' said Tony, as he scrolled through settings on a touchscreen, which I'd naively assumed was a microwave. 'It's a tiny home on wheels. Next week, we're going to the Grand Teton National Park in Wyoming.'

When they weren't taking holidays in Mexico or Panama, they were off exploring their own vast and geographically diverse country. Back at home, however, they flew a large American flag from the roof. Of the little I knew about Tony and Dianne, they didn't conform to the flag-waving Republican stereotype.

'We love America and we want people to know that,' said Tony. 'I have, however, had people stop here in their cars and ask me why I'm flying the flag. The Republican Party has appropriated the flag as a way of making out that they're more patriotic than us [Democrats].'

'It's my flag too,' Dianne chipped in. 'No one is going to take my flag away from me.'

During the 2020 presidential election campaign, they flew pro-Biden flags from their fences. 'People would come and slash them,' said Tony. 'But we taped them back together and put them back up. We became a target.'

Dianne retaliated with something called 'the Rock Stop', a pile of painted stones, inscribed with messages of hope and inspiration that passers-by could help themselves to. 'You have to take a stand! You can't sit back silently.'

They told me to look out for people flying American flags from pickup trucks. Namely, Fords. They had recently seen the image printed on paper napkins at a barbecue. It was, they inferred, a symbol of political passive aggression.

'They thought they were making a statement,' said Tony. By appropriating symbols like the Ford pickup and the national flag, their hosts were trying to suggest that Democrat voters were not as American as them. 'I think it's been part of creating that divide.'

For Dianne, the Supreme Court's overturning of Roe v. Wade, which in 2022 scrapped a woman's constitutional right to an abortion, crossed a political and cultural red line. The decision left her questioning the moral compass of a country she clearly adored.

'I am a graduate of 1972 and I had friends who got abortions when they were in high school. They had to fly to New York to do that, before they became legal. We've been like that for half a century, and now, predominantly men are taking that right away from women. How dare they?'

'We're going backwards,' said Tony. 'Women should have a choice.'

After an hour and three beers in the RV, Dianne threw together a delicious lunch of cheeses, crackers, homegrown tomatoes and cucumbers, and a refreshing iced Jamaican tea, made from sugar and tart hibiscus. You could clearly find fresh and wholesome food, just not in the places I'd been looking. It was the reality of living as a cycling vagabond; I had to rely upon gas stations and fast-food chains. But while I had the opportunity to stock up on vitamins and minerals, I was keen to take it. 'For as long as you're eating, I'm cooking,' said Dianne. 'Help yourself to fruit, and there's more beer if you need it.'

We spent the next couple of hours in Tony's garage fiddling with my bike. In the build-up to the trip, I'd splashed out on a professional bike fit, a meticulous process that contoured the handlebars and saddle to my body's exact shape and size. Good for my shoulders and spine. The change had, however, introduced an infuriating creak. Every time I turned the pedals, it sounded like a distressed mouse was trying to escape from deep within the frame.

If ever there was a place to have a problem with your bike, though, it was in Tony's garage. Calling it a 'man cave' doesn't do it justice. Formula One pitstops contain fewer tools and gadgets. There was an electric tandem bicycle in one corner and a Harley-Davidson in another. Half a dozen bicycles dangled from pulleys rigged to the ceiling. A stack of four alloy car wheels awaited tyres. A blue and red sticker on a tool cupboard read: 'MACHINISTS FOR OBAMA'. Another, on a stainless steel refrigerator, read: 'WE DUMPED TRUMP'. I have seldom seen a man quite so in his element. An engineer for 40 years, Tony owned every conceivable wrench, Allen key and screwdriver.

By a process of trial and error, replacing saddles, nuts, bolts and rivets, we finally found the cause: the seat post. Rather than spend the afternoon trawling local bike shops for a replacement, Tony insisted I take his. 'A little bit of us will travel with you across the country,' he said, with a warm, benevolent smile.

The three of us then went for a drive around Tacoma. It had turned into a blisteringly hot afternoon and we enjoyed the AC while seeing the sights. Tony had lived there all his life and had a story for every block. 'That's a veteran,' said Tony, pointing at a sunburned man in tattered clothes, pushing a supermarket shopping trolley. 'They've offered him help but he doesn't want it.'

Just 30 miles south of Seattle, Tacoma had its own, very obvious, issues with homelessness. Tony and Dianne were, however, proud of their city's sense of community and were eager to show me the Tacoma Rescue Mission. Since 1912, the charity has provided free meals, shelter and addiction services to people in need. It is also the site of one of Tacoma's Tiny Housing Villages, a collection of

$5,000 single-room homes. They looked a bit like wooden beach huts, set around a few raised vegetable beds. The community on 6th and Orchard Village has 39 tiny houses, plus a kitchen, toilets, showers and laundry facilities, and 24/7 onsite management to help residents find employment, healthcare and education. 'It's all about giving people the resources to recover and then thrive,' said Dianne. During her career as a real estate agent, she had watched the city's housing prices skyrocket. 'The true success of any society is surely how it looks after those most in need.'

After a couple more beers in Tacoma's sweltering downtown, we returned home for a barbecue and then I turned in for an early night, feeling rested and at ease in the company of old-new friends. As I lay in the RV, listening to freight trains sounding their horns in the middle distance, I felt sad to be leaving so soon.

I woke up at 6am and, after a quick shower, joined Tony and Dianne in the kitchen for breakfast. Black coffee, ham, fried eggs, pancakes and fresh blackberries. It was a Sunday morning and I felt bad waking them so early. But the dawn was bright and I'd managed the best sleep of the trip so far. Out like a log. Finally, my body clock had calibrated to Pacific Standard Time.

'So, did you hear the gunshots last night?' asked Tony, as I prepared my bike for departure.

'Yeah, right,' I scoffed.

'Seriously.'

I still couldn't tell if he was joking.

'About a block away. It sounded like an automatic weapon.'

'What? But this seems like an extremely safe neighbourhood?'

'You'd be surprised. This is America.'

'Shit, man.'

'Please be careful out there, Simon,' said Dianne in a motherly tone, handing me a packed lunch for the day ahead.

We said our goodbyes and I joined Highway 18, another busy road I was desperate to have behind me. Amazon Prime trucks grumbled from their depots and fanned out east across the region. And as if on cue, I spotted a Ford pickup flying an American flag.

Tacoma used to be infamous for its 'aroma of Tacoma', thanks to a paper mill that belched out rancid odours. Since its closure, however, a new smell has taken over. My first hour was accompanied by the faint scent of marijuana, wafting from warehouses in Nalley Valley, the epicentre of Washington's $1.4 billion-a-year cannabis industry.

The shoulder was, once again, a wasteland. Ropes, fence posts, shoes, rivets, nails, nuts, bolts, T-shirts, padlocks, a mattress and even a refrigerator. It took three noisy hours to reach the smaller and much quieter roads that rounded the forested base of Tiger Mountain, a 3,000-foot-high crag at the heart of the Issaquah Alps.

From its shaven crown, paragliders launched themselves into the azure sky and performed stomach-turning acrobatics in the void between heaven and earth. I watched them for a few minutes, then continued along the warm asphalt. I passed a church surrounded by a congregation in their Sunday best, enjoying post-worship glasses of iced water. A billboard on the edge of its bright green lawn read: 'SIN BURN IS PREVENTED BY SON SCREEN'. Which, at the very least, reminded me to throw on some factor 50.

Ten miles west of North Bend, the small town where I planned to spend the night, the road climbed dramatically – about a thousand feet in just a few exhausting miles. This sudden ascent corresponded with me running out of food and water.

When you're packed to the hilt with supplies, there never seems to be a shortage of sustenance or friendly people. But when you're starving and thirsty, it can feel like you're the only person left on earth. This became one of those frustrating afternoons and I was forced to ration every last crumb and drop. For more than an hour, all I could do was swill dregs of bathwater-warm liquid around the insides of my arid cheeks. All while my dehydrated brain throbbed noisily inside my skull.

For a day that had started so routinely, it quickly became a farce. I joined something called the Snoqualmie Valley Regional Trail, a wonderfully flat and paved 29-mile section of the old Milwaukee Road, a railroad that spanned the Midwest and Northwest of the United States between 1847 and 1986. On first impressions, it was heaven. I entered a cool tunnel of fir trees, which kept me out of the sun's direct and searing rays. I was taking a shortcut. Or so I thought. After three miles, I arrived at a tall, padlocked gate, preventing me from travelling any further and forcing me to double back.

Eventually, I found another human being, a flustered-looking mother about my age, yelling at three kids bouncing up and down on a trampoline. 'Busy pickling,' she told me, as she handed me back my bottles clinking with iced water. 'Beets. It's been a big year for beets.'

Rehydrated, I pushed on, up another 1,000-foot climb to the small town of Snoqualmie, adjacent to a river and waterfall of the same name. Feeling ravenous, I fell into the first convenience store and gorged on two ice-cream sandwiches, a family-sized bag of tortilla chips and a banana, all washed down with a litre of cold chocolate milk. More than 1,500 calories consumed in less than three gluttonous minutes.

Snoqualmie was a green, pleasant and wealthy town. In fact, it exuded such a sense of blossoming splendour that many of the exterior shots of David Lynch's 1990s television series *Twin Peaks* were shot there. I cycled slowly past restaurants filled with lazy Sunday patrons quaffing glasses of white wine. I counted three Ferraris and four chihuahuas on just one street.

When I stopped to check my phone, a man clutching a poodle with a cone around its head kindly offered advice for the days ahead. A fellow cyclist, he'd been sucked in by the sight of my chaotic panniers and generally exhausted demeanour. Remarkably, he was heading to the Cotswolds on holiday, and to my hometown of Woodstock, in just a few days' time. We bonded over the smallness of the world and the steepness of the local hills. He was eager to help in any way he could. However, I stopped short of asking him to deliver a bunch of flowers to Alana. It was our first wedding anniversary the next day and a pang of guilt followed me like a bad smell.

I spent the next hour in a strange state of déjà vu, weaving along the same forested roads I'd used on my first day out of Seattle seven years before. I followed a trail beside a golf course. Dappled in spots of shade from the intermittent clouds above, men in bright polo shirts smacked tiny white balls off tees and then watched them fade out of bounds, much to the amusement of their opponents. On a nearby green, a local cat sunbathed, legs akimbo. Or maybe it was lining up a putt.

I finally made it to North Bend at 3pm and found the house I remembered so fondly. It belonged to Nancy Hutto, an 82-year-old widow who had given me a place to stay on my first trip. Not much taller than five feet and with a crop of short silver hair, she wore a T-shirt that read 'CHANGE IS GOOD. LIFE IS GOOD'. She found me staggering around her two-acre, mostly forested property, looking beaten up and sunburned.

Before we'd even exchanged a hug, I had an ice-cold beer thrust into my hand. I necked the lot within 90 seconds flat. 'I barely drink these days,' said Nancy, as she walked with me into the forest. 'So, you're welcome to as many beers as you can find.'

Shadowed by hundreds of hemlock and big leaf maple trees, I could either camp, sleep in a 1980 Monaco RV or take the little cedar cabin festooned with prayer flags and Buddhist chakra banners where I'd slept seven years before. About the size of a six-man tent, it held a special place in my heart. So, of course, I chose the latter.

Inside, I found trinkets, crystals, and one of those lucky Chinese cats with a waving paw. Since my last visit, Nancy's sister had moved in from the East Coast when she was diagnosed with terminal cancer and had lived in the woods for her final few months. 'It was a place we used to meditate in and reconnect,' said Nancy, before leaving me to get settled.

After the rumble and roar of the filthy road, the forest was an Eden. In the canopy above, I could hear a dozen different chirps and cheeps. I even saw a pair of big, stocky elk crashing over fallen branches like fatigued Olympic hurdlers, their proud, cinnamon-brown antlers garlanded in moss and vines. I then joined Nancy for dinner in the kitchen, along with her neighbour, Dianne, an equally kind and talkative 70-year-old woman who I'd met during my last stay. Nancy had cooked us steamed Pacific salmon, brown rice, salad and freshly harvested sweetcorn.

Since my last visit, they told me, America had changed

dramatically. The pandemic in particular had created social and economic fault lines, locally and nationally. 'Covid changed everything,' said Dianne, who contracted the virus twice and had been suffering with long Covid ever since. She still spoke through a hoarse throat and blocked sinuses. 'Some people said it wasn't a thing. And that was all down to Trump.'

For Nancy, however, America had been on a downward trajectory since the 1980s. 'This all started with Reagan and his supposed trickle-down theory. The idea of lowering taxes on the rich and that they, in their largesse, would let everybody benefit. And, of course, it doesn't work. That's how we've ended up with a country where the top 1 per cent owns about half of all the wealth.'

Nancy and Dianne took great delight in my ravenous appetite and encouraged me to eat until bursting. Because to feed a weary traveller is a universally human trait. I did my best, going back for seconds and thirds.

North Bend used to be a lumber town, a Republican stronghold. But when the logging industry wound down, Seattle's tech entrepreneurs – who often lean left – moved in. Nancy and Dianne felt aggrieved by the political power of oil, gas and pharmaceutical companies. They conceded that for congresspeople elected on the back of donations from those industries, it was hard to stand up against issues such as the opioid crisis or climate change.

'I'm pretty negative because I don't see the will to turn things around,' said Nancy. 'However, I'm a little bit hopeful by the next election cycle because so many young people are going to be able to vote and they are so done with the conservatives. Actually, they're not even conservatives. They're crazies. I just worry that it could be too little, too late.'

In the lulls of our conversation, we petted Nancy's dogs – Frodo and Coco the Norwegian elk hounds – and Mel the cat. 'She's a Buddha cat,' said Nancy. 'She's got a small head and a big belly.'

They no longer discussed politics outside of their immediate friendship group, for fear of unnecessary conflict. 'There's no in between,' said Dianne. 'If I hear that someone likes Trump then that's the end of my—'

'They're nuts,' Nancy chipped in. 'There's no logic there.'

'You can't even start to have a conversation because they believe everything they hear on Fox News. It's scary shit.'

I was curious to find out where they got their news from. 'MSNBC is the one I depend on,' said Nancy, as Dianne nodded in approval. Which, according to research conducted by the Pew Research Center in 2019, was viewed by 33 per cent of Democrats, in contrast to just 14 per cent of Republicans. 'I feel like you can trust all the people they get on as consultants,' said Nancy. 'I also read *The New York Times*, the *Washington Post*, the *Seattle Times* and the *Guardian*.'

After dinner, we took a short stroll down their quiet, fern-lined street and sat in deckchairs beside the Snoqualmie River, which trickled gently over a bed of fallen branches and shingle. 'This is our beach,' said Dianne, as we watched a great blue heron swoop overhead like a pterodactyl, followed by a palm-sized belted kingfisher, which hovered over, and then dived into, the minnow-rich waters.

They were both highly concerned for my wellbeing. Dianne looked me in the eyes and told me, unequivocally, to 'avoid all our major cities. Don't go anywhere near them. If you do, then I seriously fear for your safety.'

There was also the issue of air quality, which I'd naively ignored. According to an app on Dianne's phone, Washington State was enduring the fifth-worst air pollution on earth, thanks to the Canadian wildfires that had greeted me a week before. On reflection, my chest did feel like I'd chain smoked 50 cigarettes. The app warned to 'avoid all unnecessary outside exercise'.

There was, however, hope on the horizon. Rain forecast for the day after next would reduce toxins in the atmosphere and return it to 'normal' levels. So, with dusk descending, I decided that the following day would be a rest day.

5

THE HILLS HAVE EYES

In reality, there was hardly any rest at all. I washed my clothes, cleaned out my panniers and gave the bike a once over with a multitool. I then spent six laborious hours editing the first in a YouTube series I'd committed to making. At home, it had seemed like a good idea, but now all I wanted to do was relax, not fiddle around with audio levels and colour corrections.

Alana and I chatted on FaceTime for 20, somewhat techy, minutes. Rather than looking back fondly on our first year of marriage, I confess to spending most of the call complaining about the maddening idiosyncrasies of Final Cut Pro and the unreliable battery life of my new microphones. Far from sweet nothings.

Thankfully, Nancy and Dianne were on hand with snacks to keep me going, and when I was finally finished I collected half a dozen peaches and apples from their trees and made myself four enormous sandwiches for the following day. By 9pm, I'd fallen into a deep but occasionally startled sleep, with squirrels scuttling over the hut's roof, an owl hooting in the distance and the thought of my pregnant wife sleeping alone back home.

Nancy and Dianne waved me off the next morning, pointing towards the Palouse to Cascades State Park Trail, a 2 per cent gradient walking and cycling route that would take me up and over the North Cascades mountain range on a gravel pathway entirely free of traffic.

The landscapes, if I remembered correctly from my first visit, were stupendous. If only you could see them. The weather was gruesome: heavy rain combined with thick fog. It was tempting to turn back and spend another day at Nancy's, but within 20 minutes I was as wet as I could get and resolved to keep pushing forward, rewarding myself with half a sandwich or an apple every hour or so.

Mercifully, the toxic air had been washed clean. Icy, fresh and green, it nourished my lungs and bloodstream with every remedial inhalation. Surrounded by lush rainforest, packed tightly with ferns and towering trees, their knotted branches dripping in lichen, this was fast becoming my favourite day so far. With no risk of being hit by a passing car or succumbing to heatstroke, I had a single, mediative focus. Maintaining a constant speed and body temperature, I swerved around fat green slugs that resembled slimy pickled gherkins.

For two hours I didn't see a soul. Until I stopped at a creosoted old railroad bridge to fly my drone and capture the ethereal fog lifting from the forest canopy. Startled by the presence of another human, I was quickly put at ease. Mountain biker Monte Olsen greeted me in cargo shorts and a multicoloured cycling jersey.

'There's surely no leveller quite like it,' he said. 'The bicycle, and long-distance cycling especially, is a great way of bringing people together.' On a week-long holiday from Colorado, Monte saw an optimism in the cycling community that he struggled to see in wider American society.

'This country seems like it's just one step away from some sort of catastrophe,' he said, as the rain finally abated and we admired a scene of incomprehensible vastness, a million sodden fir trees, fighting to emerge from the soup. 'It's very unnerving sometimes but then there's beauty like this, and people riding bikes, and it gives me hope.'

On closer inspection, I could see his cycling jersey was adorned with the acronym RAGBRAI (Register's Annual Great Bicycle Ride Across Iowa), the week-long, 30,000-person bike tour that crosses the Midwestern state every July. It is, in many American cyclists' eyes, an institution, a bastion of everything that makes long-distance bike touring so life-affirming.

'You can be riding next to a Republican or an Independent. Black, white, it doesn't matter because you need to keep pedalling. It restores your faith in humanity.'

Talking with Monte, I was reminded of my conversation with

the sailing military veteran John Price. Both believed modern America lacked a 'common enemy'. Without one, the country was struggling to establish a sense of identity – and unity.

'A kind of boogeymen,' said Monte. 'Be that religion, or different types of government, or different ways of thinking. When I look back to 9/11, there was this kind of "yay for America" kind of thing. It used to be whoever was wearing the wrong uniform. But today it's someone attacking our cyber security or something like that. So, it's almost an invisible enemy.'

Monte was, however, hopeful that Americans could come together via a shared love of sport, music, museums and national parks. 'Maybe we can rally around some of those cultural things and move past some of the pettiness that divides us,' he said, before we shook hands and continued on our separate ways.

At lunchtime, I stopped at a trailhead, as a billion droplets of water continued to fall from the forest's branches. It sounded like static fizz on an old cassette tape. After four hours of climbing, it was a good place to rest for a few minutes. It had a long-drop toilet, a wooden bench and a map of the trail. I was about halfway into my day's ride and not far from the summit, Snoqualmie Pass. From there, it would be downhill for the rest of the day.

There was, however, an alarming poster stapled to the toilet door. It read:

CAUTION. BEAR IN THE AREA. A BLACK BEAR HAS BEEN ACTIVE IN THE ALICE AND CARTER CREEK CAMPSITES FOR THE PAST WEEK. PLEASE USE CAUTION. STOW FOOD IN HANG BAGS AWAY FROM YOUR TENT SITE OVERNIGHT. DOGS MUST BE LEASHED AT ALL TIMES.

Of course, the chances of encountering a bear were extremely slim but the possibility still delivered a jolt of sobering fear. One's perception of expansive wilderness really can flip in a heartbeat. What had started as a paradise, bursting with natural splendour, now possessed a sinister, foreboding edge.

Before setting off again, I strapped the canister of bear spray to my front right pannier – an easy arm's reach. For the next few miles, I practised my quick draw: the cowboy-like skill of grabbing a gun from its holster and pulling the trigger with just a split second's notice. I sang loudly, too. Incomprehensible, gobbledygook mostly: 'Bear! Bear! Mr Bear! Go away, you big fat bear!' Over and over, as loudly as my larynx could muster.

I must have looked and sounded like a prize idiot to the other cyclist heading towards me, with front and back panniers, a sleeping bag strapped to his handlebars and a mud-splattered American flag dangling from the rear of his frame. We greeted each other like long-lost friends. Or, at least, battle-hardened cyclists who knew an empathetic face when we saw one.

Twenty-year-old Ben Yao was on his very last day of an 80-day, 4,000-mile cross-country bike ride from Washington D.C. to Seattle. He had steamed-up glasses and a neck buff wrapped around his freezing nose and ears. After leaving college that summer, he had decided to explore the USA 'before properly becoming an adult'. He'd faced extreme heat, ferocious dogs and fractured his wrist along the way. Nevertheless, the young man exuded an infectious enthusiasm – not only for life but towards the country he had just discovered at the gentle pace of a bicycle.

'We really just want the same things,' he told me. 'We just want our kids to have a good time and to live in a better world. We disagree about how to get there, but at the core we are really just watching different news and getting different ideas. But I honestly haven't seen people going after each other. People are good.'

The summer-long journey, unlike anything he'd done before, had clearly expanded Ben's horizons. I'd only been in his presence for a few minutes but I saw a lot of myself in him. He had a yearning to escape the humdrum and push the boundaries of a so-called 'normal life'. Not in an arrogant or macho way, simply with a philosophy of: my life is incredibly short and I'm going to grab it by the balls.

'I now have a feeling of being able to get things done,' said Ben, as he took a deep breath and placed his right palm across his chest, as if comforting a quivering heart. 'There's this reoccurring theme among the touring cyclists that I've met that from now on, anything you encounter in normal life is manageable, because you've biked over the Rockies, slept in the rain, and dealt with all these things like racoons and bears.'

At the start of his ride, he'd been thinking of pursuing a career 'that maybe felt a bit safer', but now, with the entire country behind him, he was eager 'to dive into the deep end and explore new things'. He was thoughtful and insightful with his comments, probably because he'd had thousands of hours to mull them over. Time most people never get. On his very last day cycling across America, he was desperate to help me out in any way he could. He gave me a bottle of water, a pair of flipflops and a bag of cookies. He would have given me his sleeping bag, roll matt and probably even his entire bike if I'd needed. Such was the making of the man.

Serendipity had thrown us together on an otherwise lonely byway. As Ben crunched down the gravel trail, I pushed upwards. My mind naturally drifted to my own memories of being 20 and hitchhiking around Australia and New Zealand. That trip didn't just change my outlook on the world, but seemed to rewire the structure of my brain entirely. I returned from that journey and threw myself into a university degree with an enthusiasm I'd never had before. From the glint I saw in his eyes, I could tell that Ben had been altered, unequivocally, too.

Half an hour later, I finally reached Snoqualmie Pass, the 3,015-foot summit I'd been inching towards all morning. In late August it was already fresh and frigid; winter was setting in. As the gradient levelled out at the summit, I entered a channel of spruce and Douglas firs. Named, somewhat alarmingly, Avalanche Avenue, this section of the old Milwaukee Railroad was particularly vulnerable to landslides.

The deadliest avalanche in US history occurred on the next pass to the north, Stevens Pass, in March 1910, destroying two Great Northern trains and killing 96 people. In the aftermath, a huge snowshed was erected at Snoqualmie Pass, and I rested for a few minutes in its cavernous shadows. Built on the higher side of the tracks, it was designed to allow snow to race over it and save the trains beneath.

I then noticed a pair of hooded figures emerging from a concrete tunnel a little further down the trail. With their faces obscured by scarves, they cut an eerie shape. Trolls, cave people, living on the edge of human civilization? As they approached me, they said nothing.

'Hey,' I said, as they walked past.

'Hey,' they replied in unison.

In the remotest place I'd been so far, I'd found the country's least talkative people.

They continued silently down the track, then I shouted back at them: 'Excuse me! Is this the Snoqualmie Tunnel?'

'Yeah.'

'Do I need a flashlight?'

'Yeah.'

And that was that. Alone again.

Abandoned since 1980, the Snoqualmie Tunnel is a 2.3-mile-long shaft that cuts deep through the Cascade Range. Fascinating and terrifying in equal measure, there are no lights inside, or alternative routes around or over the pass. Instead, I had to rely on a combination of headtorch, bike lights and smartphone, which I used more out of a craving for calm than a genuine hope of seeing my way.

I edged cautiously into the void. It was blacker than the Mariana Trench; I could see less than ten feet ahead of me. The sound of my breath and turning wheels echoed ten-fold. Petrified, I could neither see light behind me or ahead. This was a dank, subterranean world with greasy concrete walls and a bumpy potholed trail.

Unsurprisingly, my eyes played tricks on me. Could I see flashing lights darting around in the distance? Without a horizon, or any other visible bearings, it was impossible to know if I was riding up or down. My mind ran away with itself. This was the archetypal horror scene. I couldn't shake the 2005 film *The Descent* from my mind's eye. It follows the less-than-rosy escapades of six cavers as they're preyed upon by hungry albino humanoids with razor-like front teeth.

About halfway, I found two hikers walking in the opposite direction. The lights I'd seen ahead of me had been their smartphones bouncing up and down in their hands. They were just as mute as the people I'd seen on entry. Everyone was clearly as scared as me.

'Cool place,' I said, expecting to ignite some sort of conversation. 'Yeah. Cool place.' That was it.

After 12 minutes, I was relieved to see light at the end of the tunnel and raced towards it like a moth to a flame. On the other side of the mountain, rain fell heavily again. A glorious deluge. The forest bathed in life-affirming green.

I spent the rest of the afternoon screeching downhill, struggling to stay on track, wet grit caking my exposed shins. By the time I reached Cle Elum, I was soaked again and ducked into the cheapest motel. The shower ran either icy cold or scalding hot. The colour scheme, if you could call it that, occupied a tiny spectrum between brown and beige. Four out of the six plugs didn't work. The waste pipe from the bathroom above ran behind my pillow. But it was, at least, dry.

From the soles of my feet to the back of my head, everything ached. When I looked at myself in the bathroom mirror, I saw a grizzly, forlorn figure. Shoulders fixed in a painful shrug from cycling uphill all day. Wind-burned cheeks. An angry-looking cold sore in the corner of my mouth. Feeling so beaten up, I didn't make it far that night. There was a burrito restaurant across the street, so I refuelled my screaming loins with one convenient handheld bundle.

When I opened my bedroom curtains the next morning, the rain had passed but pond-sized puddles covered the parking lot and reflected flying ducks back into the rich blue sky. A few inches of oily water pooled in the beds of pickups. A woman and her confused Alsatian tiptoed along the greasy sidewalk, as though balancing on a tightrope strung between two skyscrapers.

I rolled out into the cool air. Interstate 90 grumbled to the south. But to the north, Highway 10 was delightfully empty and followed the Yakima River, a 214-mile waterway that would soon join up with the much longer Columbia River. It was an almost perfect morning to ride – blazing bright sunshine and a stiff 20–30mph tailwind. The road followed a mostly flat escarpment above a railroad frequented by the occasional noisy freight train.

Much of the Northwest had been battered by overnight rain

but no one was complaining. Especially not the farmers. In 2023, drought emergency areas were declared in 12 Washington counties. According to the state's Department of Ecology, May 2023 had been the fourth warmest since 1895.

On the east side of the Cascades, the landscapes were immediately and profoundly different. There were small corridors of riverside forest but it was mostly sprawling agriculture. As it was late in the growing season, the region's wheat had already been cut, but occasionally a truck would thunder towards me, stacked high with wooden boxes filled with blushed pink apples.

Washington's apple farmers grow more than 90 per cent of America's crop. In recent decades, however, climate change has caused problems for the $1.95 billion industry. According to a Washington State University paper published in 2021, hotter summers have resulted in sunburned apples, reducing yield by up to 40 per cent. Across the contiguous United States, summer 2022 was the third hottest in 128 years. The National Oceanic and Atmospheric Administration (NOAA) reported temperatures 2.5 degrees Fahrenheit above average.

Summer 2023 had offered little respite, and after the lushness of the Olympic Peninsula I was stunned by the land's aridity. Brown and golden in some parts, mottled in scorched spots in others. It was remarkable that anything could grow at all.

I saw my first ever tumbleweed – an object I'd only ever seen in cartoons but as much an icon of the West as a buffalo or cowboy hat. About the size of a modest Christmas tree, the desiccated Russian thistle flew down the road with abandon. I ran alongside it with my camera while bemused farmers drew level, watched me with intrigue, then drove off in their pickups.

Forest fires were also a clear and present risk. On the roadside, billboards read: 'BURN BAN IN EFFECT'. Others had rainbow illustrations outlining danger levels. Green = low. Blue = moderate. Yellow = high. Orange = very high. Red = extreme. After a heavy overnight drenching, though, this resplendent morning felt like a unique and ephemeral moment. A parched land enjoying a much-needed drink.

*

I reached Ellensburg in early afternoon and called it a day. The manager of the Hotel Windrow, the biggest and best in town, had got wind of my arrival and offered me a room free of charge. It was a kind and generous gesture, so I made the most of an espresso machine and a shower with a working thermostat, then spent the rest of the afternoon watching mindless cable television.

First up were the banal talk shows, with their tedious chitchat and Botox smiles. It was impossible to comprehend how teeth could be polished quite so bright or how many minutes could be spent feigning interest in subjects as lightweight as nail varnish or cupcake sprinkles.

I flicked over to the hunting channels, where men in army fatigues and balaclavas shot deer with crossbows. The 'hunt' seemed far from humane, with some wounded animals taking hours to track and kill. Nevertheless, it was all accompanied by a peculiar atmosphere of back-slapping bravado. Whoops and high fives followed every shot, as though they were the last hungry humans left on earth.

And then I found the sport (or sports, plural, in American English). Seemingly, every conceivable match in America had a cameraman in situ, from professionals on hundreds of millions of dollars a year to a few teenagers lobbing a tennis ball around their local park. There were dozens of 'football' matches to choose from (a sport which only rarely requires someone's foot), as well as lacrosse (a kind of yobbish quidditch for the people who didn't make the football team) and volleyball (played on a screechy floor by men and women wearing kneepads and shorts tight enough to reveal the outlines of their reproductive organs). There was also baseball. Lots and lots of baseball. Broadcast from every sunkissed corner of the nation. A sport so sedentary that it was hard to tell the difference between athletes on the field and spectators eating footlong hotdogs in the stands. And I say that as a lifelong cricket bore. I watched. And watched. And watched. Waiting for something to happen.

In England, there is a recurring discussion that too much cricket is played each summer. Spare a thought, then, for the journeyman baseball player. In a standard six-month Major League Baseball season, 30 teams play 162 games each – 81 at home, 81 away. By October, when a further 'post season' begins, a total of 2,430 matches have been played, or survived, across the United States.

At risk of falling into a very deep sleep, I turned off the baseball and went out to wander the streets of Ellensburg, a town that boasted a walkable centre, a few bars, sporting goods stores, a bike shop and the Central Washington University. I'd landed on the Thursday before Labor Day – a national holiday at the start of September – and found the town gearing up for the Ellensburg Rodeo, the biggest in Washington.

To kick things off, a hoedown was taking place in a pedestrianised corner of the downtown. I found a four-piece skiffle band under a pagoda performing the 1954 Big Joe Turner hit 'Shake, Rattle and Roll'. A few hundred people sat on bales of golden straw while a few dozen more danced with young children. Almost everyone wore blue jeans, starched denim shirts, cowhide leather boots and wide-brimmed cowboy hats. I was the only person in flipflops.

I tucked into a plate of exceptional Mexican food, produced by two strapping New Zealanders studying at, and playing rugby for, the university. Oddly, attendees could buy a beer but only if they stayed in the 'beer garden'. Surrounded by a wire fence, it looked more like an exercise yard in a maximum-security prison.

All very wholesome. Ellensburg exuded a strong sense of community, but without any friends or family to enjoy it with, I admit to finding the event somewhat heart-wrenching. On the bike, moving from place to place, I had a focus and a goal to achieve, but when I stopped, there was always a risk of descending into melancholy. Thankfully, though, the executive director of the Ellensburg Downtown Association, Brenda DeVore, was eager to share a beer. It was the start of the biggest weekend of the year and a celebration of the town's unique 'cowboy' culture.

'A lot of our descendants have come from our Yakima nation and our local surrounding Native American nations,' said Brenda. 'For this region, some of our earliest cowboys and cowgirls were from those communities.'

Like many people, I grew up watching the cowboys and 'Indians' films of the 1940s, 50s and 60s, many of which regurgitated hackneyed narratives about brave, white-skinned gunslingers of European descent and their skirmishes with violent 'savages'. In Ellensburg, however, through its annual rodeo and museum, there was a drive to redress this history and its stereotypes.

'The rodeo was happening with our Native American nation,' Brenda told me. 'And then of course the settlers began doing it as well. Our rodeo is a hundred years old, but they [Native Americans] were here long before that.'

A keen cyclist, Brenda and her friends were fascinated by my journey and what I might find. In her opinion, Ellensburg was an anomaly. With its strong Native American heritage, a buzzing university and a population of just 20,000 people, the town – unlike some – was accepting of all.

'When you come to a smaller town, where we really build ourselves on community, I don't think you feel the division that you get in bigger towns. I have never been in a community where there are so many people willing to help you. There's hardly any traffic, so people aren't angry and irritated. We have a very low crime rate and a very low homeless rate. And we also get 300 days of sunshine a year. People are happy.'

I have interviewed hundreds of tourism executives over the years, people whose job it is to convince travel writers like me that their town or city is the next big thing. It can feel like you're being read a script devised in a boardroom. I'm often left wondering if those people really mean it. Brenda's words sounded genuine, though, and Ellensburg seemed completely at ease with itself. Not too big and not too small, it was one of those thriving mini cities that had bookshops, cafes, a movie theatre and independent stores. I didn't spot a single chain fast-food restaurant. The town was also surrounded by world-class hiking, biking and skiing. And every September, a new cohort of 18-year-olds arrives with a fresh dose of youthful exuberance.

'There's this thing about Ellensburg, it's a magnet,' said Brenda. 'People might leave but a lot come back to raise families. It has a spirit about it that I've not found in any other town.'

*

I was sad to leave the next morning. Nevertheless, a lifetime of travel has taught me that it's better to feel like you're departing early than to be counting down the minutes until escape. Well rested and eager for the open road, I meandered through the university campus. With its red bricks and porticoes, it reminded me of umpteen coming-of-age Hollywood movies, but also left me dwelling on the past. I almost spent a year studying in the United States but the opportunity fell through at the eleventh hour. Who knows how things might have played out differently if I'd lived an entire year in the country while so young. Would I have developed the same infatuation? Or perhaps killed the romance dead?

On the eastern edge of town, the rodeo grounds heaved. Thousands of men, women and children were camping alongside hundreds of horses, each one being polished, scrubbed and brushed like a Lamborghini. A temporary trailer city, it reverberated with the sound of clinking horseshoes and smelled of damp fires and haylage. Apart from the bright white trailers used to house humans and horses alike, this quintessentially Western scene had barely changed in centuries. I stopped to catch my breath and watched two boys, aged just three or four, dressed in full cowboy outfits, launch lassos at an unsuspecting fencepost. It seemed like a shame to be leaving on the biggest day of the year. However, I'd been invited to the Ritzville Rodeo, some 140 miles to the east, and I had two days to get there. Thankfully, I was going against the traffic and had most of the eastbound highway to myself.

A largely monotonous and uneventful morning followed, until I cycled over the mangled carcass of a skunk. My nose flinched in horror. The stench of its rotting limbs mixed gruesomely with the pungent odour of its notorious anal gland.

Thankfully, the moment was short-lived and soon gave way to an earthy, autumnal air, which tasted bitter on the tongue, something like stewed English breakfast tea. At times, I was joined by shapeshifting starlings, dancing in rhythmic murmuration on the horizon. I passed farmyards filled with rusting tractors, quadbikes, fishing boats, forklifts, pickups and motorbikes. It doesn't matter where you are in the world, there is a typically rural tendency to never throw a vehicle away. Just in case you might one day need a spark plug for a 1947 Studebaker Champion. Some of these places were museums but didn't quite know it. However, I didn't dare take a closer look. Most had 'Beware of the dog' signs and I didn't fancy having my Lycra-clad genitals ripped off by a cranky bloodhound. Nevertheless, from the safety of the road, I could admire a hundred years of American engineering slowly oxidising.

In awe of my surroundings, I turned to Spotify and a playlist of ROAD TRIP USA CLASSICS. I wouldn't advocate cycling around central London with headphones in, but out here, in sparsely populated rural Washington, music added an extra sprinkling of fairy dust. By the time I reached the 'town' of Vantage, on the Columbia River, with a population of just 74, I'd hummed my way through 'California Dreamin'' by the Mamas & the Papas, whistled along to 'Welcome to the Jungle' by Guns N' Roses and startled a herd of bemused dairy cows with my lung-busting rendition of 'Take It Easy' by The Eagles.

Perched on the western bank of America's fourth-largest river, Vantage triggered a strange sense of déjà vu. Because seven years before, I'd arrived there in a similarly confused state, wondering how on earth I might cross the mile-wide span of water in one piece. The small conurbation sits in a bare and rocky gorge with the look of a grey lunar valley, with barely a tree, and is the confluence of the old Vantage Highway, which I'd been following all morning, and the much busier Interstate 90, a road that weaves across the northern tier of the country. Right here, though, both narrow to just one lane in either direction across Vantage Bridge, a 1,640-foot-long cantilever bridge. There is no hard shoulder or footpath.

In 2016, I convinced a truck driver to follow me across the bridge with his hazard lights flashing, while I cycled as fast as possible just a few feet ahead of him. It was one of those quickly devised ideas that sounded plausible in theory. In practice, however, I was lucky to reach the other side with my life and limbs intact. Vehicles queuing behind my 30-tonne chaperone couldn't see me on the other side and assumed the articulated behemoth holding up the traffic was struggling with a heavy load. At one terrifying point, about halfway across the bridge, an SUV made a break for it, almost knocking me to the road.

This time, I decided to hold out for a lift across. While I was determined to cycle every single mile across the country, sometimes I had to park my ego and remind myself to live to tell the tale. This wasn't a world record attempt but a silly journalistic endeavour. Moreover, I was about to become a father. Cycling across the USA was already an extremely dangerous undertaking. If I had to mitigate the occasional risky pinch point, then so be it. Alana had made me swear to it.

I ducked into a small coffee shop, Riverview Espresso, overlooking the bridge. It had only been open a few months and, fortuitously, they had a proper coffee machine and knew exactly how to use it. Out of the wind, I savoured a triple-shot Americano and settled into a wide-reaching conversation with the owner, Katrina Fernandez, who worked alongside her two teenage daughters: Noelle, 18, and Natalie, 15. They all had long blonde hair and bright blue eyes. When they weren't making coffee for passing drivers, Katrina homeschooled the girls. They had just completed an assignment on the American Constitution. She identified as being somewhere in the middle of the political spectrum but had friends who were both 'very liberal-leaning' and 'very conservative-leaning'. She wanted to live in a country that celebrated differences of opinion, provided there was some form of shared charter. E.g. the American Constitution – a document ratified in 1788.

'Even if we disagree, the American way is that it's OK to disagree,' said Katrina, as she warmed milk for a trucker's latte. 'But there are certain truths and ideals that we should not stray from. It allows for a more civil country, versus an eroded chaos.'

'The Constitution?'

'Sure, things like freedom of speech, freedom of religion and the right to bear arms.'

How relevant was that document now, I wondered. In Britain, most people didn't have the faintest clue about their laws or rights. In America, meanwhile, it seemed impossible to go a day without a news channel citing the Constitution, or someone at the end of a bar quoting the Bill of Rights.

For Katrina, the right to bear arms remained an American birthright. 'The majority of people who improperly use firearms have not gone through the proper channels. Guns don't do bad things, right? People with mental illness, with desperation, use these tools improperly. It's no different to having good doctors and bad doctors. Or good teachers and bad teachers. It doesn't mean that the entire teaching profession has gone to crap or that you should never see a doctor.'

Katrina wanted to live in a country where it was safe to raise a family, and within an economy that encouraged personal and entrepreneurial growth. Case in point: her decision to open a cafe on the edge of a tiny crossroads town with only a gas station for company. Her goal? To make the same coffee people associate with Europe, not America.

'People are surprised by the quality and flavour of our espresso,' said Katrina. 'It's smooth and rich, without the burnt flavour of American coffee. This business has stretched our family but it has also brought us much closer together.'

Where did Katrina and her family get their news from, I wondered. From what I'd heard so far, it was hard to guess a particular channel or newspaper.

To improve her mental health, she had taken a step back, she explained. 'The less I have paid attention to the news, the more at peace I have become as a person. That's not so say I live under a rock and have become oblivious, but there's so little that you can control. You have all this information and it leaves you with this very chaotic feeling, which I don't think is beneficial to anybody.'

Katrina and her husband had grown disillusioned with the state's mainstream school system. In particular, Washington's liberal attitude towards sex education.

'They were aggressively pushing a particular mindset,' said Katrina. 'Within a lot of the public schools, especially in Washington, they had a huge push for wanting to introduce everything from how to have sex to sex toys, and that you could do it whenever you want, with whoever you want.'

These teachings went against the family's Christian values. Katrina and her daughters were pro-life. They had recently returned from a Christian conference and had discussed the subject of abortions with their religious leaders and fellow parishioners.

'People say that it's just a clump of cells. Or it's just a foetus. But this is a full-grown, almost human being,' said Noelle. 'I think that sometimes people don't want to believe it is a baby or that it is human life. We read about many women who regret having abortions because they were lied to and told what they were doing was OK. So, from my standpoint I would say I believe that life should be given a chance to live.'

Considering that some random British vagrant had just appeared from over the hill on a bicycle and doorstepped them out of the blue, Katrina and her daughters were exceptionally generous with their time and opinions. I could have spent hours in their warm cafe drinking their delicious coffee. But my journey had to continue and I was still without a ride across the bridge.

'I'm praying for you,' said Katrina, as they waved me off with big bright smiles. 'God bless you.'

Perhaps he did, because it took less than five minutes for a pair of friendly construction workers to haul me, my bike and panniers across the bridge in their pickup truck. They dropped me off on the other side, told me I was 'totally fuckin' insane' and gave me what was quickly becoming a routine send-off: 'Stay safe!'

6

MY FIRST RODEO

I followed the sandy banks of the Columbia River, then clicked into my highest gear and hauled myself steeply eastwards, along the shoulder of Highway 26, leaving the bulbous, silvery serpent behind me. Thankfully, the drizzle had passed but the greasy road now shimmered and smelled like a wet Labrador.

Roadworks back in Vantage meant that traffic was held at temporary stop lights, only to then be released in sporadic, fast-moving waves. I couldn't relax for fear of being squished by apple lorries travelling west or corn trailers heading east. Occasionally, I would need to swerve around bright yellow cobs that had wiggled free and were about to become lunch for the crows.

It took me a couple of hours to reach the outskirts of Royal City (neither regal, nor much bigger than a village), where the road turned sticky with chocolatey mud, and distant human figures tended to pumpkins, onions and melons in the adjacent fields. In the verge, a big wooden sign read 'BLUE LIVES MATTER', a pro police movement that emerged in 2014 as a countermovement to Black Lives Matter. A few minutes later, I passed the gruesome sight and stench of a long-dead dog.

According to the 2010 census, almost 90 percent of Royal City's population, who largely work in the agricultural sector, is of Hispanic or Latino descent, mostly from Mexico, Puerto Rico, Cuba and El Salvador. When I entered the town's gas station desperate for food, everyone there spoke Spanish and half a dozen brawny men in steel-toecap boots and high-vis jackets clutched 12-packs of Corona under their sunburned arms. Ironically, for a region where so much produce was being grown, fresh food was – once again – scarce. Instead, the shelves bulged with beige, mostly fried or super-processed goods. Sugary carbohydrates in garish packets.

Thankfully, there was a small Subway counter in the corner. As fast food goes, it is the ultimate touring snack. All the food groups – including much-needed fibre – an exhausted cyclist could ever need bundled into a handy carbohydrate baton. The sensible thing would have been to pace myself – eat half there, then the other half later, allowing my stomach to digest slowly and propel me efficiently forward for another 30 miles. Instead, I consumed the whole foot-long monster sandwich in less than five minutes and washed it down with a litre of fizzy soda.

The remainder of the afternoon became a gruelling ordeal. My body struggled to process more than a thousand calories in bread, turkey slices, cheese, tomatoes, salad and jalapeños, sending my blood sugar level haywire. It's no wonder lions can sleep for 24 hours after hunting and eating. The mammalian body still struggles with the simplest of multitasks. I'd never been one for energy gels but as I laboured along the lonely road, my eyes growing sleepier with every mile, I could appreciate the appeal. Before lunch, I'd felt like a sharp, well-oiled machine, fuelled solely by peanut M&Ms and Powerade. Now, I felt heavy, drowsy and grotesque. Desperate for the day to be over.

I finally made it to the small town of Othello and went straight to the Sacred Heart Catholic Church, where I had arranged to meet Father Alejandro Zepeda. The Mexico-born religious leader had lived in this semi-rural community for 13 years, filling a vacancy for a Spanish-speaking priest to work with the migrant population. Dressed in a black cassock, a bright white clergy collar and a baker boy cap, he resembled a clerical Peaky Blinder, just without the potty mouth. Instead, he was a quiet and considered man, who paused for several, somewhat awkward seconds between each sentence.

'We have problems with drugs. Young people are getting involved with that,' he told me as we sat down at a large wooden table, in a vestry lined with leatherbound books. 'But it's not like Chicago or LA. It's a peaceful community. A united community. When we have problems, I think we gather and help each other.'

Christianity was the glue that held Othello together. The town had 26 churches and, due to its large Hispanic population, Catholicism was by far the most popular denomination. Father Alejandro did, however, face challenges. He struggled to align his religious teachings with laws passed at a state and national level.

'We are having some issues with the value of life,' he said, as a large clock ticked loudly on the wall behind him. 'We in the Catholic church believe that an embryo has the same rights as a person and the country is now allowing more abortion for young people. In this state, we have some very difficult differences between the view of the government and the view of the Catholic church.'

Same-sex sexual activity was legalised in Washington in 1976, followed by same-sex marriage in 2012. In 2018, bishops representing 1.3 million Catholics sent letters to the state governor, Jay Inslee, asking him to veto a new bill – the Reproductive Parity Act – which would require health insurance companies to offer abortion coverage where maternity care was also in place. These laws, Father Alejandro told me, went against the values of his faith.

Washington and the Catholic church had reached a similar impasse on the issue of gender identity. In his parish, he had seen an increase in children transitioning from one gender to another.

'Families come to me and ask me, "What can I do with my child?" And I say to tell them, "This is wrong, but you still love them." We [the Catholic church] respect the decision of the people but we don't accept the decision of the individual. We can't tell you that we accept your decision to do a transition, but we still respect you as a person.'

'Can someone who makes that transition still be a Catholic?' I asked. 'Does their relationship with God break down?'

'No, it doesn't break down. Everyone is a child of God. We all do mistakes. We all do wrongdoings in our lives. But if you decide, for example, to make that decision to change your gender then you are in great sin, according to the morals of the church. But we don't reject people.'

After half an hour at the church, I retired to the only motel in town – a single-storey abode with cardboard-thin walls and a parking lot filled with beaten-up pickups. I took a quick shower then re-emerged to find food. Othello at dusk felt much dodgier than when I'd arrived. A block away, the side of a convenience store was illuminated with blue police lights. The motel was fully booked with men sleeping four or five to a room. They spilled out on to the sidewalk clutching big spliffs and bottles of Modelo.

Pursing my lips, I walked quickly past their bedrooms. A man with crazy eyes and a tattooed face barked loudly at me like a dog, intent on intimidating me and amusing himself. This was a sketchy corner of town and I didn't feel like dawdling, so I ducked into the closest place I could find, a Chinese restaurant doing a roaring trade in big piles of monosodium glutamate.

Many American restaurants pride themselves on an ethos of quantity over quality and this establishment was certainly no different. When my 'small' portion of sweet and sour vegetables with rice was plonked down by a mute teenage waitress, it spilled across the shiny red table. Even for someone burning 5,000 calories a day, the size of my meal left me feeling slightly grossed out. Guilty for mankind. Around me, people shovelled in comical mountains of food. And none of it was as cheap as it should have been. The family of three sat beside me must have ordered $200 worth before they'd even added a tip.

According to a 2023 study conducted by the Oxford University information platform Our World in Data, 'the average American buys 3,868 calories a day'. You don't need me to tell you that the overconsumption of food is linked to obesity, heart disease, stroke, cancer and diabetes. However, the particularly interesting takeaway (pun intended) from this report, and many others like it, is that not all this food gets eaten. According to Feeding America, a nationwide network of food banks, around 38 per cent of the country's food gets wasted. That's 80 million tonnes, 149 billion meals, valued at a staggering $444 billion. These numbers are hard for the human brain to comprehend, but when I looked around the room they became more plausible. At almost every single table, I saw people scraping leftovers into squeaky polystyrene boxes destined for the fridge. In fact, when I ventured to the bathroom, I saw that six entire booths stored thousands of takeaway boxes. When I returned to my table, one had been placed next to my plate, seemingly out of routine rather than request.

In my vision of utopian America, I wondered if food could one day be served in smaller portions and cost half the price. Or maybe improve the quality a bit. It was a nice idea. But in America, the producer seemed to lead the consumer. Bigger was always better. And the notion that any restaurant owner might produce a smaller product for less money was a supersized slice of pie in the sky.

I retreated to my motel room, double locked the door and massaged my aching stomach. The night echoed with souped-up exhaust pipes, police sirens and arguments in Spanish. At one point, I woke to hear ominous slow footsteps pacing outside my curtains, followed by cigarette smoke drifting through the small gap under the door. My feeble response? To turn on my TV and pretend I was making a phone call.

I woke up again a few hours later to the sound of hungover men loudly opening and slamming every door between them and a new day's work. Crashing beer bottles and lengthy debates about mislaid work boots. Almost every single pickup was left to idle for at least 20 minutes ahead of departure. By the time I finally rolled out, just after sunrise, the air was warm with unleaded.

The morning sky was dark and brooding. A hard grey, like slate. But the forecast for the afternoon promised blue and broiling. I was eager to make ground before the mercury climbed, so I joined a long, straight road without a single bend for 17 miles. To my left, acre upon acre of lush green alfalfa, ready to be cut and fed to beef cattle. To my right, great swathes of potato plants swayed gently atop little pyramids of cocoa-fine earth. Othello produces more frozen French fries that anywhere else in the world. Approximately 1.5 billion pounds a year, roughly 15 per cent of North American production.

Both crops, however, are thirsty. So much so that there are fears that Othello could run out of water. The government-funded Columbia Basin Project transformed this otherwise desert-like region into an agricultural heartland in the 1950s by damming the Snake and Columbia rivers and constructing a network of wells and irrigation channels. Three quarters of a century later, though, and local water experts have warned they could run dry by 2028. One organisation, the Columbia Basin Development League, has described it as 'a looming economic and environmental catastrophe'.

Cycling along the empty black road, with a mustard yellow stripe down its centre and barely a manmade object on any pastoral horizon, I was left spellbound by the epic scale of American agriculture. Not only did these fragile breadbaskets feed millions of American mouths, but this land also kept motels fully booked, Chinese restaurants busy and churches packed. A trickle-down effect? In more ways than one.

I sat on that empty road for two or three hours, contemplating farms the size of small English counties and grain silos accessed only by railroad. At one point, I thought my eyes had deceived me, but on closer inspection, an orange-blue biplane, A.K.A. the 'Farmer's Air Force', soared gracefully up and down the green undulations, farting out plumes of brilliant white pesticide from a hundred feet above the earth.

The cycling was neither hard nor easy, but just enough to feel fit and interested. And, after almost two weeks in the USA, that open, empty landscape made me feel at ease. I had adjusted to the routine and rigour of the expedition and was itching to find out what person or place came next. Landing in this happy place, this sweet spot, with barely another soul in sight, was enough to make me feel like I could ride and ride. Forever.

The potatoes lasted for about 30 miles, then the powdery soil grew coarser and turned into lumpy scrub the colour of golden straw. I had entered the Channeled Scablands, an immense natural wonder, captivating in its sheer sparseness and aridity, barely known in Washington let alone in the rest of the United States. A mostly barren and soil-free region formed by mega floods during the last ice age, it covers an area of around 2,000 square miles and is crisscrossed by about 150 ravines, some up to 60 miles long.

It was impossible to imagine anything, apart from maybe a few humans with air conditioning, living in such an inhospitable place. But when I stopped to take on calories beside a rusted old railroad track, a youthful grey coyote, a little bigger than a red fox, climbed between the desiccated sleepers and silhouetted itself against the cloudless blue sky. This is, perhaps, the greatest of all cycle-touring joys – the ability to move silently and almost invisibly. The animal sat serenely for more than a minute before spotting this wheel-footed alien munching trail mix and scurried off into the camouflage of the graphite land.

The afternoon sizzled and the asphalt swirled with a fuzzy heat mirage. I slopped factor 50 sun cream across every patch of exposed skin, turned up my collar and pulled down my sleeves. At the tops of exposed hills, I found a welcome, albeit warm breeze, but in the windless pits of deep ravines, the sun-scorched stone radiated fiercely like a pizza oven.

I'd been invited to stay on the outskirts of a small town called Ritzville, with Morgane and Damon Plager-Roth, a fun and friendly couple about the same age as me who I'd met while cycling across the country seven years before. All I had, however, was a postcode for their farm and a very patchy memory as to what it looked like.

About ten miles southwest of Ritzville, the solid road became a loose sandy shingle the colour of Cotswold stone and an absolute bitch to ride on. With almost no grip going downhill, and even less when going up, I was left with no choice but to get off the bike and push. With the sun beating down on me, in 35 degrees centigrade heat. For over an hour, I trudged beside freshly cut wheat fields, a never-ending expanse of golden stubble. A few patchy corners had been left untrimmed, where the combine harvester had been unable to reach. Like a pair of barber's clippers missing a few hairs behind an ear.

Totally out of food and water, I stopped at the end of a long drive. It led to an oasis-like home, surrounded by tall trees, a green lawn and outbuildings. According to my phone, though, I was still three miles from the Plager-Roth residence. So, I slogged on further, and further, and further, for about 90 minutes more. Finally, I reached the address, which wasn't a house but an octagonal road sign. I slumped into its meagre shade. My parched tongue throbbed.

My phone had just a single bar of signal. But through a lot of frantic waving, I managed to get hold of Morgane.

'What can you see?' she asked.

'I can see hills. A farm. And, well … that's about it.'

'Anything else?'

'I passed a small cemetery a couple of miles back. It had a white picket fence around it.'

'Oh, you've gone way past us! I know exactly where you are, though. Wait there and I'll come fetch you.'

After about ten minutes, I could see a pickup way off in the distance, racing towards me in a cloud of yellow dust. Five minutes after that, Morgane pulled up, handed me a big bottle of iced water and then we cruised all the way back to her house with my bike bouncing around in the back.

That oasis-like home that had looked so inviting and familiar? The one I'd seen 90 minutes and a whole load of swearing, sweating and suffering before? That was Morgane and Damon's place. Google, however, thinks they live three miles away. In a ditch. Beside a stop sign.

In 2016, we had connected via a friend of a friend of a friend and they'd generously offered me a place to crash. We spent a memorable, albeit fleeting, evening together, drinking whiskey and toasting marshmallows beside a campfire, under a canopy of effervescent stars. Once again, it would have been remiss of me to cycle on past them without saying hello. Plus, my return wasn't entirely at random: I'd planned to arrive on this specific day, 1 September 2023, because it marked the start of the Wheat Land Communities' Fair and Ritzville Rodeo. Events not to be missed.

At the house, we found Damon waiting with a cold beer. And after I'd had a quick shower, the three of us and their four children – Rudy, 12, Freya, 11, and eight-year-old twins Willa and Josephine – bundled into two cars and headed straight to the Ritzville rodeo grounds.

The showground was busy with horses, cows, trailers and hundreds of people wearing plaid shirts and blue jeans. Within five minutes, I'd seen a real-life cowboy spit tobacco into the dust. Enough to leave me giddy with excitement. It was a wholesome, family affair with the hum of chatter and the aroma of horse faeces, cheeseburgers and beef tacos hanging in the warm air. Morgane and Damon had been enlisted to do a shift on the bar overlooking the rodeo arena, so naturally I bought a handful of beer tokens and let the good times flow.

Rodeo, they told me, was at the heart of this rural community. As quintessentially American as the village fete is British. Albeit with fewer giant leeks and more giant cow pats, or 'pies' as the locals affectionately called them. 'Just hang around here and you'll have no shortage of people wanting to talk with you,' said Damon, as he handed me a can of Coors Light.

I must have been at least four beers deep by the time the rodeo officially kicked off at 7pm, under a pinkish sky flecked in creamy, raspberry-ripple clouds. In the other direction, an enormous super blue moon pompously hogged the horizon, lapping up the admiration of its onlookers. The event started with the national anthem, sung by a teenage girl from the local high school. Everyone, without exception, paused their conversations, removed their hats and sang along. Some held their right hands against their hearts. Others, with a military background, saluted an American flag, held aloft by a man on horseback.

'The Star-Spangled Banner' rang out, proud and loud.

Oh, say can you see by the dawn's early light
What so proudly we hailed at the twilight's last gleaming?
Whose broad stripes and bright stars through the perilous fight,
O'er the ramparts we watched were so gallantly streaming?
And the rocket's red glare, the bombs bursting in air,
Gave proof through the night that our flag was still there.
Oh, say does that star-spangled banner yet wave
O'er the land of the free and the home of the brave?

Spanning an octave and a half, the American national anthem is notoriously hard to sing in tune. And – no offence – this crowd struggled. Nevertheless, the song, followed by rousing applause, gave me goosebumps. This was the country I'd come to see, taste, touch and hear. I was also clearly the only tourist in town and loved it. My accent cut through the local chatter and turned heads. I was, once again, the only person in a 50-mile radius wearing shorts and flipflops. It was a battle not to stub a toe on all the leather boots.

'Hey, you're not from round here, are you?' I was asked every few minutes by the next curious person. Routinely, Morgane and Damon would remind anyone who had forgotten that 'It is, actually, his first rodeo!' Which stirred great delight among the locals. By 8pm, I'd been bought three more beers and was loving every rambunctious second of it.

One local man, Scott Wilson, dressed in a red plaid shirt, jeans and a cowboy hat, talked me through the events. There was the barrel racing, which involved riding a horse in a cloverleaf pattern in the quickest time possible. Then bull riding, on the back of a bucking bronco. Followed by several events that involved lassoing cows of different ages, shapes and sizes, either around the legs or horns.

Prominent animal welfare groups such as People for the Ethical Treatment of Animals (PETA) campaign against events like these. The rodeo page of their website reads:

Countless animals have paid with their lives to satisfy humans' desire to play cowboy in events such as calf roping, bull riding, steer wrestling, and bronc riding. Cattle and horses may be zapped with electric 'hot shots' so that they'll charge out of the chute, calves' necks are twisted as they're violently slammed onto the ground, and horses are viciously spurred into bucking.

Proponents, however, argue that rodeo and its offshoot subcultures are a celebration of the Great American West, and that animal injury, cruelty and death are extremely rare.

'This is our normal,' said Scott. 'People in other parts of the country probably look at this and see it as being abusive, or whatever polarising word or agenda they want to call it.' Scott grew up in Texas but had lived in rural Washington for 23 years. He even met his wife at a rodeo.

'This is our culture. But I don't fully expect someone to really, truly understand this. But I also don't expect them to stomp on me or my thought processes. It's the same with people living in the heart of New York or Baltimore. I'm not going to judge them or change their way of life because I don't understand it.' Scott believed social media has made Americans quick to judge people with different lifestyles. There was, he said, an increasing lack of tolerance.

Did rodeo swing in one political direction more than another, I wondered. Statistically, I was surrounded by mostly Republican-voting men and women. Scott included.

'It probably leans a bit more to the right than it does to the left. But I've got guys I've travelled 100,000 miles with, in the truck, who are the most liberal, left-sided people. But they're still some of my best friends. We just don't talk about politics.'

This was a response I'd already heard several times and I hadn't even left the first state my journey would take me through. Politics had become such a loaded issue that many people avoided the subject for fear of – or perhaps fatigue from – conflict. 'I think we've lost the ability to agree to disagree,' said Scott.

The rodeo finished at 10pm and I left the bar in high spirits alongside the Plager-Roths. After the stifling heat of the afternoon, a cool breeze tingled my clammy, sunburned skin. On the 10-mile drive back to their house, the super blue moon resembled a giant bronze tuppence. Free of almost all light pollution, the undulating stubbled wheat fields now shimmered sepia. Smoked-mackerel-coloured waves, rushing across an ocean in the dead of night.

We were met at the door by their two sheepdogs, Meriwether and Garmyr – who were just puppies on my last visit – who gave us a good sniff and lick before allowing us turn in for the night. Freya, Morgane and Damon's eldest daughter, had kindly given up her bedroom, and I fell asleep in a single bed, overlooked by cardboard cut-outs of Elsa from *Frozen*, plus Princess Leia, C-3PO and R2-D2 from *Star Wars*. A unicorn nightlight shone on my bedside table beside a baseball, a posey of freshly picked lavender sprigs and a welcome card signed by the whole family. I slept peacefully, safe in the knowledge that I was surrounded by good friends with generous hearts.

When I stirred early the next morning Morgane was already brewing coffee and scrambling eggs. 'Meriwether was out last night chasing coyotes like a jackass,' she said, handing me a brew. 'And now he's sat on our bed sleeping!'

Even by 7am it was hot and sunny again – a good day for a rest – and we spent an hour catching up on their back porch, looking out across a barren yet beautiful scene. It reminded me of southern Africa's often desolate Kalahari Desert. We had the dogs, a pudgy tabby cat and a dalmatian-spotted house rabbit for company, plus a big box of glazed donuts to keep us going.

Morgane and Damon grew up on nearby farms, started dating after college and married in their mid-twenties. Both had experienced life elsewhere in the USA but decided there was no better place to raise a family than beside the golden wheatfields of home. Despite the apparent sparseness of the landscape, and the distances between homesteads, they lived in a close-knit community. 'Even if someone doesn't know you specifically, they'll certainly know your parents, grandparents or father-in-law,' said Morgane.

There were, however, drawbacks to living in the country. For example, no same-day deliveries. Instead, they travelled to Moses Lake, a large town about 45 miles away, once a month to stock up on groceries. 'When the pandemic hit and everyone started panicking about buying stuff, almost like "prepping", I was like well, this is how we live normally.'

Ostensibly of a more left-leaning political disposition, swimming in a sea of Republican rural red, how did the couple fit in culturally? Or was I jumping to lazy conclusions?

'I think with the decline of local reporting [the widescale closing of regional newspapers and TV networks], the misconception is that everyone out here is conservative. I hate to say it, but you get these big media organisations like Fox News constantly pushing these awful concepts of straight-up racism and "othering" people. If you're constantly "othering" everyone, then pretty soon, you don't end up aligning with anybody.'

The mother of three daughters, Morgane believed passionately in a woman's right to an abortion. 'We've had 40 or 50 years now of politicians demonising women. And the end goal is a loss of bodily autonomy. If we cannot have bodily autonomy, then we cannot have a republic. We cannot have democracy.'

The couple had built their home from the ground up, working hard to afford every last brick. Morgane was, however, keen to remind her children that they had benefited greatly from inherited privileges. Her German and Russian ancestors had been encouraged to migrate west by the US government's 1862 Homestead Act, a law that awarded 160-acre plots to anyone who farmed the land for five years. More than 160 million acres, or nearly 10 per cent of the total area of the United States, was eventually given away to 1.6 million, mostly white homesteaders. Land that had previously belonged to North America's indigenous people, who had been evicted from their ancestral homelands.

'I want my kids to understand who and where they are in the world, but also their privileges. As far as America is concerned, we are deeply middle class. We have a lot of privilege that a lot of people will never have because of the colour of our skin and because of generational wealth. We are coming from a starting point on the game board well ahead of most other people.'

I spent the next few hours doing all the chores I saved for rest days. Editing that week's YouTube film, including an epic aerial shot of the Plager-Roth house and their rural surroundings. Washing and drying my clothes for the week ahead. Charging every gadget and battery. And giving my bike a much-needed hose down, after the hot and dusty day before.

We then all headed back to Ritzville for another afternoon of festivities. First, there was a parade. Floats moved slowly through town, carrying firefighters and prom queens. Then came farmers on bright green John Deere tractors, throwing candies to the thousand or so onlookers, followed by a handful of wannabe mayors on the backs of pickups pledging election promises through loudspeakers. Ritzville exhibited a strong sense of community. However, this was the biggest weekend of the year and I got the impression that the high street was rarely so busy. The nearest Walmart was about 45 miles away, which gave the town's small businesses some hope of survival. Nevertheless, there were at least half a dozen boarded-up shopfronts and closed-down bars.

While the kids filled buckets with multicoloured sweets, Damon pointed out stores that had once thrived but were now no more. There used to be a bakery, two drug stores, a video store and four restaurants. 'We went to that bar the night we got married,' he said, pointing to a dark room covered in dust sheets. 'That building down there used to be a movie theatre. And that one was a bowling alley.'

Not dissimilar to the modern British town centre, the American high street has been in steady decline since the advent of online shopping and the rampant proliferation of supersized stores like Walmart that have driven down prices and devoured the mom-and-pop. It's hard to picture what small towns might look and feel like in a decade, let alone a generation.

However, Ritzville did hold a jewel in its crown: a Carnegie Library, built in 1907 and funded by the Scottish-American philanthropist Andrew Carnegie. Not only was it delightfully air conditioned inside but the librarian, Heather Carruth, was eager to tell me about the challenges facing American libraries. According to a 2023 report conducted by PEN America – an independent organisation that defends poets, essayists and novelists against the rising threat to free speech – during the 2022–2023 academic year, 1,557 books were banned in US public schools.

'I feel like the school librarian is going to become almost obsolete,' said Heather. 'The way book banning is going, its astronomical.'

In an act of peaceful protest, she had curated an entire shelf dedicated to either formerly or currently banned books, bordered by large paper letters that read: 'LET FREEDOM READ'. 'I did this in response to all the resistance people are being met with.'

'What types of books are being banned in American schools?' I asked.

'Typically, we see LGBTQ as the biggest ones. Anything that people consider sexually explicit. There are also people of minority, like Black authors, Native Americans and Asians. Anyone from a minority, there is pushback against their books.'

On the shelf, I saw *The Color Purple* by Alice Walker, a novel banned in schools across the United States in 1984 due to its sexual content and domestic abuse. Also, the 2017 book *The Hate U Give*, written by Angie Thomas, which was removed from school libraries due to its depictions of racism and anti-police views. And other notable titles, including *The Perks of Being a Wallflower*, *The Catcher in the Rye* and *The Diary of Anne Frank*.

Book banning is not consistent across the country. There is no standardised law or legislation. Instead, bans are often enforced by parents, right-wing campaigners and religious groups. In fact, just under half of all the 2022–2023 book bans occurred in Florida, Texas, Missouri and Utah, indicative of the political and religious stances of these states and their governors.

In Washington, meanwhile, Heather and her fellow librarians had adopted a procedure known as the 'line of defence', which required anyone wishing to ban a book to first fill in a form. It was a less knee-jerk approach, which resulted in fewer bans. 'People then meet and discuss it, and we try to make it difficult for people to ban books,' said Heather, who was keen to stress that she and her fellow librarians still followed a code of ethics.

'Technically, as a library, we are supposed to make everything available to everybody. If a little kid says they want to check out *Fifty Shades of Grey*, then I can't say, "No, you can't check that out." But what I can do as a librarian and an adult is to help sway them in the right direction, towards something that is more age-appropriate.'

Every month, Heather received statistics on what types of books people in Ritzville liked reading. Physical audio books had fallen out of favour in recent years, due to the rise in online and smartphone versions. 'Cosy mysteries', however, were as popular as ever. Hundreds of Christian fiction and Western titles, such as *The Half-Stitched Amish Quilting Club* and *The Renegade Gun*, occupied four hefty shelves.

What made this library even more special was that local people could borrow things like backpacking equipment and sporting goods. A tent and fishing rod, for example. There was also an alphabetised seed library, allowing members to share seeds for flowers, fruit and vegetables.

I almost skipped to the rodeo grounds, fortified by the scent of ink and paper. The elation was, however, short-lived because I soon started to fade in energy. I'd now been off the bike for 24 hours, and without the buzz of adrenaline I felt hungover, lost, out of sorts. In a desperate bid to recalibrate, I sought the shade of a tree and propped my head against one of its big bulbous roots.

If only I could snooze for a while. But my mind was elsewhere. Back at home, Alana was sleeping, and the thought made me feel lonely and homesick. I was surrounded by families enjoying picnics, grandparents chasing toddlers, friends laughing over drinks. But none of them were mine. Damon, Morgane and the kids tried their best to keep me entertained with bingo, the livestock sale and a raffle. I ate three cheeseburgers and half a roast chicken. But by the time we ventured home, I confess that my mind was already on the road.

It is an affliction of these long-distance endeavours. Mindfulness is so seldom achieved. Especially at the end of a rest day, when the guilt sets in and the call of the wild grows louder. *I could have cycled today*, I thought. But had to remind myself to take it slow. Rest was medicine and this wasn't a race. I was here to speak and learn. Not impress myself, or you, with speeds and miles.

Nevertheless, talk is cheap, and I barely slept that night. Instead, I tossed and turned in that single bed, surrounded by fluffy toys, listening to the honks of distant freight trains. Every time I closed my eyes, I saw a giant map of the USA, with dozens of multicoloured states melting into the eastern horizon. A trippy, Salvador Dali-like depiction of North America.

7

OFF THE RAILS

After a few hugs, I left the Plager-Roths and rejoined the empty road. It ran parallel with a railroad used by the giant orange-black locomotives of the Burlington Northern Santa Fe Corporation (BNSF). The largest of six freight railroads in the United States, BNSF runs 8,000 trains along 32,500 miles of track. I had heard their horns throughout my journey but had rarely seen them up close. Out there, though, amid the overcast expanse of eastern Washington, I cycled less than 50 feet from hundreds of screeching wheels, all covered in a layer of rust and dust.

In a normal year, BNSF hauls 1.2 million carloads of agricultural commodities. Enough grain to supply 730 million people with a year's supply of bread. Sugar to bake more than 144 billion cookies. Without these trains, the USA would, quite literally, grind to a halt. The company transports 1.5 million coal shipments, enough to power 29 million homes for a year. And as for America's unquenchable lust for automobiles? They move 2.5 million new cars and trucks per year, approximately five a minute.

I spent the morning in their noisy company, wondering why, in somewhere so empty, did the drivers need to sound their horns so frequently. Perhaps to ward off absent-minded fauna from wandering on the tracks? I spotted another silver-backed coyote and a small herd of mule deer. They had antlers and big ears like southern African kudu.

There were also birds of prey aplenty. Kestrels hovered about 40 feet above the ground, waiting for an unsuspecting snake or mouse. Jet-black turkey vultures with lipstick-red faces and flashes of white wingtips soared high in the gloomy heavens. Their sense of smell is so good they can detect carrion from eight miles away.

Couple this with powerful stomach acids – capable of withstanding pathogens such as black plague, botulism and anthrax – they are the garbagemen of America's open roads. About 20 miles in, I stopped for a glug of water and disturbed four of them with their bloodied heads and shoulders deep inside a freshly roadkilled white-tailed deer.

My favourite companion was a plucky red-tailed hawk. Flaunting ochre-coloured plumage, it seemed to exhibit an oddly human trait of not wanting to be alone. For about five miles, it skipped between the liquorice-hued pylons lining the road. It would wait for me to catch up, then flutter down to the next one. Though I was surely just its stooge. It hoped I might startle a tasty rodent. Nevertheless, it was nice to think – albeit briefly – that in such a barren landscape two sentient creatures craved the company of another living soul.

Despite having barely slept, I felt light and energetic. I had the breeze at my back and the road was blissfully flat. By mid-afternoon, I'd arrived at the busy outskirts of Spokane, the biggest city since Seattle, with a population of 229,000, wondering if I should throw in the towel for the day or keep plugging away.

I chose the latter. But the city was a nightmare to bisect on a bicycle. Even on a Sunday afternoon the roads were snarled with traffic. It was impossible to determine where the city centre was. Or at least some sort of cultural hub where, maybe, there might be a pedestrianised street or two. Where were the people wandering to the pub? Or perhaps down to the park? Spokane felt eerie and empty, just one prefab superstore after another, each surrounded by parking lots the size of British postcodes.

The only people I saw on foot were a few dozen homeless people living in tents. Their shanty towns occupied underpasses and slivers of wasteland beside the deafening freeway. I pushed on past boarded-up homes with children's toys still strewn in their yards, long strands of ivy choking out the last of their memories. The houses in between had high wire fences and rottweilers testing their defences. I passed a man smoking a bong in his clapped-out station wagon. A woman sleeping in the shadow of a trash can.

I was eager to reach the eastern edge of town and pastures green and new. But then, in Spokane's semi-industrialised outskirts, I was stopped by two young men dressed in bright white shirts, grey suit trousers, neat ties and black name badges. Sat on a bench in the blazing sunshine, sweat streaming down their rosy faces, they couldn't have looked more out of place.

'How are you?' one asked politely, as I pursed my lips and slowed. 'You look like you're headed on quite the journey?'

Elder Miller, aged 19, and Elder Davis, 18, were members of the Church of Jesus Christ of Latter-day Saints, the fourth-largest Christian denomination in the United States. Headquartered in Salt Lake City, Utah, the church has more than 16 million members worldwide. They had met in Spokane as part of their two-year missions – excursions to spread the gospel and expand the church's membership. 'People think we're paid to be here,' said Elder Miller. 'We actually pay to be here.'

'Is the word Mormon a pejorative?' I asked, not wishing to cause offence.

'It's not offensive but it's a nickname. It's what we've been referred to as.'

'OK, so what would be the correct way?'

'The Church of Jesus Christ. Or LDS [Latter-Day Saints].'

Fresh-faced, polite and eloquent, the teenagers had grown up in Utah and Arizona respectively. They could have been sent anywhere; the church has missionaries stationed in more than 400 locations around the world. They had friends in Alaska, the Philippines and Italy. Their assignment, however, had been Spokane. And now they found themselves sitting on a bench, talking to me.

'We do the same thing as what Jesus Christ did when he was on the earth,' said Elder Davis. 'We go and teach people, and help them on their path towards being baptised, like Jesus Christ. We share messages from both the Bible and the Book of Mormon [a religious text which, according to Latter Day Saint theology, contains writings of ancient prophets who lived on the American continent from 600 BC to AD 421].'

As two similar-aged teenagers walked by in hoodies, smoking a joint and listening to rap music, Elders Davis and Miller told me that their church, and their work as missionaries, was often misunderstood. 'They [passers-by] see the white shirt and tie and often have a preconception about what we're here to do.'

That preconception, I confessed, had been held by me, too.

'People think we're trying to take them away from their faith, but what we're trying to do is build their faith.'

The Articles of Faith – 13 statements published in 1842 – steered their belief in God and set out the basic doctrines and practices of the Church of Jesus Christ of Latter-day Saints. Elder Miller took out his smartphone and read article 11 aloud.

'We claim the privilege of worshipping Almighty God according to the dictates of our own conscience, and allow all men the same privilege, let them worship how, where, or what they may.'

As I reran the words through my mind, I was taken aback. 'That seems incredibly ... open minded,' I said. 'For a church. There are some faiths that denounce other religions but that's not what you do?'

'Yeah, a lot of churches do. Because if you're not with them, then you're against them. That's how they see it.'

My prior awareness of the Church of Jesus Christ of Latter-day Saints had been restricted to billboards in London, mostly on the tube, advertising *The Book of Mormon*, the musical that lampoons the missions of two young men who travel to a Ugandan village. Elder Miller and Elder Davis, however, were instantly likeable and amiable young adults. They certainly didn't come across as indoctrinated or brainwashed. And I say that as an atheist who is generally wary of all religions. On a purely human level, we were very much the same. Sure, we were living vastly different lives. Principally, they believed in a deity and I didn't. They expected a second coming of Christ and I didn't. Moreover, the Church of Jesus Christ of Latter-day Saints preaches dogmata that I struggle to reconcile with. For example, the church does not fully affirm LGBTQ believers or recognise same-sex marriage. It also teaches the abstinence of alcohol, coffee and premarital sex, which immediately rules me out.

Halfway through their two-year missions, the young men were starting to consider careers. Elder Miller wanted to become a firefighter, while Elder Davis had the ambition of becoming a search and rescue helicopter pilot. Both spoke passionately about wanting to make a positive difference in the world.

They were keen to stress that their words did not, in any way, represent the political standpoint of their church. But before I climbed back into the saddle and we took a few selfies, Elder Miller told me: 'Satan had drawn lines and sought to separate people where possible. We have country borders, city borders, state borders. But we are all God's children.'

These words stayed with me for the rest of the afternoon as I pushed on eastwards to Liberty Lake, a suburb of Spokane, less than five miles from the Idaho state line. By the time I found a cheap motel on the side of Interstate 90, I'd covered 78 mostly flat miles. I knew, however, that the following day would mark a stark change, a transition I had been dreading. The terrain of eastern Washington was about to rise, and sharply so. I'd climbed less than 800 feet that day on roads that ran in efficient straight lines. For the foreseeable future, though, I'd either be climbing up or screeching down.

When I ventured out for dinner – another plate of overpriced fried food, plus a 20 per cent tip – I fiddled with Google Maps. For about the next thousand miles, my route wiggled in one direction, then waggled back in another. This was the start of the Continental Divide and the foothills of the Rocky Mountains. The next day promised more than 3,000 feet of climbing. And to add another element of discomfort, a storm was rolling in. A big one. So big, there was no use in trying to wait or ride it out. I was going to get wet. Most likely, very wet.

Thankfully, I managed a decent night's sleep and began the day by taking full advantage of the 'complimentary' motel breakfast. The room was filled with well-wishers, unable to take their eyes off my bike and panniers. A man about my age, with his wife and two young daughters, studied every nut, bolt and weld as though signing off a NASA space rocket ahead of launch. I spotted an unmistakable glint in his eye, a desperation for adventure. He scared me a little. Would that be me in three years? His wife noticed us sharing a flirtatious glance and jealously thrust nappies in his direction.

A couple of long-distance motorbikers sat on an adjacent table, looking slightly perturbed that I was stealing their thunder. Beside them, a quiet couple consumed waffles with the enthusiasm of prisoners just released from solitary confinement.

Just as I thought about leaving, a Christian pastor, Mark Allen, sat down beside me. The head of a local church, he was living in the motel while his home underwent renovations. Bespectacled, in jeans, sneakers and a sleeveless blue shirt, he placed two slices of toast and a bowl of oatmeal beside a gilt-edged leather bible. With a military dog tag around his neck and a tidy silver haircut, Mark had served as an officer in the US Army, specialising in ammunitions, before answering a calling from God. In his opinion, America was worse off since 'the misdeeds of the current [Biden] administration'. In his view, the 2020 election had been 'stolen' from the Republican Party.

'How do you know that?' I asked. 'Can you prove it?'

'There are well-known people that have adequate evidence, and they have all the internet traffic information that shows connections from voting centres in the United States to China and Europe. They have individual records that show there was manipulation.'

According to a Monmouth University poll, published in June 2023, three in ten Americans, including two thirds of Republicans, believe that Joe Biden only won the 2020 presidential election because of voter fraud. In Mark's opinion, senators and 'political elites' were 'paid off' to achieve a Democratic Party victory.

As a military veteran, it had been instilled within him to protect the American Constitution. The so-called 'Stolen Election' had therefore been an assault from within. 'There are those of us that see that election as an attack on the United States, just as Pearl Harbor was an attack on the United States.'

Mark told me he was 67, and I was curious to learn how the country had changed in his lifetime. He'd grown up during the Civil Rights movement (1954–1968) and the Vietnam War (1955–1975) – periods of enormous cultural and political change.

'The United States has gone past the precipice and we are on the decline because there are no forces speaking about unity. When I grew up in the 1960s, if someone asked who you were, more people would say "I'm an American". But now we're Asian Americans or

African Americans. I feel that we've been intentionally fractured so that our individual groups are more important than our collective identity.'

'Divide and conquer?'

'I think that's exactly what's happening.'

'What will America look like in, say … 20 years?'

'I'm a pastor and I'm not so certain we are going to exist in 20 years.'

'OK?'

'There are indications that our timeline here is coming to a close,' said Mark. He believed that humanity may have already entered the Great Tribulation, a seven-year period marking the end of the world. 'I think it's happening relatively soon. When you look at all the things happening. All the fires, the earthquakes and natural disasters happening all around the globe, in proportions that have never been seen before, I think they're warning signs.'

'A Doomsday?'

'Well, it depends on which side of the argument you're on,' said Mark, as we shared a sardonic smile. 'For those of us who know the Lord, we're told that we will be taken out and we will be spared.'

'And what about the others?' I asked sheepishly.

'They're standing in for seven years of a very tough time. When you do the math, half the world's population is going to die.'

With the clock ticking, in more ways than one, we shook hands and I rolled out into a gloomy morning. The sky was shrouded in off-white clouds. They resembled cottonwool pads, dirtied with the previous night's mascara. It took less than half an hour to reach the state line and cross over into Idaho. At times, it had felt like a fabled land, a Narnia somewhere over an unassailable horizon. To my British sense of size and scale, Washington had seemed gargantuan. At 71,362 square miles it is, after all, roughly three quarters the size of Great Britain. Ahead of me, though, lay a state even bigger. With an area of 83,570 square miles, Idaho is about the same size as Austria but has a population of just 1.9 million. Roughly the same as Kent.

The border was marked by an unassuming bronze plate set into a giant hunk of granite. I felt compelled to mark the occasion with a selfie that would probably never see the light of day. It was good to celebrate these milestones, however seemingly arbitrary.

Aesthetically, nothing much had changed yet. Politically, however, I was now leaving the 'Blue Wall' – a bloc of eighteen US states won by the Democratic Party in each presidential election between 1992 and 2012.

Idaho is at the heart of the so-called American Redoubt, a political migration movement first proposed in 2011 by James Wesley Rawles. The survivalist novelist and blogger designated Idaho, Montana and Wyoming as a safe haven for Christian Nationalism – the belief that America should be governed as a Christian nation. No one knows exactly how many people have moved to the region, where more than 90 per cent of the population is white. However, hundreds, maybe thousands, of newcomers are believed to have purchased easily defendable, off-grid rural ranches that they believe they could hold out in should America descend into anarchy. According to a Sky News report published in July 2023, one Idahoan real estate agency specialising in survivalist properties offers buyers a semi-automatic AR-15 rifle as a 'closing gift'.

Idaho has some of the most relaxed gun laws in the nation. Open and concealed carry of a firearm is permitted without a permit or license. There are just two rules: gun owners must be over 18 and citizens of the United States. According to Everytown for Gun Safety, the largest gun violence prevention organisation in the country, the state has the fourth-highest rate of household firearm ownership and the sixth-highest rate of gun suicides.

I emailed James Wesley Rawles in the hope of visiting either him or one of his disciples to better understand the ideologies of the American Redoubt. Unsurprisingly, I didn't receive a response. So, instead of entering Idaho with some semblance of a plan, I was now heading east into the unknown. I cycled past a silver Ford pickup. A Stars and Stripes bumper sticker read: 'YOU'RE IN IDAHO NOW ... SUCK IT UP!'

From now on, there would be no familiar or friendly faces from yesteryear. Every character and encounter would appear at random. Partly liberating, somewhat terrifying, I was now fully at the whims of fate, the kindness of strangers and Mother Nature. And didn't she let me know it.

By midmorning, I'd reached Coeur d'Alene, a wealthy-looking city on the conifer-lined north shore of a lake by the same name. I stopped for a quick coffee in its quiet suburbs and watched the sky grow hard and miserable. By the time I jumped back on my bike, the morning's gentle breeze had transformed into a full-blown headwind.

I followed a cycle path around the lake. As the surface churned into an eddying ocean, four-foot waves crashed into the coastline and sprayed fishy foam across my path. At least every other house had an American flag flying in its front yard. Against the brooding sky they shone brightly. Gusting directly on my nose, the wind was so unrelenting that their fabric stood horizontal in the wind as though starched. I could barely cycle at 5mph.

Just as the trail started to climb, it turned into gravel and then the rain began. A trifecta of discomfort. For the first half an hour it was just a fine mizzle. A bearable, albeit cold mist of rain. After that, the heavens truly opened. Intense and unrelenting, it was the sort of deluge that left me wondering if human skin really was that waterproof and if my panniers had the muscle to keep £5,000 of electronics dry.

I was desperate to find shelter but had no such luck. The only sign of human life came via passive aggressive roadside signage: 'POSTED. NO TRESPASSING. KEEP OUT. BEWARE OF THE DOG.' All I could find was a freshly creosoted wooden lean-to housing half a dozen post boxes for homes somewhere deep in the saturated green. I stood there shivering for five minutes, hoping for the sky to clear or a thunderbolt of fortune to come my way. Wishful thinking. Life is rarely so kind when you need it the most.

A postman stopped to drop off mail and didn't say a word. When I resolved to continue on my way, a car whizzed past and sprayed an entire muddy puddle across me, soaking everything from the waist down. I was drenched. The wettest I'd ever been on a bike ride, anywhere in the world. My only option was to keep going, for as long as the day required.

My plan had been to follow a route suggested by the navigation application Komoot. It wiggled through the Coeur d'Alene National Forest, a 726,362-acre expanse of dense wilderness. On a perfect weather day, it would have posed a stiff challenge. But on a day like this it was clearly impossible. After two hours, and just five miles east of Coeur d'Alene, I begrudgingly turned north and hit tarmac. Interstate 90.

Idaho is one of 11 US states where you can legally ride a bicycle on the hard shoulder of a motorway. Unsurprising, really, for a state that often dances to the beat of its own drum. There are only two rules for cyclists to abide by:

1 Clinging to motor vehicles while bicycling is not permitted.
2 A bicycle may not carry more than the number of persons for which it is designed, except adults carrying a child in a sling or backpack.

This, therefore, ruled out any 70mph 'backies' (to anyone other than a baby) but it did provide me with a plan B. I could now climb 1,500 feet in less than 20 miles to reach my first Rocky Mountain pass: Fourth of July Summit.

Nevertheless, cycling on the side of a motorway, not unlike the M40 or M25, is a dirty and noisy experience. Efficient, yes, but I would need to spend the next two hours with articulated lorries grumbling up behind me, wondering if I was about to be decapitated by a flailing cargo strap or a five-litre bottle of piss.

'Cycling on the side of a motorway!' I hear you screaming at the page. 'This guy's a bloody fool!' Yes, maybe. But this was one of those mountainous bottlenecks where and I had no option. The cycle trail was impassable. And from previous experience, there was also a part of me that felt safer on a freeway. Not only could drivers see me at a greater distance but I also had an entire shoulder to myself, sometimes as wide as ten feet.

That's not to say it didn't feel extremely dangerous. As I edged up, taking one gruelling pedal stroke at a time, heavy rain lashing down on me, I couldn't stop thinking about the British Olympian James Cracknell. In 2010, he was knocked from his bicycle by a petrol tanker in Arizona while attempting to cycle, row, run and swim from Los Angeles to New York for a Discovery Channel documentary. He suffered a frontal-lobe brain injury, forcing doctors to put the dad-of-three into a medically induced coma. For ten days, his wife sat at his bedside, not knowing if he would ever wake up. Miraculously, he did. But he was left with damage to the part of the brain that controls mood and motivation, leaving him with personality changes and prone to epileptic fits. In 2015, he told the *Mirror* newspaper: 'My kids had one dad for six years and another for the last five; it was very difficult for them to come to terms with.' The accident, and the strain his injuries put on his marriage, eventually contributed to divorce in 2019.

These are not useful thoughts to have swirling through your brain at about the same time of day your pregnant wife is going to bed back home. But I was in deep and all I could do was keep swimming. About halfway to the summit, I stopped to make sure that my gear was still dry and that my helmet remained firmly fastened. The inch-thick layer of polystyrene and polycarbonate was feeble protection but it was all I had to save my life.

The rain was so heavy and visibility so poor that most cars passed with their headlights on full beam. Some even flashed their hazard lights. A few beeped their horns. It was hard to determine if this was done out of derision or support.

Eventually, at just after midday, I reached the top, 3,069 feet above sea level. I took a quick photo for posterity: I look washed out and jaundiced. Clothing heavy. Hair greasy. Eyes sunken. Face gaunt. I was unsure of how much energy I had left in the tank and my iPhone was also on the verge of death. When I plugged it into my power bank, with just two percent of battery left, a notification read: 'CHARGING IS NOT AVAILABLE BECAUSE LIQUID HAS BEEN DETECTED IN THE LIGHTNING CONNECTOR. DISCONNECT TO ALLOW THE CONNECTOR TO DRY.'

It had just enough energy to receive one final message from Alana: 'WHERE THE HELL ARE YOU?'

Then it died.

The next pass – Lookout Pass – was 45 miles away to the east, via a few small mountain towns on the way. There was no chance I could do two climbs in a day, so I threw on an extra layer and tried to savour the descent: 25mph, with the brakes firmly grasped. By the time I stumbled into a small interstate-side diner in the sparsely populated 'unincorporated community' of Cataldo, my hands were fixed solid like claws from gripping the handlebars.

The small restaurant was warm and cosy, rammed mostly with truckers and construction workers. The men sat shoulder to high-vis shoulder around shiny wooden tables, eating big plates of stodgy carbs and salty meats, washed down with coffee in chunky white mugs. After the morning I'd just had, it was exactly what I needed, too. So I squeezed myself onto the only table with a free seat and ordered three fluffy pancakes, two fried eggs, four rashers of sticky smoked bacon, a black coffee and half a litre of maple syrup. With plumes of steam rising from my sodden clothes, I could feel two dozen eyes on me.

'Hey, you're not that guy we just saw on the freeway, are ya?' said the lady sat next to me, who was out for a drive with her husband and two friends. 'Oh, you poor thing. That rain is terrible.'

'We saw you and said how awful it must have been,' said her husband. 'It's been bad enough to drive in!'

For the next half an hour, the five of us chewed the fat like old friends, as sideways rain lashed against the diner's wooden panels. All in their late sixties or early seventies, they were gobsmacked by my sense of adventure, or perhaps miffed by my abject stupidity. If they hadn't seen me on the side of the road with their own eyes I think they would have called me a phony, faking an English accent.

'Where are you staying tonight?' asked Alice, who was married to Geoff.

'As it stands, I have no idea. But I'll find a motel or campsite.'

'Well, how about staying with us? We live in Wallace, about 20 miles east of here.'

It was hard to tell if she really meant it or if she felt put on the spot.

'Don't worry, I really wouldn't want to impose upon you. And I'm in a rotten state. I can work something out.'

'We insist. We'll be home in a couple hours, and we'll get you fixed up.'

And before I knew it, I had a scrap of paper forced into my

hand with an address and phone number on it. They left about ten minutes ahead of me and wished for better weather that afternoon. Then, when I got up to pay my bill, the manager told me not to bother. 'It's all sorted. They paid it.'

The next few hours were spent in a state of exhausted rapture. Albeit with a slight tinge of concern that Alana was back home worrying about me. Thankfully, though, I was no longer on Interstate 90 but following the car-free Trail of the Coeur d'Alenes. The tree-lined bike path followed the Union Pacific Railroad through deep ravines cloaked in thick mist. With my stomach stuffed and the rain easing, I was overcome with optimism brought on by the simple, benevolent act of strangers buying me lunch.

At about 5pm, I rolled into Wallace and found Alice and Geoff's beautiful clapboard home. Painted lemon cream and pine green, it sat on a wide residential street lined with weeping willow, conifer and linden trees. Almost every house had a small patch of lush green lawn. Theirs had fairy lights twinkling on the porch. And when they opened the door to greet me, I was met by my two new human friends, plus Ollie the border collie. The three-and-a-half-year-old still had a puppy's energy and a temperament that melted my heart.

By 6pm, my clothes had been washed and were spinning around the drier. My phone was drying out in the airing cupboard and we were drinking potent pints of 7 per cent IPA in the local brewery, just a few minutes' walk down the road. For a town of less than a thousand people, Wallace boasted a staggering number of amenities. Hotels, independent restaurants, bars, bookshops. It was, in many ways, not very American at all. Preposterously, you could actually wander from store to store without needing an automobile.

Hemmed in by misty-peaked mountains, dense with pines and huckleberry bushes, Wallace is the silver mining capital of the world: since 1884, 1.2 billion ounces of the precious metal have been produced in Shoshone county. It is also famed for its role in modern firefighting. In summer 1910, a three-million-acre forest fire – the largest in US history – swept through the Wallace area, destroying a third of its downtown. One heroic man, Forest

Service Ranger 'Big Ed' Pulaski, saved 38 men by guiding them to safety in a mine tunnel. In 1911 he invented the Pulaski axe, a hoe-like contraption still used all over the world which allows firefighters to both chop wood and dig trenches with the same convenient tool.

I was entranced by Wallace's redbrick buildings and Ferrari-red fire hydrants. A piano sat on the street outside an art gallery. American flags fluttered above old coal trailers planted up with shrubs. The town is so delightful that every downtown building is on the National Register of Historic Places. And as if that wasn't unique enough, in 2004, the mayor of Wallace audaciously proclaimed the town as the Centre of the Universe, because, well, no one could prove otherwise.

Originally from Florida, Alice and Geoff shared their time between the Sunshine State and Idaho. Geoff had run a successful construction business, while Alice had worked as a professor of audiology at the University of Florida. They were keen skiers and had bought a second home in Wallace in 2003 'to be close to the slopes', and drove back and forth a couple of times a year. Geoff had run the numbers and their carbon footprint was about the same as two return flights.

'We get to see the country,' said Alice, as we settled into our beers. 'It's about 2,800 miles if we go in a straight line, or about 3,900 if we go to see our kids in Tucson [Arizona] and Houston [Texas]. It does make me feel guilty, though. But we just couldn't do it in an electric car. America doesn't have the infrastructure.'

In the two decades they'd been living and skiing in the region, had they witnessed climate change, I wondered. 'We haven't seen it on the mountains,' said Alice, 'because we get some odd things [snowstorms] coming down from Canada. But we have seen it in town. We're not seeing as much snow.'

Summers in Wallace, they told me, felt considerably hotter. For the first time in 20 years, they'd seen squirrels coming down from the mountains to find water. 'We did a hike and didn't find any water in the little gorges,' said Geoff. 'It's definitely hotter here in the summer than it was 20 years ago.'

Alice was concerned about what America might look like for

her grandchildren, blaming habits that go unchallenged. 'I worry about what it's going to be like for them,' she said. 'I think we are terrible in this country. It's like "soccer moms" driving a Suburban [a nine-seater SUV made by Chevrolet] or people living in the city driving cars that are far too big for their needs.'

After an exhausting day and two pints of strong beer I practically floated back to their house. Ollie was eager to be cooed over and my clean clothes came out of the drier hot to the touch and fizzing with static. My phone was also dry enough to check in with my – understandably quite peeved – wife, who desperately wanted to go to bed.

'SORRY. SORRY. SORRY.' Read my first communication in 12 hours. 'I'M FINE. GOT SOAKED. STAYING WITH LOVELY KIND PEOPLE. GO TO SLEEP. LOVE YOU.'

Alice threw together a delicious chicken and vegetable stir-fry, while Geoff strummed a few chords on his acoustic guitar. Over dinner, they told me that most of their news came from the Public Broadcasting Service (PBS). 'They do slant to the left,' said Alice. 'But I feel like they teach facts. I also read *The New York Times* and occasionally the *Wall Street Journal*. I also have the *Guardian* on my iPad.'

Geoff, however, 'challenged' himself to watch ten minutes of Fox News every week. 'Just to say I'm watching it. But I don't do much more than that. I'm worried it would suck me in!'

In their lifetimes, they had watched political debate grow messier, partisan and polemical. 'I think the lack of knowledge comes from talking heads on cable news channels,' said Alice. 'And they infer that everything you hear on other channels is false.'

What about the story of some Idahoans preparing for anarchy? Maybe even looking forward to it. Was that hyperbole or grounded in truth?

'We had a guy come round to put in our cable TV and he was in this really strong cult,' said Geoff, who owned a shotgun and rifle, strictly for hunting. 'And he told me that he and his sons had everything they needed to protect themselves.'

Geoff cracked a joke with the man. If America descended into lawlessness, maybe he could visit and borrow some munitions?

'Well, in that case,' the man replied, 'I may have to cut off your hand.'

The next morning was deliciously crisp. Sunshine streamed through my bedroom windows as the scent of coffee, toast and scrambled eggs drifted under the door. By 8am, Alice and Geoff had waved me off with another full stomach and a handful of snacks to keep me going. Just a few waking hours in their company were enough to invigorate my soul. Kindred spirits? More like adventure gurus. I promised to look them up in Florida – if I made it that far.

This was, on paper at least, set to be one of the toughest days of the entire cross-country ride. To cover just 50 miles that day, I would need to cycle 4,150 feet up, then 4,250 down, and reach a maximum altitude of 4,725 feet at Lookout Pass, the lofty border between Idaho and Montana.

Just east of Wallace, I began the climb to its summit. Sunny, 16 degrees centigrade, no wind. Perfection. Or so I thought. Everything was going to plan, but after an hour of slogging up, and up, and up, on the shoulder of Interstate 90 – BANG! My first puncture, 650 miles in.

Thankfully, there was a layby safely away from the road and the air tasted fresh and moreish. Two pensioners stopped to spend a penny behind their RV and insisted I take a handful of cookies and a bottle of water.

'Do you need a ride?' They enquired. 'We can take you where you need?'

Tempting, but as puncture locations go, it was about as good as it got. And 650 miles wasn't a bad return, considering the weight I was carrying. I therefore sent them on their way and reminded myself to stay calm. It is easy to get flustered in these situations. Instead, I worked through the problem – a four-inch nail – and got it fixed without my pulse racing too much.

An hour later, I finally reached Lookout Pass. A place occasionally so windy that a steel signpost marking the summit had been crumpled like foil and now sat in a heap on the roadside. Other than that, there was little to look at, apart from a bridge over the interstate and a sign marking the end of Idaho and the start of Montana, my third state. It was a moment to celebrate. However, there was a somewhat more sobering blue sign, with a white crucifix and the words: 'WHITE MARKERS REPRESENT HIGHWAY FATALITIES'.

From there, it was almost all downhill for the rest of the day, following the meander of the Saint Regis River, which cut through a valley of steep-sloped mountains. Larch trees, with proud, pointed crowns, covered every last inch of hillside. About 10 per cent teased with golden fall but the majority still held on to emerald summer.

All I had to do was turn my legs over gently to keep them warm, but I didn't push too hard, to save them for the days ahead. The weather was so pleasant that I stopped off in Saltese, a tiny 'town' of just 18, and called into the store for supplies. Not much bigger than a broom cupboard, it sold fresh jerky, huckleberries, local honey, hunting knives and motor oils. In a living room behind the counter, the owner sat in a reclining armchair, watching – by the sound of it – true-crime documentaries.

Outside was a small awning covering a metal bench designed to look like an American flag. With its Stars and Stripes as a backrest, I munched my snacks and admired a dizzying array of signage which covered the store's exterior. One poster read: 'UNLESS YOU ARE THE LONE RANGER, YOU DO NOT NEED A MASK HERE'.

Another read: 'GUNS ARE WELCOME ON PREMISES. PLEASE KEEP ALL WEAPONS HOLSTERED UNLESS NEED ARISES, IN SUCH CASE, JUDICIOUS MARKSMANSHIP IS APPRECIATED'.

There was a tin placard with a picture of a Smith & Wesson Magnum revolver and the words: 'THE AVERAGE RESPONSE TIME OF A 911 CALL IS 23 MINUTES. THE RESPONSE TIME OF A .357 IS 1400 FEET PER SECOND'.

As I jumped in the saddle and motioned to leave, a final one caught my eye: 'NOTICE. THIS PLACE IS POLITICALLY INCORRECT. WE SAY MERRY CHRISTMAS. ONE NATION UNDER GOD. WE SALUTE OUR FLAG & GIVE THANKS TO OUR TROOPS. IF THIS OFFENDS YOU, PLEASE LEAVE. IN GOD WE TRUST'.

Two miles west of St Regis – home for the night – I felt a squishy back tyre bouncing beneath me, followed by the grinding sensation of rim on tarmac. It had been an otherwise delightful afternoon, under blue skies, surrounded by epic alpine scenes. So, instead of beginning the rigmarole of changing the tyre there and then, I walked the final stretch and found a motel. Some tasks are better faced with a cold beer in hand.

Situated at the confluence of the St Regis and Clark Fork rivers, St Regis was a pleasant little place surrounded by trees. Albeit, offering little to anyone without a car. Especially not an exhausted cyclist with enough lactic acid pooled in his legs to make Bradley Wiggins wince. It took less than five minutes to see the sights of 'downtown': a closed bar, a small supermarket and a gas station. Otherwise, I spent a rather enjoyable evening eating a random mishmash of foods – ramen noodles, coleslaw, three slices of peperoni pizza, two apples and a packet of sliced ham – and then treated myself to a ten-minute dose of Fox News.

8

BIG SKY COUNTRY

I awoke at 6am with a start. The people in the room next door were leaving like a troop of baboons escaping a zoo, clubbing paws against every hard surface on their way to freedom. I'd gained an hour and was now only seven hours behind the UK. Nevertheless, 6am in western Montana was considerably darker than the same time in eastern Idaho, so it left me with little choice but to spend an hour drinking coffee in bed. Every cloud.

The small breakfast room was filled with tourists making an equally early start, eating biscuits and grits – scone-like rounds covered in a bland and gloopy mush with the consistency of watery porridge. Instead, I opted for four slices of brown toast, topped with peanut butter, banana and a light dusting of salt: cyclist's rocket fuel.

I saddled up at 7.41am and emerged into a morning kissed with frost. The breakfast TV news had forecast a warm and sunny day across the nation, and Montana would be no different. First, though, I had to survive a period of sharp cold in a dark valley still untouched by the sun's rays. The sky above was metallic blue. A few blinking stars remained.

When I packed for the journey, I'd decided that warm gloves would create unnecessary clutter. But now my exposed fingers ached to the bone and threatened to crack like ice. The solution? Socks. Three pairs of used and stinky ankle socks took the windchill off at least. But as for my frozen ears, not much could be done to save them. I pulled up my neck buff and thought warm thoughts. Earmuffs made from hot biscuits. A dollop of steaming grits warming my scalp and shoulders.

The American novelist John Steinbeck described America's

fourth-biggest state as 'a great splash of grandeur. The scale is huge but not overpowering'. He also famously confessed: 'I'm in love with Montana. For other states I have admiration, respect, recognition, even some affection. But with Montana, it is love. And it's difficult to analyze love when you're in it.'

I too admit to falling in love. Spread across an area of 147,040 square miles, the state is surpassed in size by only California, Texas and Alaska. If it were a country, Montana would be the sixty-second largest on earth. It is also sparsely populated – just 1.1 million. Only Wyoming and Alaska have fewer people.

When I stopped for coffee and a second breakfast in the small town of Superior, I was left in awe. For seven absent years, Montana's horizon-defying landscapes had been at the forefront of my American mind's eye. So big, they eventually pulled me back like a dog on a retractable leash. At my school and corporate talks around the world, someone nearly always asked about my favourite US state and I would always answer 'Montana!' in a heartbeat. Now I was back, and with almost three weeks of cycling in my legs, it felt as though my adventure had returned home.

I enjoyed 15 minutes' chitchat with the employees at Superior's gas station. At $3.98 a gallon, it was the cheapest fuel I'd seen anywhere in the country so far. They had a big National Geographic map of the USA on the wall – I was still a long way from Key West – but Montana signalled the start of a truly open road.

'I came here from California 20 years ago,' said a middle-aged female employee dressed in a red tabard, indulging in a quick cigarette out of sight of the forecourt. 'I won't ever leave now. The rest of the country seems too stressful, too busy.'

Armed with a glazed chocolate donut as big as my outstretched palm and a boxed salad that would wilt and wither by lunchtime, I continued east on an empty service road sandwiched between Interstate 90 and the Clark Fork River.

Montana's rippling waterways were immortalised by the American author Norman Maclean in his 1976 novel *A River Runs Through It*, followed by a 1992 film adaptation, directed by Robert Redford. 'In Montana there are three things we're never late for: church, work and fishing,' says the character played by Brad Pitt.

Eighty-three per cent of the American population now lives in urban areas, up from 64 per cent in 1950. A great migration. Nevertheless, a cultural fascination – even fetishisation – for the country's wilderness remains, notably in its cinema. *Brokeback Mountain* (2005), *Into the Wild* (2007), *No Country for Old Men* (2007), *The Revenant* (2015), *Nomadland* (2020). Mountains, forests, prairies and deserts, all given time and space to breathe. Sadly, these 16:9 depictions are the closest to nature many Americans will ever get. Others, however, gladly lap it up. I stopped on a concrete road bridge crossing high over the river and watched six figures, packed tightly into two inflatable canoes, get thrown over rocky rapids, their oars fighting with swell. From a distance their bright smiles beamed like distress flares.

On the outskirts of Alberton, a small town of just 500, I saw my first proper firearm. Despite all the warnings, posters and mentions, it had taken this long. It marked a watershed of sorts, a moving away – geographically and culturally – from the liberal Pacific coast to the conservative mountain west. Notably, the pistol was not being carried by a police officer or hunter, but on the belt of a balding man dressed in chino shorts and a polo shirt. The only human for miles around, he was in the 'safety' of his own home, mowing the lawn.

In the local grocery store I mentioned my sighting to the friendly lady behind the cash register. 'What did he need a gun for?' I enquired, somewhat perplexed, revealing myself as an out-of-towner.

Gun ownership was, she told me, not just an American right but, for many Montanans, as normal as throwing on boots in the morning. Anyone over 18 can carry a gun without a permit. Be that concealed or on open display.

'We don't have very much happen here because we can carry,' she told me. The sight of people openly carrying guns on their belts made her feel safer in Montana than in states with stricter laws. This struck me as a bizarre paradox. Surely more guns resulted in more gun violence. Who, or what, were people protecting themselves from?

'I feel better if someone comes in with it on their side, just knowing that they're my backup, because I don't carry here [in the store].'

Outside the store, there was the risk of running into a bear. 'Brown and grizzlies come down from the mountain,' she explained, as she served a big, burly man in jeans and a leather waistcoat. He had a long-barrelled revolver resting in a holster on his hip. The sort you'd see in a Western.

'There wasn't enough fruit in the forest this summer, so a lot of them came down into town looking for food. One of them was shot.'

'Then what happened to it?'

'It was given to the high school for the kids to dissect.'

'Wow.'

'You're in Montana. We're kind of rough up here.'

As people came and went – mostly on quadbikes – the lady answered my questions between scanning items. Occasionally, an eavesdropping customer would baulk or snigger. One man told me, with no hint of sarcasm, that what local people hated most was 'tourists. And people asking stupid questions.'

But mostly the lady spoke of an outdoorsy lifestyle and a culture of people just wanting to keep themselves to themselves, who didn't enjoy being told what to do.

Before I left town, she suggested I cycle a few doors down the street, to the Montana Valley Book Store.

'A bookstore!' I yelped. 'Here?'

'Ask for Keren. She'll be a great person for you to talk to.'

Home to more than 100,000 second-hand books, the store was a basilica to literature. It was cool, tightly packed and slightly musty – everything a bookshop should be. I looked up at 15-foot-high shelves bursting with David Baldacci, Lee Child and C.S. Lewis. There must have been a thousand books on Montana alone. There was also an entire 'American Indian' section. And somewhere in a backroom, a wolf-whistling African grey parrot.

As I flicked through dogeared pages, held together by soft, stressed spines, I thought the same perverse thought I do when I enter any good bookshop: if there was a nuclear holocaust and I had to hole up anywhere for the rest of my life, then it would be here.

The store's owner, Keren Wolhart, was similarly wired. An erudite literary 'prepper' of sorts. 'If the lights go out, all the internet, the electronics, and all of that stuff, we will still have people to talk with and we still have books to read.'

Keren was raised by a father obsessed with books. He bought so many, in fact, that one of her earliest memories is of having no room to park the family car, a Volkswagen camper, in the garage. With boxes piled high, he opened his first store in 1966, in a 26-room Victorian hotel in Montgomery County, Pennsylvania. He then opened the Alberton store in 1978, and from the age of eight, Keren learned to sort, catalogue and shelve the boxes of books that would arrive most days.

'How important are places like these?' I asked as we cooed over first editions and antique atlases.

'These books remain phenomenally important,' she said. 'Because you can take a book home and no one is censoring you. It doesn't matter who it is, you can form your own ideas and opinions. A person could sit in this room for ten years and read a little bit of everything.'

In the 50-plus years she had been selling books – at the coalface of cultural, social and political discourse – were Americans more, or less, interested in books now? In contrast to, say, 30 years ago? Moreover, how much of an appetite was there to have one's views challenged in the long form?

'People are more inclined these days, and all ages. But I think people still veer off to their comfort zone. I am a conservative person politically, but I'm not closed-minded at all. I encourage people to read the history of America and make their own minds up.'

Keren worried, however, that books could only be so powerful. In her opinion, the US higher education system favoured a particular way of thinking. 'In America, college-educated kids are told to open their minds, but then they're indoctrinated in a way of believing in more government and more control. But America was founded on the freedom of the people. You could have 28 different opinions and they're all valid.'

She believed that left-leaning Americans found it harder to accept the views of those, like her, who veered to the right.

'They just get pissed off, flip you off and say, "Screw you, you're stupid."'

This went against the stereotype that liberal people are more willing to accept, or at least respect, opinions different to their own.

'I've had people ask me my opinion, then I very softly give it, and then I've had two different people in here throw their hands up and say, "There's just no talking to you!" And out the door they go.'

It was almost time for me to make my own – hopefully slightly less abrupt – departure. But before I did, I wanted to know where Keren, a self-confessed 'open-minded conservative', stood on the issue of gun ownership. I'd seen more in the past hour than I had in the previous two weeks.

'Do you want to see my purse?' she laughed. 'It's got my pistol in it. I had a brother who died in a car accident when I was 16, a gun had nothing to do with it. But I also had a father who was shot to death by my brother-in-law with a .22 rifle when I was 22.'

I was stunned.

'And that didn't change your opinion on guns?'

'I believe guns are a marvellous thing. Guns don't kill people. People do. I'm a sane person, I wouldn't dream of going out and shooting somebody. People who shoot people have other mental problems going on. Don't take the guns away. I love the Second Amendment [the Right to Bear Arms] in America.'

'The gun in your purse. What exactly is that for?'

'It's for me to feel safe. I hope and pray I never need it, but it's a small measure of mental comfort.'

It was hard for me to get my head around. The man mowing his lawn, the man in the store and now Keren. They all had guns at arm's reach. Just in case. But was the threat real? Or perceived? And was it possible to tell the difference?

From a distance, and as a foreigner, I'd assumed gun-carrying Americans were slightly unhinged. But in the space of an hour, I'd seen three citizens, all of sound body and mind, carrying them. In a corner of the country that seemed anything but dangerous.

Keren was also a keen cyclist and as I jumped back on my bike, she gave me some local advice about reaching Missoula. The town was 30 miles to the east and marked my next overnight stop. If I'm honest, it went in one ear and out the next. I was desperate to reach the Adventure Cycling Association (ACA), the global headquarters of all things cycle touring, before it closed at 5pm. To get there on time, I would have to cycle like the wind. I therefore re-joined the shoulder of Interstate 90. Like Idaho, motorway cycling wasn't exactly illegal, but it was frowned upon in Montana. It wasn't pretty and I felt silly, but it saved me a ten-mile detour.

Twenty miles west of Missoula, the road dipped into a vast bowl-like valley. I had reached the convergence of five mountain ranges: Bitterroot, Sapphire, Garnet, Rattlesnake and the Reservation Divide. Ahead of me, I could see mile-wide sheets of rain lashing against the distant city, but somehow a peculiar dry patch tracked perfectly overhead. For an hour, the atmosphere smelled of earthy petrichor, like cucumber, topsoil and lemon balm. A Pimm's on a damp spring day.

Ten miles from town, my luck changed and the heavens opened. Intense dumps of water boomed down from the sky. In the eye of the storm, visibility dropped to less than 50 feet. Hundreds of hazard warning lights flashed around me.

I finally reached Missoula at 4.55pm and fell through the ACA's double doors like a pound shop Shackleton, staggering in from the cold. I was the dictionary definition of 'bedraggled' – drenched in sweat from the inside, soaked in rain on the outside. I had sunburned panda eyes and gave off the unmistakable pong of eau de road.

Luckily, they had seen, and smelled, it all before. Because the ACA is the mothership of bicycle touring, a non-profit with the sole focus of championing the joys of long-distance bicycle travel. They took one look at my dishevelled figure and directed me straight to their 'bikers' kitchen' and a refrigerator packed with complimentary soda and ice cream.

With my cheeks packed with sugar, I staggered around the headquarters. This was my Lord's. My Wembley. My Madison Square Garden. A shrine to bikes. There were hundreds of Polaroid photos on the wall depicting equally strung-out cyclists who had visited in recent months. Below each picture, there was information detailing when, who, where from and where to. Some people were just on weekend jaunts. Others were crossing the state. A few were cycling cross-country; a handful were cycling around the world indefinitely.

A dozen bicycles of varying ages, with different mechanical complexities and luggage setups, had been mounted on the walls. For the bicycle touring nerd, it was like pondering twelve hominid skeletons depicting the gradual transition from ape to man. Steel bikes from the 1960s with leather panniers and down-tube shifters. Tandems ridden across America by married couples who obviously had steadfast patience and a fondness for each other's farts.

The most modern bike showed how the trend for 'bikepacking' had emerged in recent years. It was a sleek and spartan design, with a svelte saddle bag, front suspension and tribars. But my favourite had been modified with a windshield, allowing for aerodynamic progress across America's notoriously gusty Great Plains. It was the physical realisation of a design that had been dreamed up in my mind umpteen times before while grimacing into cold headwinds.

'Travelling long distance on a bicycle is a profoundly powerful experience,' said Brian Bonham, the association's vice president of community engagement, who had kindly hung around at the end of the day to offer some advice for the 3,000-plus miles ahead of me. 'You're connected to your environment and its people in a way that you just wouldn't get from driving in a car. You're much more vulnerable and that lends to you seeking out the goodness of people. There's a connection that happens inherently when you're traveling by bike and carrying all your gear.'

The ACA created its first route in 1973, the TransAmerica Trail. Since then, it's developed more than 50,000 miles of tried and tested cycling routes across America. It distributes online and physical maps and organises around a hundred guided cycling expeditions of varying shapes and sizes, mostly for people who prefer to travel in small groups rather than slum it on their own like me. The TransAmerica Trail, however, remains the longest of the lot: a more than 4,000-mile, coast-to-coast route from Astoria, Oregon, to Yorktown, Virginia. If I made it to Key West in one piece, then it would certainly be on my radar. One day.

Every week, Brian and his colleagues met people from all over the world. For many, cycling long distance was more than just a physical challenge. Riding that far, for that long, was a life choice. A chance to reset. To see America, and the world, differently.

'For most people, it's safe to say that riding your bike across the country, or even just pushing yourself outside your comfort zone, shows you what the human body and mind are capable of. With 54,000 members in the association, I'm optimistic. For as long as the bicycle exists, there will be people who want to explore on it.' Brian was preaching to the converted and this was our church.

When the rain eased, I headed across town to the Bicycle Hangar, a small bike shop with rock music blaring and the smell of chain oil in the air. I'd lost a bolt that connected my kickstand to the bike's frame, and Eric Leutz – the resident mechanic – kindly dropped what he was doing so that I could continue on my way as swiftly as possible.

Eric was a keen cycle tourer himself. Long-distance, offroad stuff, mostly. And though we barely exchanged a word, he knew exactly how I was feeling, what I'd been through that day, and could empathise with all my worldly needs.

'You want a beer?' he asked.

'Ah, man. Yes please. I've had a big day.'

For Eric, as it is for me, travelling by bike is the perfect speed for body and mind. Moreover, his desire to help me out, with a bolt and a beer, was done for karma's sake. No money was exchanged; Eric just wanted to play a small – but not insignificant – part in my huge adventure. He had been on the receiving end many times before.

'The bike is the best icebreaker out there,' said Eric as he tightened the kickstand, pumped up my tyres and gave the rest of the bike a once over. I then watched his brow furrow with puzzlement.

'Your tyre is on backwards,' he said.

'Is it?'

'Yeah.'

'Ah, that must have been the puncture I fixed on the side of the road.'

'Don't worry, man. You'll be fine.'

How had people treated him on his adventures around the country, I wondered. Had those journeys changed his perception of America?

'It blows people's minds. They live in one town, and you've biked two towns over, and they're like, "You just rode a bike there?" American culture is too focused on cars. Americans still see bikes as a children's toy, whereas if you look at a lot of European cities, they're built around cycling infrastructure. They're seen as a genuine mode of transportation.'

We threw my panniers back on and shook grubby hands.

'Eat lots of food. Be free. And have fun,' said Eric, as he watched me cycle the wrong way down a one-way street.

'What way to Draught Works?' I shouted.

'Two blocks over! You can't miss it!'

Missoula emitted an obvious and intoxicating buzz. With dozens of independent stores, cycle lanes and pop-up restaurants, it seemed a near-perfect size. Not so small as to feel parochial or over-familiar, yet not so big that it was awash with franchised fast-food joints and department stores. As I made my way across town, I saw pride flags fluttering from apartment balconies and a crosswalk painted like a rainbow.

The college town is a political anomaly in the context of Montana, a 'blue island' in an ocean of red. In January 2023, Missoula sent Zooey Zephyr, the first openly transgender legislator in Montana's history, to the state capitol. She won 80 per cent of the vote in her liberal, mostly student, district.

Sometimes journalism just falls into your lap. When I staggered into Draught Works – one of 13 craft breweries in a town of 75,000 people – to meet my host for the night, Bill Watson, a Democrat mayoral rally was in full flow.

'We'll chat later,' said Bill. 'I'd like you to see this.'

About 20 people stood in the corner supping pints of IPA, cream ales and pilsners, listening to a speech from Jordan Hess, one of five candidates challenging for the city seat. I grabbed a beer and settled into a chair, feeling my muscles tightening. I wouldn't be moving for a while.

Hess spoke of aiming for a 100 per cent clean energy goal by 2030. 'We're a city of people who really want to do something meaningful about the climate crisis,' he told the group. He was an ardent believer – as one would expect – in the power of local government but conceded to being somewhat hamstrung by Montana's state-level Republican leadership on issues like gun policy. At the end of his address, he joined me for a pint.

'A lot of the negative impact is around decisions made at a state level being imposed upon the locals,' said Jordan. 'But I am pragmatic about incrementally trying to move us in a direction. Missoula has become more liberal, while the state has become considerably more conservative. We are reliably 60–40 Democrat, which is a landslide by American election standards.'

Of all the big issues, however, housing was 'the issue of the day'. Homelessness had contributed to a growing number of people suffering mental health problems. The city faced an affordable housing crisis. Between 2012 and 2022, the median home sales price in Missoula had risen by 158 per cent. Meanwhile, the city's average income had only grown by 59 per cent.

'There's a lot of picking up the pieces from the state's missteps,' said Jordan. 'For instance, the state cut mental health care case management a few years ago in the legislative session and that has precipitated out this incredible impact of homelessness and untreated mental illness. So, a lot of what we are doing is reacting to the inaction at other levels of government.'

Six days later, Hess came third out of five candidates.

Montana has the third-highest number of breweries per capita of any US state, lagging only behind Maine and Vermont. If you like your craft brew, as I do, then you're never too far from a pint of porter or pale ale. Nevertheless, the state's idiosyncratic brewery laws caught me off guard. Not only did they call last orders at 8pm but there was also a three-drink limit. When I'd bought my first pint on arrival and been informed of this by the barmaid, I'd laughed it off as a rare case of American sarcasm, a funny joke. But no. Three beers in and my glass was dry.

It was, however, a blessing in disguise, because after 80 miles in the saddle, a can of beer at the bike shop, followed by three strong pints of ale, I was – to use British parlance – totally bollocksed. Thankfully, I had Bill Watson to guide me on my way. A keen cyclist in his sixties, we'd connected via the website Warm Showers, a worldwide community of 190,000 cyclists and 57,000 hosts. I discovered it for the first time in 2016 and had used it about a dozen times to connect with wonderful people across the nation. It is, essentially, Couch Surfing for bicycle tourists. Or Grindr, just with marginally more chains and lube. Friendly folk offer up a spare room or a garden for camping, for no other reason than to help a weary traveller on two wheels. No money is exchanged, just good vibes. And for added peace of mind, both parties have an online profile, complete with testimonials written by previous guests and hosts. As a rule of thumb, I only ever approached hosts that had welcomed guests relatively recently and had at least a handful of positive reviews.

Since 2016, Warm Showers has been developed from a rather clunky website into a smartphone app, allowing users to zoom in on different geographical regions. It has also been monetised – £2.99 a month – but for any would-be tourer, it is the best three quid you could ever spend, costing less than the fabled fifth beer.

Bill personified exactly what makes Warm Showers so special. He had been on his own long-distance tours, had benefited from the kindness of strangers and now wanted to pay something back to the community. When I eventually have the time and space to do the same, then I too will register as a host. I owe it to the world.

We got caught in an almighty storm. The biggest Missoula had seen all summer. Deafening claps of thunder reverberated against the Bitterroot and Rattlesnake mountains. Forked lightning cracked through the black sky, like the filaments of giant lightbulbs. The rain grew so intense and scary that we took refuge in a bar and refuelled with more pints of IPA and burritos the size of newborn babies.

The bar was wonderfully Missoulan; there was a peace flag flying in one corner and a taxidermied buffalo bust in the other.

A poster depicting a giant hand read: 'MISSOULA RESISTS. ONE HAND CAN CAST A VOTE. ONE VOTE CAN PROTECT DEMOCRACY. MANY HANDS CAN CHANGE THE WORLD.' The ladies' and gents' toilets were adorned with lino prints of John Lennon and Yoko Ono.

When the rain eased we finally made it back to Bill's. He could tell that I was shattered and made up a bed for me in the basement, a cosy snug filled with records, CDs and tapes. A keen muso for 'rock and prog, mostly', Bill had worked as a roadie for bands all over the world, enjoying stints on Bob Dylan's 1978 World Tour. In fact, he was working that very night. The folk-rock band The Lumineers had just headlined Missoula's KettleHouse Amphitheater and their stage needed to be dismantled and shipped to the next venue. As he laced up a pair of work boots and departed for a six-hour shift, I dropped onto the bed and closed my weary eyes. Exhausted and intoxicated, the next light I saw was morning.

I didn't see Bill again. He returned in the dead of night. But I did bump into his partner, Annette, as I tiptoed out of the house at dawn. We enjoyed a quick coffee together and she told me about some of the fascinating people they'd hosted in recent years. It took a special type of character to go to bed at night not knowing what random person was coming home from the pub to sleep in the basement.

She had short dark hair and bright, kind eyes. Their kitchen-lounge was lined with house plants, books and band posters.

'I'd say most of the Warm Showers cyclists we have staying with us tend to be a bit more … progressive. Politically and culturally.'

Since the pandemic, they'd seen an uptick in international cyclists crossing the country.

'We had this guy from France. He stayed with us several days. He was awesome. We also had a group of four Belgians – the Flemish Flyers – they were a lot of fun. And this guy called Ben a few weeks back. My goodness, was he tired!'

'Ben? American guy, with glasses?'

'Yeah.'

'I met him in the Cascades, just outside Seattle.'

We laughed. It was one of those 'small world' moments, a stroke of serendipity that had brought the four of us together, sort of.

'Why do you do this?' I asked. 'You don't have to do this.'

'It's really heartening for me because ...' Annette thought for a few seconds. 'I watch the news. But when you get one on one, people strip away that dichotomy and just become human beings.'

I could hear consternation in her voice. She told me that she could talk politics with the random strangers passing through her home but seldom her own family. Most of her relatives were 'pretty conservative', while she leaned much more to the left. So much so that, once again, politics had become a divisive issue.

'We get into big family arguments and it's really uncomfortable. We just choose not to go there.'

Guns, abortion, gay rights, racial issues and economic policy were off the table. Having more liberal perspectives on these topics had seen her branded 'woke'. In particular, she believed in a welfare state that helped those less fortunate.

'In the West, there's this mentality of pull yourself up by your own bootstraps. In my family, there's this sense that some groups [racial and cultural minorities] are getting favourable treatment, but what they really need to do is pull themselves up by their bootstraps. There's a feeling that people are playing the system.'

I could feel myself getting comfortable. Good conversation and great coffee. But comfort wasn't the best sensation for the start of a day, so I gave my thanks and dragged myself out into the morning. The storms had passed but it was humid and overcast, and a frenetic tingle lingered in the atmosphere. I headed east on a bicycle trail beside the Clark Fork River, then zigzagged through a leafy university suburb.

Every other building belonged to a fraternity or sorority. Palatial homes, more French chateaux than student digs. Some had grand Roman columns, most sported ostentatious Greek lettering. They looked like the party houses I grew up watching in Hollywood student movies like *Road Trip* (2000), *Van Wilder: Party Liaison* (2002) and *The Butterfly Effect* (2004). If the silver screen was to be believed, then these were the sorts of places where you'd see freshmen chugging beer bongs or swigging tequila from bright red plastic cups. A far cry from my £3,000 a year polytechnic degree and £50 a week student house on Liverpool's so-called 'Murder Mile', the average cost of a college degree in the United States is $108,364 spread across four years for out-of-state students, and only marginally cheaper for those studying in their home state.

Critics claim that frat and sorority houses create a culture of nepotism in wider American society. A 2013 report by Bloomberg found that fraternity connections were influential in securing lucrative jobs at top Wall Street brokerages. Proponents argue, however, that these institutions offer camaraderie and networking opportunities.

There is also the controversial culture of 'hazing' – a kind of rugby-club-style initiation, and some. In some states the practice is legally forbidden, but it almost certainly still exists, and most focus on physically and emotionally degrading rituals, regularly involving alcohol. Between 2000 and 2021, there were more than 50 hazing-related deaths in the US. In 2021, 19-year-old Virginia Commonwealth University student Adam Oakes died due to alcohol poisoning. In February 2023 his family sued his fraternity for $28 million.

By lunchtime, the sun had burned away 90 per cent of the grey cloud and the sky was now all but pure electric blue. On the open road, I had found a rhythm and was moving quickly: 14mph on a gloriously flat 'frontage road' – a much quieter thoroughfare that ran parallel to Interstate 90.

I had four bananas and a family-sized bag of M&Ms, of which I could scoff down a handful without stopping, charged with adrenaline and E numbers. My only restriction was water: I couldn't carry as much as I needed for a whole day, and therefore had to rely upon the drab concrete rest stops built on the side of America's highways. They were, however, brilliant places to meet people. In a parking lot filled with idling SUVs, my bicycle and red panniers caught the eye of almost every motorist making a pitstop to empty their bladders.

'You're catching up with us!' exclaimed a woman as I emerged from the toilets. 'We saw you miles back. Boy, you're moving fast!'

Septuagenarian sisters Dee and Patty were travelling east across the country to visit their 99-year-old mother who lived in South Dakota. They were, as I'd come to expect, overwhelmed by the notion of someone riding a bicycle in a land where the car was king. Especially a person who they had just seen sweating beside them as they cruised in the comfort of their air-conditioned bubble. Wearing sweatpants and baggy sweaters, they were dressed for a long drive.

Dee and Patty had grown up in the 1950s on a North Dakotan farm and were two of eight siblings. Passionate about traditional family values, they believed in hardworking parents who set good examples for their children. 'We were raised with a strong work ethic,' said Dee.

'I just wish we could go back to the time when we were at school,' agreed Patty. 'It's just sad. On a farm. North Dakota. No indoor plumbing. I wish things could go back to that kind of living.'

Over the course of successive governments, they had seen America become 'an easy touch' on crime. In their opinion, the current Democrat government was the easiest touch of them all.

Dee had recently retired from a 32-year stint as a loss prevention manager at a department store. 'We controlled losses. Theft and shoplifters, all that kind of stuff. Before I exited out, laws were getting very lax. It was like it was OK for people to come in and steal. We couldn't even detain anybody. It's a free-for-all!'

They wanted to live in a country with 'stiffer laws' and jails that worked harder to reform drug users, inside and outside. And they were speaking from experience. Patty's son used marijuana as a pain medication, but Dee's son was currently incarcerated for harder drug dealing. He had been in and out of jail for most of his adult life.

'Was it right that your son went to jail?' I asked, expecting to be fiercely and loyally rebutted.

'Absolutely,' said Dee. 'For the crimes he committed, yes. But there is no rehabilitation in our prison systems. It's a vicious, revolving door. To me, it [America's drug culture] has just taken on a life of its own.'

I wondered what her son would say if he were stood on that roadside with us, with the sun on his face and the breeze in his hair. Enjoying the trappings of 'freedom' that many Americans held so dearly. As a felon, in and out of the system, had the country done good or bad by him?

'That's a deep question,' said Dee with a pause then a shudder in her voice. 'I think sometimes he feels that the world owes him. That he didn't deserve this. But on the other hand, he has had our family's support to help him through those tough times and he will accept responsibility for that.'

I continued on my journey in a state of admiration for Dee's openness. For discussing, so candidly, with a stranger, an issue that must have caused so much pain and heartbreak. Her son was one of the 1.8 million Americans in jail. No country on earth has more prisoners. But behind these gargantuan figures were real people, their families, mothers and aunts.

With the scent of manure hanging in the warm air, I rolled into the small town of Drummond just before 4pm. 'HOME OF THE TROJANS' read a freshly painted welcome sign just off the interstate. A cattle grid prevented livestock from invading the road.

I almost checked into the Drummond Motel, the only accommodation in town. It was shabby chic, with little of the latter. I enquired as to the cost of a room – $90 with a credit card or $80 cash. About $50 too much, either way. 'I'll go down to the gas station and get some cash,' I told the woman behind the desk, unsure if I'd ever actually return.

I was torn. Physically exhausted and mentally ready to finish for the day, all I wanted to do was collapse on a bed and have a warm bath But this really wasn't the place. On the side of a rusting truck trailer was a giant painting of a baseball field, a batter hitting a home run and the words: 'PLAY BALL. DON'T PLAY WITH METH. IT'S NOT A GAME. NOT EVEN ONCE.'

The worst advert for the motel, however, was a freight train that rushed past the front door sounding its horn. Less than 100 feet away, the earth shook beneath me. 'They go all night,' said a man at the nearby gas station, who was skilfully managing to speak out of one side of his mouth while spitting tobacco out the other.

I decided to push on. The weather was hot and sunny, and, armed with three litres of ice-cold water and a fresh pack of M&Ms, I continued east towards the intriguing-sounding town of

Deer Lodge. Thirty miles more tonight, I reasoned, would be 30 miles less tomorrow.

The land southeast of Drummond was the biggest of big sky country. I had mountains on both sides, cradling peaks of epic grandeur and fanciful names. To the north, I could see the twin summits of Old Baldy. At 9,156 feet, it was the king of the Sawtooth Range. To the south was Mount Powell, even bigger – over 10,000 feet – and the highest point in the Flint Creek Range.

Thankfully, I had another frontage road almost entirely to myself, sandwiched on one side by Interstate 90 and the railroad on the other. Occasionally, a train, about a mile or so long, would grumble by, pulling trailers of oil, logs and sometimes cattle. It was a beautiful road but with an ominous sight on the horizon: a gargantuan cumulonimbus. It was hard to tell if the cloud was getting closer or moving further away. Nevertheless, the clock was ticking to get back to civilisation.

For the first time on my journey, I raced and raced. Head down. The clouds were closing in. I thought I was beating the rain but 15mph was no match for a thundercloud the size of a city. About ten miles from Deer Lodge, I noticed a few spits on the back of my hands and neck. Then, five miles from town, the deluge consumed me. Even bigger than the storms before.

After the flashes of intense forked lightning in Missoula the night before, I felt exceptionally exposed. No shelter whatsoever. All I could do was keep moving forward. Within five minutes, I was soaked through again. This was late summer in Montana and a pattern was emerging: cool mornings followed by hot afternoons, rising heat, then an explosion of pent-up energy.

Being struck by lightning is rare, but not impossible. Around the world, approximately 2,000 people are struck every year. Ten per cent of whom die. In the US alone, about 40 million lightning strikes hit the ground each year. Between 2006 and 2021, 444 people died from their injuries. Alarmingly, men are four times more likely to be struck than women, while the average age of a person hit is 37. As a 36-and-a-half-year-old male, I had the odds stacked against me.

Despite the intensity of the storm, though, and the perceived level of danger, it was up there with the most spectacular things I had ever witnessed. When the raincloud moved slightly to the east, the westerly setting sun refracted horizontally through its prism-like heart, creating a perfect double rainbow. It was so arresting and I was already so wet that I felt compelled to stop and take a photo. With my bike propped up on its kickstand and the road black with rain, I hastily snapped an image that will stay in my mind's eye – and likely sit in a frame on my writing desk – forever.

Just as I was about to leave, a tiny rental car stopped 20 feet ahead of me. 'Dude, this is insane!' shouted the male driver, as he jumped out and started taking photos. He was on a road trip with his teenage daughter, who seemed significantly less enthused.

'Let's take a selfie together. What are you doing out here, man?'

I told them.

'What! That's unreal, man. God bless you!'

As the wind and rain howled, we enjoyed a few minutes in each other's company before conceding that our respective journeys needed to continue. They were almost as soaked as me when they slipped back into their car. It was one of those dreamlike, ephemeral moments – not experienced with my best friends, wife or family, but with a pair of strangers, never to be seen again, who found themselves equally caught up in the timeless wonder of a great big storm.

I reached Deer Lodge long after dusk. The streetlights were on and the black sky twinkled. I was now deep within the Rockies and surrounded by mountains on all sides. It had been an intense and epic day, but somehow, through dogged perseverance and a little bit of stupidity, I wound up in the hot bath I'd promised myself. And at $60 for a clean room far away from train tracks, it was a bargain.

Dinner was McDonald's, the only option. A Big Mac and ten chicken nuggets, followed by a beer in the adjacent bar-casino, which also doubled up as a liquor store. The room blinked like a mini Las Vegas and echoed with the sound of virtual cash registers. KA-CHING!

At $4 a pint, beer was a steal. Unlike in Washington (6.5 per cent) and Idaho (6 per cent), Montana is one of five US states without a sales tax. The price you see is the price you pay. Excluding a tip, of course.

'You gambling?' asked the bartender, as I pulled up a stool and ordered a pint.

'Oh, no thanks, mate.'

It took me half a pint to realise my error.

'If I'm gambling, does that change anything?' I enquired.

'If you're gambling, then drinks are free.'

'Well, in that case, yes I am gambling!'

For a seasoned traveller with a penchant for a bargain, I'd already hit the jackpot. There was no minimum bet, so I threw $5 into the nearest fruit machine and ordered a refill. *I am, basically, getting paid to drink beer*, I thought. *I am a ... 'professional' pisshead.*

I had no idea what I was doing. But there was zero skill involved, beyond simply pressing a button every few seconds. The screen flickered in front of me and I watched my money grow. $5 became $6, which soon became $6.50. Within 90 seconds, I had a balance of over $10.

After a bit of warming up, the barman was brilliantly opinionated and great company. He didn't seem remotely bothered that I wasn't really gambling, knowing the house would always win. If not with me, then against someone else.

'America is full of spoiled brats,' said 31-year-old Cody, as he rested his elbows on the counter and began fiddling with the peak of his baseball cap. 'No one likes living here. Everyone is spoiled. It has become anti-American.'

Originally from Chicago, he had met a local girl, coincidentally from Drummond – the town I'd decided not to stay in – and got married just a few weeks prior. He had backpacked across Europe and travelled extensively around the USA, visiting a whopping 47 states.

'Americans have it very good, but we like to look at things like we don't. And it makes things worse because you kind of manifest your own downfall.'

In his lifetime, he had witnessed the housing market and the US dollar 'going to shit'. He also believed the country spent far too much on its military ($877 billion in 2022) and foreign aid ($60.4 billion in 2023, rising to $63.1 billion in 2024). He was in elementary school in 2001, when the 9/11 terrorist attacks took place, but vividly remembered the jingoistic aftermath: 'After 9/11 it was like "America! America! America!"' Since then, he conceded, the country had been on a downward trajectory.

We spent over an hour chatting, as a steady procession of locals came and went. Most were lonesome men with big white beards. They wore fertilizer-branded baseball caps, denim shirts and leather boots. Everyone was courteous and nodded as they entered, but Cody and I were the only people talking. The rest just grabbed their routine tipple – mostly shots of tequila and bottles of Coors Light – and then set about feeding five- and ten-dollar bills into machines that buzzed and blinked.

After four pints, I decided to do the immensely boring thing of cashing out. Fifteen dollars. I was $10 up and had enjoyed $20 of 'free' beer. So I left Cody a $10 tip and stumbled back to my room, which was conveniently just a few hundred feet away.

9

ACROSS THE DIVIDE

The next morning, I was jolted into life by next door's yapping dachshund in need of its morning crap.

Despite my early alarm, though, I'd slept soundly. And when I tiptoed out into a new day, the storm had passed. Half day, half night, the morning was sharp like glass. Most of the sky was tinged in an amethyst wash, but to the south, an immense and brilliant light dazzled.

'Montana State Prison,' said one of two friendly cleaning ladies on reception. 'Sixteen hundred felons, all living in a compound of 68 acres.'

'It's our claim to fame,' said the other.

My bike and accent were met with wide eyes and flapping hands. I was eager to get out of the door but they were so charming, and keen to tell me of their English, Irish and Scottish heritage, that I stopped for an extra coffee. Perhaps they were sisters. It was hard to tell. Their brown eyes suggested they had at least one of the same parents. When I told them I was from Oxford, 'Where *Inspector Morse* is set,' one of them all but fainted.

The weather was almost perfect for cycling and it couldn't be wasted. On the southeast horizon, a few fluffy clouds had appeared, but they were hours away from becoming the ominous cumulonimbus of the night before. I was almost three weeks in and sitting pretty. Feeling fit and rested, I threw on a playlist – hip-hop classics – and let Tupac, Jay-Z and Snoop Dogg propel me forward at 85 beats per minute.

Fifteen miles south of Deer Lodge, I stopped for brunch on the edge of the intriguingly named town of Anaconda, home to one of the tallest free-standing brick structures in the world: the Anaconda smelter stack. Taller than the Washington Monument (555 feet) – the pointed obelisk on the National Mall in Washington, D.C. – Anaconda's smelter (585 feet) is a giant monument to industry, surrounded by the undulating, but not jagged, Anaconda Range. It was built in 1918 by the Anaconda Copper Company and until its closure in 1981 processed copper ore mined in the nearby city of Butte.

Totally at odds with its surroundings, from a distance it resembled a giant clarinet, or an extra-terrestrial craft that had landed from a distant galaxy. It was, without doubt, the most sensational sight of the entire journey so far. In its heyday, the stack belched black smoke across the surrounding region. Examined through squinted eyes, it possessed a fantastical Tolkien quality. Something like Barad-dûr, fortress of Sauron, set deep within the black volcanic plains of Mordor.

I didn't make the detour into Anaconda's downtown, opting instead to perch on a fence, far away from humanity, and take in the immensity of the landscape around me. Sprawling plains of green engulfed every horizon until mountains blocked their way. Once upon a time, these empty grasslands were dotted with the muscular hides of American buffalo. In the late eighteenth century, there were between 30 and 60 million roaming North America. Within a hundred years of European expansionism, fewer than a thousand remained. These days, their numbers have recovered to around half a million.

As the sun warmed my ears, I tucked in to a new and highly calorific culinary creation. I called it the M&Ms pizza: a tortilla wrap, smothered in crunchy peanut butter and a sliced banana, garnished with a dozen multicoloured peanut M&Ms. It was the sort of meal that no other human being should see you eating, especially those not *au fait* with the energy-sapping realities of extreme exercise and its guilt-free excesses. I posted a photo on Instagram and at least three people branded me a psychopath.

With my brain fizzing with sugar, I joined a quiet road running parallel with Interstate 90 – there were still no other viable options – and watched a tiny sharp-shinned hawk, the smallest hawk in North America, zoom over my shoulders, complete a delicate pirouette against the azure sky and come to rest on a fencepost ahead of me. Chocolatey brown, with shiny yellow eyes like marbles, it let me get to within five feet of it before bolting off into the pure green.

Below the seemingly bucolic surface, however, a sinister poison remained. A few miles down the road, I passed through Opportunity, not so much a town, or even a village, but a sporadic collection of clapboard homes, farms and self-storage companies. Opportunity is stigmatised as one of the roughly 1,300 so-called 'Superfund' sites in the United States – places where hazardous waste was dumped or improperly managed by manufacturing facilities, processing plants, landfills or mining companies. Cancer-causing arsenic and other heavy metals have penetrated the land and its nearby streams.

Many local people benefited economically from the Anaconda Copper Mining Company plant, once the lifeblood of Anaconda and its surroundings. Since its closure, though, locals have reported pet dogs developing tumours, the mass deaths of livestock and patches of once-fertile grassland becoming suspiciously impotent.

It took me another couple of hours to reach the outskirts of Butte, a mining town known locally as 'the Richest Hill on Earth' thanks to its abundant copper ore, or 'the City of Widows', due to the 2,500 men who lost their lives in its mines between 1870 and 1983.

On the far side of a giant billboard advertising 'WORLD FAMOUS EXOTIC DANCERS', I could see the aforementioned 'richest hill'. Framed by moss-green mountains, a giant wall of ochre-hued copper ore had been exposed and cut into house-sized blocks. From afar, it resembled an enormous slice of Battenberg cake.

More than 6 billion tonnes of copper have been extracted from Butte's mines, with the metal helping to electrify the USA during the late nineteenth and early twentieth centuries. At the mine's peak, some 8,000 men were on the payroll. Their riches helped transform Butte into an attractive town, famed for its Victorian architecture, such as pretty Queen Anne cottages with their steep roofs, cross gables and large dormers. Sadly, however, Butte was also the site of the worst hardrock mining disaster in United States history. A fire at the Granite Mountain mine on 8 June 1917 killed 168 employees.

The town boasts a strong Irish heritage. Thousands migrated from the Emerald Isle to prosper during its boom time. It was also the birthplace of the world-famous daredevil Evel Knievel. The motorcyclist travelled the world wowing audiences with his death-defying stunts, dressed in his hallmark Stars and Stripes spandex suit.

These days, Butte is better known for two-wheeled thrill seekers of a different kind. It is a major stop off on the Continental Divide Trail, the 3,100-mile bike route that runs between Mexico and Canada, following the spine of the Rocky Mountains. It is a bike tour of epic proportions. With over 200,000 feet of elevation gain, it is regarded as the longest off-pavement cycling route in the world. It is a journey for another day, another book or perhaps another lifetime. But as I intersected its path, I was eager to meet a Warm Showers legend, a man who has welcomed over 400 cyclists to his home. In fact, I was his four-hundred-and-first.

'I host people doing the Continental Divide, mostly,' said John Babcock, a thin and athletic man with short brown hair, as he beckoned me in off the suburban street and into his cosy home. 'But you're the first I've ever had doing this particular route, from Cape Flattery to Key West – that's pretty cool.'

Thankfully, John had room for me. Or more accurately, a garage, complete with bunkbeds, as much electricity as I needed and tools aplenty. By September 2023, he had already welcomed 140 touring cyclists that year. So much so that – unlike some Warm Showers experiences that can start a little awkwardly – there was no standing on ceremony. John had hosted so many cyclists that he knew exactly what I needed even before I did.

'The shower's down the hall,' said John. 'I've left a towel on the bench and I'll do us pasta for dinner. I've only got one beer left, but you're welcome to it.'

John worked as a hydrogeologist, restoring streams after severe floods and ensuring public safety at collapsed coal mines. He lived with his two teenage sons and their two dogs: Roux, a friendly Catahoula leopard dog, and Flipper, a yappy dachshund-chihuahua mixed breed that had been born with deformed, flipper-like front feet.

To John, cycle touring epitomised the American Dream: 'Irrespective of where you might be politically, there is one thing that all Americans can agree upon, and that is freedom. The freedom to ride your bike is the most liberating thing. Once you're on the bike, you're down to the bare essentials.'

John spoke of the 'little microcosm of cyclists' he lived within. He travelled vicariously through the people who stayed over. The world, and America, came to him and slept in his garage. Their stories of adventure inspired him, and his sons. 'The world is pretty ugly, because of its politics,' said John. 'But this is the community I want to be a part of.'

A man after my own heart, John took great pride in using up the refrigerator's various leftovers and managed to rustle up a big saucepan of veggie spaghetti, rich with tomato sauce and grated cheese. One of his sons, Henry, joined us briefly to scoff down food before roaring off across town on his motocross bike to watch the Friday night high school football match: Butte Bulldogs versus Glacier Wolfpack. The visiting team was travelling 250 miles for the fixture.

Butte, John told me, was a different kind of Democrat town. In contrast to Missoula, it was more working class, blue collar. 'Missoula was always the kind of hippy, progressive, liberal town. Whereas Butte is kind of unique in that it's a Democratic town but it's more a union stronghold. The labour movement was really strong here because of the mining. It's very Democratic but it's not progressive. In fact, it's very anti-progressive. Which is kind of part of its charm.'

For people who enjoy an active lifestyle, Butte is a hub for mountain biking, hiking and skiing. In the winter, John and his sons were on the nearby slopes most weekends. There was perhaps no person better placed to give me advice for the days ahead. The following morning, I would cross the Continental Divide.

I spent the next couple of hours in his garage workshop, faffing around with my bike and panniers. I pumped up my tyres, charged all my gadgets and played around with that week's YouTube video.

For a short time, at least, it felt like mission control. Everything I could possibly need, all under one 250-square-foot roof.

A bright dawn bled through a chink in the garage door. John was already sat in his living room tinkering around on a laptop, but I declined the offer of coffee. He directed me to a cycle route that would take me around the mountains, rather than directly up and over them, running the gauntlet on Interstate 90 and crossing Homestake Pass as the sun rose blindingly from the east, directly behind the mountains.

That's not to say there wasn't any climbing. There was lots and lots of climbing. An ascent of about 2,000 feet. But the joy of the road was in its emptiness. First thing Saturday morning and I had it almost entirely to myself, with barely a car for company. Verdant and aromatic, thousands of aspen trees creaked and groaned. I was lulled by the purity of the forest, its lushness cleansing my lungs and soul.

This epic, beautiful road did, however, possess danger. After an hour, I stopped to pay my respects at a metal crucifix and a bicycle-shaped stencil, painted in a bright white emulsion. In July 2019, a 70-year-old cyclist was killed by the wing mirror of a passing motor home.

I had barely seen a vehicle, but 650 feet from the summit a Ram pickup screeched around a corner behind me, the driver wound down the window and screamed a tirade of profanities in my direction. Until now, American drivers had been reasonably considerate – Montanan motorists especially so. Nevertheless, there will always be the occasional dickhead. Back in Britain, if someone yelled at me from a car window, my instinct was to yell back, maybe with a hand gesture or two. But in Montana, where I had seen guns, I was keen to keep my head down. Especially at 8.30 on a Saturday morning, on a quiet road in the middle of the mountains. You have no idea if someone might be driving home from a late-night party in an intoxicated bad mood.

As I inched towards the summit, I passed stop signs that had been peppered with bullets. This was a trend in the United States, especially beside rural roads. Were people shooting them from their moving cars? When I stopped for a rest at the top of Pipestone Pass, the 6,453-foot pinnacle of my entire cross-country ride, I asked Google. The best response, found on a forum, read: 'Dude. They don't move very fast and they are always in season. Why *wouldn't* we shoot them? Dang.'

Descending down the other side of the Continental Divide was one of the greatest hours of my life. Smooth switchbacks wove through the forest. In some places, the trees were so dense they cast thick shadows across the jet-black road, creating brooding dark patches like shivering cold spots in a swimming pool. In other places, the view opened up, revealing undulating hills the colour of steamed cabbage leaves. They rambled for dozens upon dozens of miles, before being swallowed up by intense cobalt blue.

With 35 miles on the clock, I stopped for a rest in Whitehall, a small town created by the Northern Pacific and Montana Railroad companies as a train depot in the late nineteenth century. A redbrick downtown remains, and I spotted a bakery, a few pawn shops, a couple of thrift stores and a movie theatre. I overshot most of the town but was intrigued by the flea market – essentially a barn clad in corrugated iron the colour of custard.

Inside, I found a handful of traders selling all manner of bric-a-brac. Everything from peacock feathers and Native American dream catchers to bird cages and fur coats. Embarrassingly, I was the only customer – and a browser, at best – but as soon as they heard my accent, I was offered a wooden rocking chair and a polystyrene cup of 'coffee'. Two of the traders, Bruce and Gillian, did most of the talking, while the rest of the room listened in. I told them I was curious to understand the real America. The America behind the headlines.

'I believe that America is going to come to an end,' said Bruce, a tall, bespectacled man in jeans and a bright blue T-shirt. 'Civilizations, countries, places with large amounts of people, they go strong for about 200 years and then something happens – a natural disaster or a plague – and it wipes them completely out. We are just beyond 200 years old, and I believe the end is coming.'

The end, Bruce reasoned, might not be a global doomsday extinction but a significant loss of American supremacy on the world stage. This might come from a civil war or in the form of attacks from foreign powers. 'I believe that we've beat our chest too many times and the rest of the countries are going to go: "OK, we're calling your bullshit and fuck you." I'm waiting for nuclear war.'

Having just stumbled in from the mountains, into a random flea market on the side of the road, this was dynamite. If ever there was an example of an American citizen exercising the First Amendment – the constitutional right to free speech – then this was it.

'I know this is going to sound stupid, but *The Simpsons* have predicted nuclear war and *The Simpsons* have predicted so much dumb stuff. It just keeps happening.'

America, Bruce told me, was still reeling from the Covid pandemic. A period that had intensified angry wounds already present in American society. For example, widening the gap between rich and poor.

'People are starving, our veterans are homeless, our economy is shit. Covid killed everything. Nobody made money during Covid, except Walmart and the superstores. I just feel that people hate people too much here.'

Our conversation then took an unexpected turn. Bruce believed that in order for America to save itself from itself, large swathes of society would need to rebel against the government, the police force and the military.

'Big group,' he said. 'Millions need to march into the White House, march into the Senate and take out everybody.'

'Surely that would be anarchy?' I responded. 'You can't have an insurrection of that degree. You need an active, democratic society to live in.'

'Democratic would be perfect. We have some good people, but they are few and far between. The people in office now do not care about America.'

Gillian had been listening politely but she took exception to my suggestion of anarchy and argued that the incident at the US Capitol Building in Washington D.C. on 6 January 2021 was not an 'insurrection'. She believed that the real story had been covered up by the mainstream media. Protesters hadn't forced themselves into the Capitol, but 'the CIA and FBI let them in ... It was an inside job, just like 9/11 was an inside job.'

I was slightly stumped as to where the conversation went from here.

'Where do you get that information from?' I enquired, trying not to patronise or belittle.

'It's out there, you just have to dig really deep,' said Gillian, who believed Twitter was once run by 'the Deep State or the New World Order' and that a small handful of extremely wealthy people – 'the 1 per cent' – ran the world. 'They don't want the rest of us to know what is going on, because the rest of us would say "what the heck?"'

She was also undecided if 'America was still under the control of England' and believed that before her death, Princess Diana was 'trying to expose it'. Moreover, President John F. Kennedy wasn't killed by Lee Harvey Oswald, as the history books suggest, but 'assassinated by the US government'.

'Unfortunately, the information isn't just handed out to you,' said Bruce. 'They would never do that. You have to dig for it.'

You could deride the pair as 'conspiracy theorists', 'anti-establishment', 'tinfoil-hat-wearing wackos'. But to them, these words were gospel. They had grown so disaffected by 'mainstream society' that they turned to the internet for answers. They told me about social media platforms I'd never heard of and 'influencers' with tens of millions of followers being 'ignored' by the conventional news channels. The three of us were on different planets entirely. But behind all that, they were kind and hospitable people. And, once again, remarkably generous with their opinions. Especially towards a journalist who had dropped in unannounced. Nevertheless, I could tell that I made them feel slightly uneasy. A conflict existed between them wanting to be nice to a weary traveller and the distrust they had for what I represented.

During my career, I had worked for most of the major British news outlets, spanning the entire political spectrum. But they were fervently suspicious of the 'mainstream' channels and by their definition I was one of 'them' – part of the cabal.

Just before I left, I plucked up the courage and asked, 'Do you think I'm in on it too?'

'I think there are good people in all of the areas,' said Gillian diplomatically.

The afternoon passed by in a state of head-down, focused forward motion. I listened back to my flea market recording twice, agog at what I had just heard first-hand. Bruce and Gillian were the real-life embodiment of an underworld existing in the shadows of the internet. One that is rarely given a platform offline. Some of their theories seemed fantastical, borderline bonkers. What had surprised me most about our meeting, though, was how other traders watched on and let them speak openly, without heckling or contradicting. It was hard to tell if they remained silent out of scorn or muted in agreement.

The pair shared a unanimous belief that America had gone downhill. And while the Musks, Bezoses and Waltons among them prospered, they collectively suffered.

Seven years before, when I met the shaven-headed farmer who believed there were 'secret' messages in YouTube videos, his ideas felt clandestine, under the radar, off the wall. It was as though he was slightly embarrassed to say them out loud. His opinions were delivered in an erratic, scattergun style. Sure, it might have been the crack he was smoking. But it might also be because these ideas were less well formed back then. Still gathering momentum. We were, remember, still four years before the so-called 'stolen election'. The phrase 'fake news' was only just entering our shared vocabulary.

Now, though, a clear and defined thread seemed to exist. An entrenched distrust of 'they' – a hard-to-define 'elite' or illuminati – but a bogeyman all the same. Even in this relatively short interim, it felt as though the conspiracy 'theorists' had found a home, a confidence to speak up on the outside, in the real world. Their ideas had, paradoxically, gone mainstream.

10

MILITARY BRAT

I reached Bozeman just before nightfall, checked into an Airbnb, threw my clothes into a hot wash and gave myself a double deep clean. Because I was about to welcome a very special guest to the expedition: support crew. Snack manager. My wife.

At the few events I speak at each year, the post-talk Q&A follows a predictable line of questioning. Up first is usually 'What's your favourite country?' Followed by a handful of queries about saddle sores, punctures and defecating in awkward places. This plays out for around 20 minutes, but towards the end, there is often a little chirrup from the back. Naughty students, or adults, encouraging each other to ask one final, almost taboo, question: 'I can see you're wearing a wedding ring. What the hell does your wife make of all this?'

The short answer is that we make it work because this is all we've ever known. Travel has been hardwired into our relationship from the get-go. And while my occasional absences from weddings, family dinners and friends' birthdays have certainly caused their fair share of arguments, we subscribe to the notion that absence makes our hearts grow fonder. On balance, jobs that routinely take us away from each other bring us much closer together.

That's not to say that me being thousands of miles from home doesn't cause us great heartbreak and inconvenience. For Alana especially, who often needs to hold the fort while I'm swanning around on the other side of the world. But for every tearful goodbye, there is an ecstatic reunion. And when we got married in August 2022, we enshrined a non-negotiable prenuptial into our vows: wherever we are in the world, we'll never go more than three weeks apart.

My expedition across the USA would be the greatest test, logistically and financially. Not only was Alana dragging herself to Montana while pregnant, but we'd spent the advance for this very book on keeping to our word. But what is the point in doing these things if you can't share them with the people you love? And as I stood at Bozeman Airport, my legs growing weary from the day, I bounced excitedly.

At 11pm, she finally appeared and we rushed into each other's trembling arms.

Not much happened for the next 36 hours. There was no sightseeing or dancing in the moonlight. Instead, we just enjoyed the sweet, mundane joy of being together in the same room. We binge-watched a series on Netflix, read our books in bed and listened to our favourite playlist. The boring, normal stuff that most people take for granted. There were a few chores I had to complete, like editing my next YouTube film and decanting a fresh supply of pills and powders into my panniers – my drug mule had delivered. Otherwise, we just loafed around doing extremely little.

Predictably, as the adrenaline dropped, the hangover kicked in and my brain grew foggy. I felt so out of sorts, I took a nap – an extremely rare event for someone so highly strung. Then, in the early evening, we drove to a nearby pizza restaurant for dinner. It was only a few miles away, but moving at 50mph rather than 10mph made my head spin with vertigo.

Alana was my biggest concern, though. She was still suffering from morning sickness. In the seven years we had been together, I had never known her to have more than a tickly cough for a day or two. But now her immune system was taking a battering. When she wasn't throwing up, she mopped her blocked nose with raggedy tissues soaked in Olbas Oil.

'This baby is sucking the life out of me,' she groaned, as I, somewhat callously, left her in bed and continued my journey.

'Rest up for as long as you can,' I said. 'I'll see you this afternoon.'

By 7.30am, I was on the road and cycling towards the rising sun. It was a terrible time to travel, as thousands of vehicles rushed in and out of Bozeman. All I wanted to do was turn around and get back into bed, but this wasn't a holiday and there were miles to cover.

About five minutes into the day, a concrete mixer surprised me from behind and almost ripped my body in two. Its filthy chassis passed within a few inches of my neck and handlebars. With my wife and unborn child now in tow, the danger levels of the journey seemed to multiply tenfold. 'What the fuck am I doing?' I growled to myself, as I imagined Alana driving the same route in a few hours' time and being met by a traffic jam and flashing blue lights.

It wasn't pretty, or enjoyable, but in order to reach the other side of Bozeman, I jumped back onto Interstate 90. On paper, I know it sounds like madness, but the interstate was the only road I could trust to have room for a cyclist – especially at rush hour.

The shoulder was, as usual, filled with all the trash I'd come to expect. Bottles of fluorescent urine, used nappies, discarded hypodermic syringes. It is not the sort of place you expect company, especially of the human variety. But as I pushed away from the city and back into the forested wilds of Montana, I spotted a bearded man, probably in his mid seventies, living in a tent just 20 feet from the cacophonous craziness of the interstate. We shared a few friendly thumbs up – I just wanted to know he was OK – but decided that neither of us had the time or energy to pass further pleasantries.

At times, Montana felt like a cycling nirvana, blessed with wide open spaces and straight roads. Directly east of Bozeman, though, it felt like perdition. The route became so hemmed in by steep slopes that the air was churned thick with acerbic fumes unable to escape. Throw a stiff headwind into the mix and you have a recipe for a particularly challenging morning. It should have taken me three hours to reach Livingston but I eventually needed five.

Perched on the banks of the Yellowstone River, Livingston – Montana's windiest city – started life as a railroad town in the late nineteenth century. Now it's better known for its quirky and eclectic vibe, and for having become something of a celebrity hotspot. Jeff Bridges – A.K.A. 'The Dude' Big Lebowski – has a home nearby.

Actor Dennis Quaid lived there for more than 25 years, and so too did the film director James Cameron. The late novelist and poet Jim Harrison adored Livingston and lived in a cabin in nearby Paradise Valley. The singer-songwriter Jimmy Buffett also had strong links with the mountain town and passed away just a week before my arrival.

I'd been invited into the offices of the local newspaper, the *Livingston Enterprise*, to tell them my story. On the front page of the previous week's newspaper, the headline read: 'FAREWELL JIMMY BUFFETT', alongside a black and white image of the moustachioed musician with shoulder-length hair and a wide-brimmed leather hat.

The newspaper occupied the ground floor of an office block and had clearly seen better – or, at least, busier – days. There was no one else in there, apart from me and the paper's local reporter, Sean Batura. He had been born into a military family and spent most of his childhood in Utah and Texas. Aged 45, he wore a suede flat cap, aviator-style glasses and a red polo shirt tucked into sand-coloured chinos. A holster on his brown leather belt housed not a gun but a smartphone – poised for recording interviews. He reminded me of a sober Hunter S. Thompson.

'The American term for what I am is "military brat",' he said. 'I think that the rootlessness of many people like me has become a significant part of the fabric of the country, for good or ill. I'm inclined to think it's mostly a detriment, but that's just my opinion.'

The *Livingston Enterprise* published a print newspaper every Wednesday and Saturday, but had a website that was updated daily. Like local newspapers all over the world, its readership had declined significantly in the past few decades. Nevertheless, it still occupied a vital role in the community.

'I think it [the local newspaper] is very important,' said Sean, as we sifted through old copies. 'There's been a declining confidence in the national news media and I think local news can really bridge that gap. Our readers can form a rapport with us. It keeps us even more honest.'

I am slightly biased on the issue of local news media because it's where – like many young journalists – I cut my teeth. Sure, it can feel a tad parochial at times. Some news days are considerably slower than others. But without local newspapers, radio and TV stations, Britain and the United States would be poorer places.

Sean reported on a small western town and felt accountable to its residents. He bumped into his 'stories' in the grocery store and passed them in the street. The same cannot be said for most journalists writing for the nationals, talking heads on TV, or 'commentators' hidden behind avatars on social media. He was an old-school newshound and still – however anachronistic it can now sometimes feel – adhered to a code of practice and ethics.

Moreover, the big issues discussed at a macro, national level were beginning right there, with him. 'For example, the issue of library books,' said Sean. 'People from different perspectives disagree to what extent they are appropriate for children. Election issues have also come up locally. People trying to change how elections are administrated.'

The following week's front page replaced an image of a smouldering Jimmy Buffett with a photo of yours truly, looking a lot less cool and a lot more dishevelled. The headline read: 'A BRITON UNDER THE BIG SKY. UK JOURNALIST PAUSES IN LIVINGSTON DURING HIS CROSS-COUNTRY CYCLING TOUR.'

Somewhat alarmingly, though, another headline on the front page read: 'MAN RECOVERING FROM BEAR ATTACK NEAR BIG SKY. GRIZZLY BIT OFF VICTIM'S JAW BEFORE BEING SHOT AT BY SOMEONE ELSE, DAUGHTER SAYS.'

I usually shared this sort of thing with Alana and my parents but opted to hold this one back. There were quite enough anxieties in camp already.

The landscape east of Livingston was spectacular. Warm sunshine collided with a creamy late summer haze which pooled in an immense valley divided into town-sized ranches. Where you could see far enough, there were mountains on every horizon. To the north was Crazy Peak – at 11,214 feet it is the highest in the Crazy Mountains. To the south, I could just make out the 9,295-foot summit of Livingston Peak, in the heart of the Absaroka

Range. Both awaited their first dusting of ice and snow. But for now, they had hundreds of fuzzy cirrus clouds floating about their summits.

I pushed on through a shortgrass prairie, an epic expanse of – you guessed it – short grass. Once grazed by huge herds of bison, it is now a mostly golden-brown biome reserved for pampered thoroughbreds. I stopped to admire a pair, their freshly brushed loins glistening in the sunshine. They were inquisitive enough to come and say hello, but not so convivial as to be petted. Their shoulders had been shaven with ruler-straight precision, like immaculate Brazilian bikini lines.

Sometimes close, sometimes far away, a busy combine harvester buzzed up and down a wheat field, creating messy lines. When it passed, the air tasted of after dinner crackers, the sort you'd serve with a creamy wheel of brie. It was a scene of iconic proportions. You could blindfold a hundred people, spin them around a dozen times, teleport them to this very spot and all would utter the same three words: the Wild West. And to make things even more special, Alana caught up with me, armed with a sandwich and a cold can of pop. Her first three words: 'What the fuck?'

She had been charged with the task of finding me a flashing bike light to make me more visible in the autumnal gloom of dawn and dusk. '$75 for a bike light? Plus tax! How is that even possible? It's not even very good!'

And a 5ml tube of acyclovir – better known as cold sore cream – for the impending horror about to break out in the corner of my mouth.

'$25 for cold sore cream! It's five quid back home. And, you cheeky bugger, I couldn't put it on our joint card because you haven't put any money on it!'

'Welcome to America,' I said with a smile.

Marital bliss well and truly restored.

After a quick pitstop, Alana departed east to try to find us somewhere to stay. I followed a bumpy gravel trail that ran on the northern banks of the Yellowstone River – a chilly looking waterway, about 200 feet wide. It flowed northwards around rocky islets roughly the size of half-sunken hatchbacks.

April 2016. Arriving in Seattle after crossing the Pacific Ocean.

August 2023. Fellow cyclists Dave and Julie on their way to Vancouver Island.

Starting out in the Pacific Northwest.

Nancy's cedar cabin in North Bend, Washington.

My first rodeo in Ritzville ... much to the amusement of the locals.

All part of the adventure, on the side of Interstate 90 in Idaho.

Roadside support for the Republican presidential candidate. Not an uncommon sight.

It's hard to find any land in the USA that isn't: 'Posted. Keep Out. Private Property.'

Epic Western grasslands, where bison once roamed.

Trains kept me company (and awake) for most of my journey across the USA.

Entering my fourth state, Wyoming. The least-populated in the USA.

Caught in one of several almighty storms. This one just outside Deer Lodge, Montana.

The open road,
Wyoming. No cars
for hours on end.

An averagely enormous American vehicle. And my bike.

The Oil Bowl, Casper, Wyoming. Small-town pride at its vociferous best.

Keeping my head down in Oklahoma.   Cotton farmer Crump Britt near
                                    Clarksdale, Mississippi.

It's a struggle to find nutrition in America's 'food deserts'.

Even the punctures are bigger in America. I kept this one as a souvenir.

The Edmund Pettus Bridge, Selma.

'Snack Manager' Alana joins for a week in Alabama and northern Florida.

Hunting for pythons in the Florida Everglades with Donna Kalil.

On the final approach to Key West, crossing one of 42 bridges.

Arriving in Key West, after ten weeks and 4,373 miles in the saddle.

Often, the hardest mornings are followed by the most rewarding afternoons. And this was one of them. Thankfully, the trail became asphalt again after about five bumpy miles – my bike couldn't take much more – and I cycled on a smooth frontage road all the way to Big Timber.

Jetlagged and feeling rotten, Alana had booked us into the 'best' of three motels. On her watch, there was to be none of my stingy ways – booking the cheapest motel just to save ten dollars. Her comfort took precedence over mine. She was fast asleep by 8pm, so I whiled away the evening watching American football on mute. When I woke at 6am, I discovered coffee brewing, a plastic bag filled with sandwiches, and my bottles washed and filled with electrolytes.

'Night shift clocking off,' she said as she jumped in the shower. 'Drop me a pin and I'll catch up with you later.'

Alana's arrival, three weeks in, was a masterstroke. Because as my route continued southeast, through rural Montana and then Wyoming, the road was set to get lonelier, and the distances between towns even longer.

Unlike in 2016, I couldn't just curl up in an underpass. America felt dodgier. Or perhaps my perception of the country had changed and I'd grown softer. I needed, or at least wanted, to find some semblance of 'accommodation' each night – to charge my gadgets, dry my clothes and wash the grime from behind my ears. Moreover, with Alana now in tow, there was only so much appetite for 'type two fun' – the theory that grim activities become enjoyable in hindsight. As such, there was to be absolutely no sleeping in the car. Pregnant or not.

It had rained overnight, turning a rural track into sticky mud. So, instead of following Komoot's sparsely populated trail through the hamlets of Tin Can Hill, Sourdough and Sixshooter Creek, I joined Old US 10, a barely used 'blacktop' highway running parallel with Interstate 90. When you can find them, these are the perfect roads for cross-country riding. And with my exorbitantly priced new bike light blinking maniacally below by buttocks, when a car did occasionally vroom up from behind, it could see me from half a mile.

With the wind at my back, I was soon achieving a blistering pace – about 15mph – so I stopped for a quick coffee at a farm shop in Greycliff. It was easily the most bijoux spot I'd found so far, oozing Western chic. Old wagon wheels had been upcycled into chandeliers. A blade rotor windmill had been repurposed as an internal fan. The antlered head of a proud, albeit stuffed, elk looked down, snootily, from the rafters.

On first taste, I thought I'd discovered more great coffee, but on second slurp I realised it had been laced with vanilla and coconut. Why, America? Why can't you just leave the coffee be, I brooded before then getting distracted by a big topographic map of Montana.

Not only was the state vast in area, but the contrast between highlands and lowlands was captivating: green and lumpy to the west, but mostly yellow and pancake flat to the east. With my index finger, I traced my route across the state, cutting through valleys and around serpentine mountain ranges. The worst of the hills were now well and truly behind me. Sure, I had a spreadsheet filled with altitudes and elevation gains, but numbers on a page are hard to comprehend. Right there, though, in front of my very eyes, I could see that I had now all but crossed the Rocky Mountains, the imposing wall of rock that had stood in my way for hundreds of miles. On a map of the USA, I was only about a quarter of the way to Key West. But not all miles are created equal. Behind me: a gruelling slog in all weathers on untrained legs. Ahead: glorious flatlands, across which I would be propelled by a heart and lungs that felt the fittest they might ever be.

With a spring in my step, I rode eastwards to the small town of Columbus. Alana was waiting in a diner for lunch: juicy cheeseburgers and crispy French fries served in baskets lined in red and white chequered paper. The joint was doing a roaring trade in chocolate milkshakes, sodas, malts and sundaes. It reminded me of the 1970s sitcom *Happy Days*. I half expected The Fonz to burst in wearing his iconic black leather jacket, amuse patrons with his 'aaaaaaay' catchphrase, and order a root beer. Instead, a pair of middle-aged sisters heard our accents and could barely contain their excitement. 'Oh, I could just listen to you talk all day long!'

said one, then gulped from a Diet Coke clinking with ice. 'You are very welcome here,' said the other, before tucking into a basket of fried chicken.

In a region so sparsely populated, having Alana there made things considerably easier. For example, she had purchased a fresh supply of sun cream, lip balm, sports drinks and beers. Trivial little things, but tasks that saved me 20 minutes traipsing around a supermarket.

That's not to say her presence didn't leave me feeling a strange sense of guilt, though. Now that I had the luxury of a 'support crew' – if only for a week – I felt like a phony. She was adamant that I throw my panniers into the car and cycle bag-free for the week. 'No one cares besides you and your ego,' she argued. But stubbornly, it was a line I wasn't prepared to cross. I had just lugged 20kg over the Rocky Mountains.

After lunch, I spent the afternoon on a lonely road almost entirely devoid of human life. Just me and a few hundred cows, munching at thick tufts of pasture on the squidgy banks of the Yellowstone River. I was also joined by a northern goshawk – a year-round Montana resident, distinguishable by its salt-and-pepper plumage and mustardy-yellow talons. Once again, we played the game of Telegraph Pole Hopscotch. This time in the company of an unlucky fish. Most likely an Arctic grayling, it had been plucked from the rapids and now squirmed as it came to terms with its imminent demise.

At times, Old US 10 squeezed between the river, Interstate 90 and the seemingly ever-present railroad track, creating an unfamiliar sense of claustrophobia. At others, the landscape opened out into sprawling corn fields, the first I'd seen, and a noticeable shift from wheat. Even people who didn't live on farms owned properties surrounded by an acre of lawn.

This sense of pastoral calm made my approach to Billings even more stressful. At the end of an 80-mile day, Montana's largest city was a giant grey obstacle that couldn't be avoided. I should have called Alana and asked for a ride to our motel on the far side of town. Instead, I obstinately persevered through rush-hour traffic, sometimes on the pavement, sometimes on the road. At one particularly hairy moment, I was almost flattened by a 30-tonne truck – a few inches from being killed or maimed.

By the time I found where we were staying, I was ashen from nerves. 'Never again,' I vowed, as I flopped onto the bed and downed a can of strong IPA. Suddenly, I was racked with self-doubt. America felt ginormous. I still had Wyoming to come, which was even sparser than Montana. Cities like Billings were impenetrable by bicycle. 'I'm going to get fucking killed out here,' I said.

As usual, Alana was the voice of brutal reason. 'This isn't a world record attempt. No one cares about this thing as much as you do. The most important thing is that you make it home in one piece.'

We went over the route, the daily distances and any potential hazards ahead of me. I just had to trust the process: 70–80 miles a day, nice and slow, and America would take care of itself.

'If we can just get you through Wyoming,' said Alana, 'then you know from experience that things will get easier. Now put those disgusting clothes in a plastic bag and make sure you stretch properly!'

My legs were fine. Residually exhausted, sure, but feeling fit. My backside, however, was sore. Really sore. Alana was adamant that I should take a day off but I was desperate to continue. As a compromise, I would do a slightly shorter ride the following day.

We then spent a less-than-romantic evening strolling the aisles of a nearby Walmart, looking for a cream or ointment to soothe my blistered nether regions. We eventually settled on a balm used to treat nappy rash in babies.

The next morning, I set off early, desperate to escape Billings before rush hour. In the half-light of a mizzled dawn, the city's eastern fringe epitomised grey and drab – a protracted concrete splurge of industrial and commercial buildings. A reality of modern life, of course. Just not a particularly nice – or safe – place to ride a bicycle.

Thankfully, within about five miles, the Old US Highway 87 looped south into squat hills, sunburned a tawny monotone, interspersed with the occasional patch of broccoli-like trees. It was a relief to have the city behind me but this really was the back of beyond. The land emitted a stark Martian 'quality' – menacing and empty. A few conical-shaped corrugated iron grain silos sat on a distant hillside, resembling the first modules of a new colony. The tagline for the 1979 sci-fi horror film *Alien* was: 'IN SPACE, NO ONE CAN HEAR YOU SCREAM'. I suspect this is also the PR motto of the local tourist board.

The Yellowstone River was now behind me, continuing its journey north. For several days I had been soothed by its ever-present ripple. Now, though, the breeze was deafening. It whipped across the parched earth and rattled long strands of barbed wire, hanging loosely between fenceposts. Something like a skiffle guitar with slack steel strings.

I saw one car in the first two hours, a pickup driven by a stubbled Clint Eastwood type. He had a cigarette and a mobile phone in one hand and a 500ml can of energy drink in the other. We nodded our heads from behind our respective wheels and handlebars, then I savoured the brief aftertaste of tobacco hanging in the noisy air.

Thank goodness the morning was cool and autumnal because the barren and shadeless route would have been suicidal during summer. I had just enough liquids to keep me going: three litres of sports drinks and three litres of water. Mints helped, too – sucking them kept my mouth moist.

Thankfully, I found Alana waiting in the random roadside layby we had pinpointed on a map the night before. I rolled in at midday, aged from the morning, my cheeks blush with breeze. Alana, meanwhile, blasted Taylor Swift from the hire car's speakers, beside a big white sign that read: 'RATTLESNAKES HAVE BEEN OBSERVED. PLEASE STAY ON SIDEWALKS'. She handed me a peanut butter sandwich and we discussed our options.

For a cyclist, this region was a nightmare for finding accommodation. Elsewhere in the country, there was at least some semblance of a motel every 50–100 miles. Not here. We therefore decided that I would continue a little further, to cover ground with a tailwind. If I found somewhere to stay, then we would call it a day there.

I made it 15 miles, to Crow Agency, the governmental headquarters of the Crow Native Americans. It is the largest of Montana's seven tribal lands, spanning 2.2 million acres. Native American reservations remain some of the poorest communities in America and Crow Agency was no different. I spent 20 minutes cycling up and down its mostly empty streets, trying hard to avoid the four mangy-looking dogs that were snapping at the hubcaps of every passing car. Given half the chance, they would have had my hamstrings for dental floss. The most obvious difference between this and other towns I had seen in the USA was the distinct lack of amenities. I was used to visiting villages of less than a thousand people with movie theatres, diners, hardware stores and public swimming pools. Crow Agency, however, appeared to have none of that. I stood in the shade of a corrugated iron administrative building, phone in hand, contemplating my next move.

'How's it going?' asked a tall man with a black ponytail, wearing a freshly ironed burgundy shirt, brown leather brogues and blue chinos held up by a multicoloured beaded belt.

'I'm good, thank you.'

'You lost?'

'Maybe. I was hoping to find somewhere to stay.'

It was a fortuitous encounter that I couldn't have set up in advance, even if I'd tried. Because Cody Chief Child Meeks was senator of the Crow Tribe, responsible for overseeing its healthcare, economic development and judiciary.

'This is the heart of America, with the true native people of the country,' said Cody. 'I can't say enough good stuff about the people, but the living circumstances, the economy and the healthcare is far less than the rest of the country.'

According to Cody, the Crow Tribe was repeatedly short-changed by the federal government. He described them as 'the forgotten people', set up to fail. A 2020 census revealed that approximately 40 per cent of the reservation's population lived below the national poverty line, almost 30 per cent above the national average.

'We have the best land in the country in my eyes. We have great rivers, we have oil, we have trees, we have coal. But with the restrictions the government has put on us, we are not able to benefit from any of this.'

Cody was referring to contracts, or treaties, signed between Native American tribes and the US government between 1778 and 1871. These agreements forced indigenous people into reservations, removing their right to live nomadically – like they had done for millennia – across much bigger areas of North America.

'We did not understand at the time what long-term effects those contracts would have on our people. A hundred per cent of our problems stem back to those agreements.'

Two centuries on and Crow Agency struggles with power cuts, a temperamental water system and a lack of new housing. Unable to find a home on tribal lands, Cody and his family lived in Hardin – 15 miles to the north.

'There are no jobs here. There's not a single fast-food restaurant on our reservation. There's really not much here. You even have to go off reservation to find a grocery store.'

In Neah Bay, right at the start of my journey, Zaliyah and Ou'axs of the Makah Tribe had spoken of a resentment towards America. Did that exist here too?

'We are ready to move past it,' said Cody, who wore the expression of a man with great weight on his shoulders. 'But at the same time, we need better representation and support from the government.'

With confirmation that we had zero chance of finding a place to stay in town, I continued south a few extra miles to the Little Bighorn Battlefield National Monument – a convenient place to reconvene with Alana. In stark contrast to Crow Agency, it was rammed with tourists, entering nose-to-tail in their SUVs, paying $25 for the privilege. Three hundred and twenty thousand people visit the site every year to see a memorial to those who lost their lives in June 1876 during the most significant battle of the Great Sioux War.

Otherwise known as Custer's Last Stand, the battle resulted in the defeat of US forces. It is, however, seen by many historians as one of the Native Americans' last armed efforts to preserve their way of life. Subsequent battles, treaties and encroachments upon tribal lands saw them squeezed into the 326 reservations now spread across the USA. If only there was an appetite to witness the inconvenient modern truths of this history, then Crow Agency might benefit from a few extra visitors.

Alana scooped me up from the carpark and drove us back to Hardin. It seemed crazy and I felt like a fraud, but it was a necessary evil. While we had the car, it made the most sense. Cycling all the way back there, into a headwind, would have been unnecessarily stubborn, even by my standards.

11

BLACK GOLD

I was booted out of the car at Little Bighorn the next morning and left to cruise south like the Lone Ranger. It made sense for Alana to leapfrog ahead of me and get on with her own working day. I could make my own peanut butter sandwiches; Alana had her own business to run remotely from a different, difficult time zone. She was also struggling physically. Significantly more than me. Not only did her morning sickness last all day, but she also had an unshakeable cold. Her eyes were puffy and red with hay fever-like symptoms. At night, she struggled to sleep.

But apart from the occasional interlude of marital bickering, we were finding a rhythm and routine. If I needed her, she was only a phone call away. I felt more at ease knowing that she was comfortable in a coffee shop in a small town, rather than loitering around a dusty layby. It also gave me something to ride towards: I looked forward to seeing her at the end of each day.

I joined a road running parallel with rusty train tracks atop a flattish, scrubby plateau. Every time a locomotive rolled through, the rails screeched like fingernails on a blackboard, enough to send shudders through my spine. My relationship with these trains was bittersweet. Loud and boisterous, they had the habit of sneaking up on me and sounding their horns. But for as long as I had them in earshot, I knew that the road would remain level, or thereabouts.

Otherwise, it was another hot and empty trail. By midmorning, I'd stripped down to a vest. Heat mirage swirled above the black tar road. Luckily, I had a stiff tailwind, blowing north to south. I zipped through the small 'towns' of Lodge Grass and Wyola at 18mph, warp speed for a heavily loaded touring bicycle.

This felt like the start of the 'flyover states' – a pejorative term used to describe the sparsely populated hinterlands of the United States, where foreign tourists, or indeed many Americans, seldom venture. These were landscapes that appeared empty from a plane window. 'Empty', however, is in the eye of the beholder. And at ground level, I can assure you, there are a handful of cows. If you look really closely. But in its bareness comes its majesty. Ruler-straight roads, dumpling clouds and four open horizons, each one flaunting every conceivable shade of green. With a tiny inkling of downhill and the wind directly behind me, I floated over the earth.

But so much of it was off limits. Pretty much everything beyond 20 feet of the verge was blocked off by a barbed wire or electric fence. Dozens of signs read: 'POSTED. KEEP OUT'. As a Briton, I am used to the joys of public right of way – the legal privilege to use footpaths and bridleways, irrespective of the land they might pass through. Of course, I wouldn't wander through someone's garden unannounced. Moreover, our British right to roam is convoluted and nowhere near as unrestricted as in Scandinavia. In the United States, though, the concept of private property seemed hardwired with what it meant to be American. Often regardless of one's political affiliation.

It was the country's first president, George Washington, who said that 'freedom and property rights are inseparable. You can't have one without the other.' His fellow founding father and second US president, John Adams, agreed: 'property is surely a right of mankind as real as liberty'. The Fifth Amendment to the US Constitution states that private property shall not be taken for public use without just compensation, and for more than two centuries, politicians have returned to this subject time and again, perhaps as a way of declaring patriotism to the electorate. In a 2007 speech, the late Republican politician and United States senator John McCain said: 'Property is more than just land. Property is buildings, machines, apartment leases, retirement savings accounts, checking accounts, furniture, computers, cars, and even ideas. In short, property is the fruit of one's labor.'

I didn't, therefore, feel like I could escape the road and explore the hills around me. They weren't mine, and they're not yours, either. Rather, they belong to a single person or family. And if the officious signage was anything to go by, then they were keen to keep it that way.

In America, unlike in Britain, fewer people seemed to wander out of their homes for a walk, into whatever green expanse they had directly on their doorstep. Instead, recreation is sought in one of the country's many national parks – 325 million visits were made in 2023. These are the places where you can go to run, ride and camp. But, of course, you have to drive there first. And in many cases, pay an entrance fee.

How had this constitutional blocking from nature shaped America, I wondered. Had it made Americans more likely to own guns, perhaps? To defend the lands they owned? Or maybe it had made them fatter? Was there a correlation between obesity and a lack of free and local recreational space?

I would have doorstepped someone with these very questions. But I didn't see a human all morning and the horses only spoke very patchy English.

The border with Wyoming was marked with a big green and white sign. It sat on the roadside next to a dozen fresh hay bales beside a less than fresh tractor. It looked as though it had hauled its last blade of grass many decades ago before being left to rot in the exact spot where it had given up the ghost. Wyoming didn't look any different. This was just an arbitrary marker. Nevertheless, I was now entering my fourth state and officially the emptiest in the contiguous USA. There were 578,000 people spread across an area of 97,814 square miles – about two thirds the size of Montana – bigger than the United Kingdom but not quite as big as New Zealand.

Wyoming did, however, seem better off than Montana. Immediately the roads were cleaner and newer. For the first 30 miles I brushed this off as conjecture, purely anecdotal. But when I rolled into our overnight stop, Sheridan, I passed a Porsche on a main drag that was aglow with banks, hotels and restaurants. In fact, while Wyoming's gross domestic product (GDP) of $44 billion is the lowest of all 50 states, GDP per capita is the twelfth highest, at roughly $76,000 – a cool $20,000 better off per person than Montana.

At the base of the Bighorn Mountains, Sheridan felt quaint, creative and wealthy. Within a short walk of our motel, we passed art galleries, gastropubs and bookshops. A bumper sticker on a station wagon caught my eye: 'I SURVIVED OBAMA, YOU SURVIVED TRUMP. GOD HELP US ALL SURVIVE BIDEN'.

The town boasted ten sites listed on the National Register of Historic Places, including the Sheridan Inn Hotel, where author Ernest Hemingway made the finishing touches to *A Farewell to Arms*. Outlaws Butch Cassidy, the Sundance Kid and Buffalo Bill Cody all called the place home.

As the heavens opened, we made a beeline for the Luminous Brewhouse – one of three downtown breweries – known affectionately by locals as 'Sheridan's living room'. Owner Megan Butler and head brewer Kyle Mueller had kindly offered to ply me with free alcohol and Alana with all the tap water and kombucha any pregnant woman could ever wish for. The brewpub had been the dream of Megan's late husband, Cooley, who passed away in 2022 aged 40. His vision was simple: to create a community hub where people could drink flavoursome beer, listen to music, play games and bring their children – the antithesis of the dingy, often windowless, vibe of many American dive bars.

'It had to be family-friendly and accessible,' said Megan. 'Somewhere you can get a good pint, good food and anyone can come and feel comfortable.'

They were also proudly pet-friendly and had a fun 'Dog Tally' at the bar – a list of all the pooches to visit that day. Two handsome pointers lapped at a bowl of water while their owners sat in a window seat watching the rain. The atmosphere was warm and buzzing; Cooley's dream had been realised.

Was Sheridan as wealthy as it appeared at first impressions, I asked.

'We've definitely had an influx from California,' said Megan.

'There's also a lot of old ranchers,' said Kyle. 'Four-thousand-acre ranchers, a couple of generations deep. They spend a lot of money, especially come the end of agriculture season. When the cows go to auction and slaughter, they walk away with a hefty sum.

The ranch hands are compensated accordingly. Those gentlemen like to drink.'

The biggest drinkers, and spenders, in town, however, were the men running Wyoming's oil and gas fields. Most worked on a shift cycle of 14 days on, five days off. 'They will drink people under the table,' said Kyle. 'Thousands of dollars at a time.'

Having a taste for craft beer and a proclivity for half-cut journalism, brewpubs are my bag. I had visited 50 or more across the USA and had enjoyed my fair share of sozzled assignments in states like Oregon and California. From experience, though, these businesses tended to lean left, attracting an edgier, liberal clientele. Wyoming, however, is officially the reddest state in the land. It has voted Republican in every presidential election since 1952, except 1964. In 2016, 67.4 percent of voters backed the Republican candidate, Donald Trump. So did a brewpub in mountainous Republican Wyoming have a different vibe to one in seaside Democratic California, say?

'Luminous: enlightenment, basically, we encourage everything,' said Megan. 'Whether it's on the far right, or the far left, whatever, we really try not to take a [political] stance.'

'The running joke is that we're your therapist. While you're drinking. But our job is to listen, not to talk,' said Kyle.

In many ways, Luminous prided itself of being the archetypal public house. It was a forum for ideas and opinions, even the ones some patrons might not agree with. Diplomacy was also good for business. Kyle knew of other breweries that had taken hardline stands on political or cultural issues and had seen their takings suffer.

'Wyoming is a very Western, cowboy state,' said Kyle. 'A lot of people here won't purchase things they don't agree with. If we take the wrong stance, then they will stop coming. Other beer brands have done that and have lost 25 per cent market share. So if you side with one direction, you alienate the other half.'

What about the heated culture wars seen in modern political discourse. 'The war on woke', 'the trans debate'. Did they see those arguments playing out on a micro, Sheridan scale?

'Nobody wants to admit that they are wrong,' said Megan.

America's brewpubs could, however, be at the centre of a brave new movement. One that actively fostered a culture of agreeing to disagree.

'There's a vast difference between someone you met and someone you're talking to [online],' said Kyle. 'You're not just a pixel on a screen. We have a human element, that connection between two separate people willing to not attack.'

Three pints deep and with our stomachs rumbling, Alana and I made a dash for a nearby Thai restaurant – the first I'd seen. My palate had grown so accustomed to bland variations of bread, meat and cheese that my tastebuds quivered into orgasm at the mere scent of stir-fried vegetables, tamarind sauces and prawns on skewers coated in lemongrass and chilli. Flavour. Rejoice! Albeit, far too close to bedtime.

Full to bursting, we fell into a sugar-and-salt-addled slumber. Alana must have got up to use the toilet half a dozen times in the night, waking me on every occasion. When my alarm sounded at 6.30am, we both felt hungover and groggy, but eager to escape our motel. Which – having had plenty of time to think during the night – we'd concluded was clearly some sort of halfway house, frequented exclusively by single men.

Luckily, there was a cosy little coffee shop open a few blocks away. The coffee machine left a delicious layer of crema atop its double espressos. A fresh batch of irresistible warm blueberry muffins had also just popped out of the oven. So, I scoffed two of each, bought my wife breakfast and hit the road.

South of Sheridan, the landscape reminded me of the Scottish Highlands. The quiet road rolled through hills cloaked in evergreens. Up and down. Up and down. The cycling was delightful, like a spin class. Ten-minute sections of flat, followed by 15-minute climbs and then five minutes down. Enough to keep one's mind excited without burning out the body.

What made it doubly enjoyable was the lack of expansive views. Counterintuitive, you might think. But in contrast to the Rockies – where I could look ahead to the horizon and see two or three hours into the future – this road undulated so regularly that my universe was only ever a mile or two wide. On a 4,000-mile bicycle journey, there is an addictive thrill in not knowing what is about to come next, much like the compulsion to keep turning the pages of a good book.

It was another typically Montana/Wyoming sort of day. For the first three hours I only saw four people and they were cocooned in cars. But a few miles north of Buffalo, on a trail sandwiched between the Bighorn National Forest and a vast grassland called Thunder Basin, I was joined by a herd of around 30 pronghorn deer. Indigenous to the American West, these even-hoofed mammals aren't really deer at all but have closer taxonomical links with African giraffes. With short black horns, bright white underbellies and fluffy cream bottoms, they raced beside me for a few full-throttled minutes. It was one of those exhilarating animal encounters that made me feel like the only person left on earth.

Buffalo would have been a splendid place to spend the night. The downtown was compact and characterful, built mostly in redbrick and with grand pastoral murals painted on the corners of its treelined streets. Equidistant between Yellowstone National Park and Mount Rushmore, the town has served as a crossroads for centuries. Namely for the Sioux, Arapaho and Cheyenne tribes, followed by Europeans in the late nineteenth century. But with only 40 miles on the clock, I was keen to keep moving.

The landscape south of Buffalo was even more stupendous in its grandeur. With cool temperatures and a robust tailwind, it turned into one of the greatest rides within a great ride.

If you're reading this book and starting to like the idea of perhaps not cycling across America but maybe riding individual sections, then may I strongly recommend the old Highway 87, which connects Buffalo and Kaycee. Not only was the road empty but its asphalt was smooth, like a bowling ball. To the east and west I had mountains. But to the south, a never-ending grassland, reminiscent of the Mongolian-Manchurian steppe. I half expected to stumble across a small village of yurts, surrounded by a caravan of gurning camels.

I fell into that fabled 'flow state', the act of becoming so absorbed by a place or activity that hours and minutes vanish. My memories of that afternoon are therefore more like intoxicated flashbacks.

The scent of road tar. The whistle of wind. The sight of immense ranches marked only by deer skulls nailed to their fenceposts. I passed one home with so much sprawling 'yard' that the owner had created a DIY nine-hole golf course. Beyond anything else, it was an A* example of sit-down lawnmowing.

We spent the night in Kaycee, in a motel room resembling a prisoner-of-war barracks. The colour scheme was best described as 'instant coffee'. The town website boasted of 'the friendliest folks you'll ever meet!' But we must have caught them on an off day. When we walked into the local pub – as smoky as a 1980s sports and social club – the barmaid was the only person who spared us the time of day. I was used to being accosted by friendly locals, but not here. It was a head-down, drink your beer and keep yourself to yourself sort of place. Almost all men, in dungarees and steel-toecap boots. If I hadn't been with my sick and pregnant wife, then I might have stuck it out for more than a single drink.

The next day started bright and clear, with a warm but autumnal feel. After a long and gradual climb out of Kaycee, I stopped to check my bike. It had acquired an annoying squeak, but I couldn't work out where from. I wiggled the seat post, then tightened my headset. Everything in order. Nothing untoward.

As I continued south, the squeals grew louder. It was driving me crazy. I stopped again but this time the noise continued. It wasn't coming from my bike at all but from the roadside. The verges shapeshifted with thousands of chubby brown rodents: prairie dogs. Members of the squirrel family, related to groundhogs, chipmunks, marmots and woodchucks, they scurried between cone-shaped mounds, colonies known as towns. Hundreds of millions of prairie dogs used to live in North America. But their range has shrunk to less than 5 per cent of its original area due to habitat encroachment from humans and livestock.

Forming a tight-knit family, each group is made up of one or two breeding males, a handful of females and their pups. The males take monogamy less seriously but the females stick together for life. Fascinatingly, they have one of the most complex vocabularies in the animal kingdom. Not just capable of alerting their kin to a threat, but also to the species, size and colour of their clothing: 'Tall ape. Wheels for legs. Orange anorak. Take cover!'

The land also stirred with robotic arms – pumpjacks sucking oil from deep beneath the earth. In 2022, there were almost 28,000 of them spread across Wyoming. Up and down they go, slurping black gold into pipes. The state's four refineries are capable of processing up to 125,000 barrels of crude oil each day. Some older wells looked like giant sledgehammers knocking six-foot pins into the scrub. New ones resembled service structures used to hold up space rockets before launch.

I made it to Casper – nicknamed 'Oil City' – on the biggest night of the year: the Oil Bowl high school football match between the Natrona Mustangs and the Kelly Walsh Trojans. An event not to be missed.

We ended up in the away end, the bleachers looking into the sun, surrounded by students and parents waving flags and eating hotdogs. About 50 feet to our right, a marching band of trombones, clarinets, French horns and drums performed a bone-shaking rendition of the White Stripes' song 'Seven Nation Army'. The level of fervour within the crowd was staggering. Almost everyone wore official school merchandise. Two in three had painted faces. When cheerleaders walked around with a big green bucket, fundraising for a boy injured in the previous year's match, locals threw in $20 and $50 bills with abandon.

At my state comprehensive, we were lucky if our PE teachers turned up for our sports matches, let alone our parents. And if some random bloke from town decided to come and watch, then he was at risk of being branded a 'paedo' – or worse, thrown on the sex offender register. Not here. This was a city-wide event of American proportions. As though all of Casper was in attendance.

The puzzled looks on our faces gave us away as tourists but at the same time made us the source of great intrigue. We were offered candy, pickled gherkins, cinnamon buns and nachos. Even a bed for the night if we needed it.

During the halftime show – a rambunctious medley of Metallica tunes played by more than a hundred student musicians dressed as oil workers – I got talking to a man called Terry. Aged 74, dressed in – you guessed it – a red plaid shirt and jeans, he owned a sport merchandise business that sold kit to high schools. Which, from what I could see, was a licence to print money.

'Are you supporting any player in particular?' I asked.

'Oh no, I'm just local!'

Terry was a proud Republican, in favour of low taxes. He wanted to live in a country with minimal governmental interferences. 'You don't bother me, I don't bother you,' he said, as the teams took to the field for the second half.

He was against a Democrat government awarding money to people who didn't deserve it. 'Out here, you earn your way. You don't just get handouts.' In his opinion, the American welfare state had been abused. Too many people were 'used to getting something for nothing, and out here [in Wyoming] that doesn't go'.

In Terry's opinion, states and metropolitan areas with Democratic leadership had failed on issues such as drugs and homelessness because they were seen as an easy ride. 'You've got to have boundaries,' said Terry. 'You've got to have law.'

It was an extraordinary evening. An immense cacophony of sound and colour. Casper was a thriving community. Sharing candy. Clapping in unison. Yelling at boys in helmets. A palpable sense of togetherness.

In America, local pride can feel almost feudal. Perhaps that harks back to the founding days of European settlement, when families marched west in covered wagons and set up villages where their legs, wheels or spirits broke, never to be moved again. Most towns in the USA are less than two centuries old. It's not uncommon to meet people whose family trees are firmly rooted in one place.

As we filed out, I was reminded of Monte Olsen, the mountain biker I met in the Cascades Mountain Range, who believed America could come together via its 'cultural things' like music and sport. Well, this was a case in point. Take away the smartphones and the rolling news channels and all you have left are the people in your direct vicinity.

Furthermore, human life doesn't get much rawer or self-affirming than 22 adolescent boys smashing the living daylights out of each other. And for 5,000 mothers, fathers, brothers and sisters, that match, and what it stood for, superseded all else.

Perhaps it was this overwhelming sense of family that made the next morning so tough. Because it was time for Alana to hotfoot it to Denver – 275 miles to the south – and fly home to England. For over a week, she had followed along with this madcap adventure, attempting to make things as easy for me as possible. And all while feeling sick and jetlagged. I couldn't have done it without her. We threw her suitcases into the car, then wrapped our arms around each other one last time.

We were there. Again. Never wanting our embrace to break. But it had to, and if she could get the time off work then I would see her again in a few weeks' time. I watched her drive away from me, my eyes aching, the scent of her just-washed hair imbued into the foetid armpit crease of my rain jacket.

This sweet reminder stayed with me for most of the day as I escaped from Casper and rode southeast, through a deserted land broken up by the occasional patch of alfalfa. I spent the day with my mind elsewhere, barely looking at the tarmac in front of me. Instead, I imagined the road, the check-in desk and passport control in front of her. By the time she walked onto the plane and we lost contact, I had cycled another relatively easy, but heartwrenching, 90 miles.

12

THERE SHE BLOWS

I spent the evening in Glendo, in a motel used mostly by fishermen and hunting parties, studying a big map of the USA. After a month on the road, I still wasn't quite halfway, geographically, but the hills were now firmly behind me. The America ahead, however, was flat. Deliciously so.

There was also the matter of wind. Above 30 degrees north, the prevailing wind in the USA tends to blow from west to east. For many Americans who have driven cross-country comfortably sat behind a windscreen, this subject has barely crossed their minds. As a cyclist, however, it can be the difference between a great and horrendous day.

Plan A had been to head south into Colorado and then turn east into the panhandle of Oklahoma, at the pinch point between Kansas and New Mexico. But sometimes you need to think on your feet. And when the five-day weather forecast predicted 30–40mph northwest-to-southeast gusts across the entire Midwest, Plan B was swiftly initiated. Next stop: Nebraska.

A restless night followed, as I played out routes in my mind, half dreaming about turning left at a stop sign or right at a fork in the road. The next morning, however, the wind rattled against dustbins and blew tumbleweed down Glendo's empty main street. Under normal circumstances, hoolies like these would leave cyclists reaching for the snooze button, but not when they're perfectly at your back. I jumped out of bed and onto my bike like a five-year-old at Christmas. Combine this wind with a flat and empty road, and I flew: 40 miles inside three hours.

I stopped for brunch at a bar and grill on the outskirts of Fort Laramie – a nineteenth-century trading post used by fur trappers and emigrants 'expanding' west. The restaurant felt more like a living room in a retirement home than a bona fide business. Nonetheless, it was a charming shrine to Americana. A feast for the senses. Almost every spare surface had been filled with an American flag. The curtains, shelves, tablecloths – all Stars and Stripes. In the corner stood a life-size cut-out of a woman in Air Force fatigues holding an A4 sign: 'ACTIVE MILITARY GET 10% DISCOUNT'.

The greasy spoon oozed unpretentiousness, and I tucked into two poached eggs on toast with a side of hashbrowns and a somewhat puzzling garnish of sliced apple. The coffee was reasonably dark, too. I couldn't see the bottom of my mug, which was a nice change.

The friendly owner, who must have been in his late seventies, had migrated west himself, from the East Coast, and had run the restaurant for 18 years. In that time, he had welcomed more than 100,000 customers. There were photos of a few dozen of them on the wood-panelled walls.

'Boy, it can get windy out here,' he said in an unmistakable, Bostonian twang. 'You're lucky it's behind you! But you be safe out there.'

The road southeast ran beside yet another railroad, busy with mile-long trains pulling trailers piled high with shimmering coal. The air was hot and dry, the skies electric blue. It felt as though Wyoming was petering out and Nebraska was beginning, even before I saw the state line. A clear shift from rolling hills to flat expanses of crops.

In the middle distance, mostly soyabeans and bright yellow sunflowers. On the verge, car-sized anti-abortion billboards with closeups of babies and the words: 'CHERISH LIFE. EYE DEVELOPMENT, 14 DAYS FROM CONCEPTION'. A few miles later, another sign warned against the risk of guns in the home: 'PREVENT SUICIDE. LOCK UP YOUR FIREARMS'.

The actual border between Wyoming and Nebraska was marked by a few stacks of hay bales, a handful of grain silos, and one of the big green and white signs I had come to love. I was entering the fifth state of my journey and one of the least-visited in the country. In fact, a 2023 report published by the Statista research department ranked Nebraska as forty-sixth on a list of 50. Just 19 per cent of respondents visited the 'Cornhusker State' in 2022, in contrast to the 61 per cent that had travelled to Florida. I was off the beaten track and loving it.

When I checked into a motel just across the border in Morrill, I collapsed onto a shaded bench just outside the lobby and downed three bottles of iced water. The afternoon was broiling. A digital sign read 99 degrees Fahrenheit – 37 degrees centigrade. It was a Sunday afternoon and the motel was packed with railroad workers hanging around outside their bedrooms, listening to country music and working through slabs of Bud Lite. Most had big beards and sunburned arms. One wore dungarees and a Donald Trump-style MAGA hat.

One man, Sean Taylor, drove the trains that had kept me company throughout the West. With a shaved head, a goatee beard and wrap-around shades, he and just one colleague drove a 300-car, three-mile train from one depot to the next. Nebraskan born and raised, he told me to expect a conservative state, comprised mostly of farming country and plenty of open road. 'Most farmers here lean to the right,' said Sean, as he lit a cigarette. 'Most say they won't stop working until the day they die.'

Working at the heart of blue-collar America, Sean was most concerned by the rate of inflation. In recent years, he had watched the cost of rent and groceries climb to unaffordable levels. Life had, he said, 'got a lot harder for people at the bottom. There's a lot of corporate greed. It's a constant battle [to make enough money].'

His work put him in a highly physical and dangerous setting, and Sean was insured to the hilt by his employers. This not only covered himself in the event of serious injury, but also his family. He told me that it was reassuring to have the plan in place because the cost of medical insurance in America had spiralled. In 2024, the average monthly premium for a 40-year-old was $420 (£330) for bronze cover, rising to $713 (£560) for gold cover. 'Eight years ago, I was looking into insurance for a roofing company, and it was $1,300 a month for me and two kids. It was ridiculous.'

Before we parted ways, I was curious to find out what – as someone who transported thousands of tonnes of coal from one

American town to the next – was his opinion on America's use of fossil fuels. 'Do you think humans are responsible for climate change?' I asked.

'I personally don't think coal has anything to do with climate change. More of it comes from the big factories that work off gas and oil. I also don't ever see us crossing over to electricity solely because our power grid can't handle it. I don't see it happening in 50 years. There are still so many untapped fossil fuel reserves in this country.'

'But just because reserves *can* be tapped, I guess the bigger question is *should* they be tapped?'

'It's unfeasible right now. You look back at incidents such as Chernobyl and that makes people pretty scared of nuclear power. We're just not there yet.'

I had flown on a plane to do this trip. I was eating red meat along the way and drinking coffee shipped in from warmer climes. However, moving slowly and (mostly) emission-free did give me plenty of time to contemplate my own carbon footprint, in contrast to many of the people around me. What was becoming evident, though, was that in much of Middle America, especially, making 'green' choices was often impossible – even if someone so wished. The distances were often so vast that electric cars simply didn't have the range. America wasn't getting any smaller anytime soon. Moreover, in the average diner, the most vegetarian meal you'll find is a portion of French fries. That very night I contemplated buying a 'salad' but knew it would be so underwhelming that I opted for the safe bet: a cheeseburger. And then there's all the idling vehicles sat outside convenience stores, gas stations, and drive-thru restaurants, belching out fumes. For many Americans, it is simply inconceivable to imagine a world in which they might leave a V8 pickup for three minutes to buy a Big Gulp and return to find their vehicle two degrees warmer.

The next morning, the wind was just as robust as the day before. It thrust me southeast, like a comforting palm resting between my shoulder blades. It took less than 90 minutes to reach Scottsbluff and take in my first sustenance of the morning: a wildly overpriced

Starbucks coffee and a croissant so stale it had the potential to cause a diplomatic dispute with France.

Outside a nearby gas station, I got talking to an 80-year-old army veteran when he challenged me to a drag race in his beaten-up Ford saloon. With his car's exhaust held on with zip ties, gaffer tape fixing the passenger-side door in place and the wind behind me, I fancied my chances. He was furious at the price of gas.

'It costs twice that in England,' I revealed.

'Is that right? Well, maybe you got to shoot the president!'

Growing up in rural Nebraska, his earliest memory was 'the '49 Blizzard' – the worst on record in the Northern Plains: 'We had these two cottonwood trees that were next to the dirt road. They were 35 foot tall, and the snowdrifts were over the top of them. The wind just blowed and howled and howled, I was amazed we were even able to go to sleep at night!'

He was a proud patriot, first drafted for the Vietnam War (1955–1975) but spent most of his time stationed in Germany and Saudi Arabia building irrigation equipment. In 1994, just 10 per cent of Americans owned passports. By 2023, that number had risen to roughly 43 per cent. The man in front of me had seen more of the planet than most. How had travel changed his perception of America, I wondered.

'Oh, it's better than most. But the gas and groceries are too expensive now. But I'm lucky, the US Department of Veterans Affairs takes care of my hospital and medical bills.'

We shook hands and he spluttered off down the road in a cloud of noxious smoke, followed shortly by me.

This felt like the day I'd been dreaming of. Not just flat, the road was actually slightly downhill. Unnoticeable to the naked eye, but gradually descending for the foreseeable future.

About 30 miles east, I passed Chimney Rock, an extraordinary 480-foot sandstone formation – a bit like Somerset's Glastonbury Tor – towering high above the otherwise empty landscape. Dating back millions of years, the landmark served as a guide for pioneers as they blazed their way across the USA. Most notably, on the Oregon, California and Mormon trails, wagon routes followed by European migrants. It signalled the petering out of the Great Plains and the start of the Rocky Mountains. On the long, hot, trudge across the New World, it must have appeared on the horizon like a cathedral. In fact, one pioneer described it as 'towering to the heavens'. Thousands of others etched their names into its dusty feet. To those weary men and women, it was the beginning of the end. To me, it heralded the start of a truly open road.

Once again, the afternoon grew sweltering, a heat I only really felt when I stopped. In the small town of Bridgeport, I paused for tacos and soda at the gas station and lapped up the praise of passers-by. If I was to use this group of random people as my sample size, then 90 per cent of Americans thought I was crazy. The idea of a human being cycling across their country was simply incomprehensible. At least 80 per cent feared for my safety.

'You got a gun?' asked a man with missing front teeth, driving a pickup pulling a speedboat.

'No ...'

'Dude, I wouldn't go anywhere in this fuckin' place without a gun!'

A hundred percent of people, however, believed that the journey was worth it. It spoke, indelibly, to that intangible American obsession: freedom.

'If I was 50 years younger,' joked a hunched woman leaning on a Zimmer frame. 'But good for you. And God bless you.'

In tremendous spirits, I reached the beautifully named town of Oshkosh with 94.4 miles displayed on my bike computer. It had taken less than six hours and I'd averaged a whopping 15.9mph – the fastest I had ever travelled on a bicycle. Sunburned and dehydrated, I checked into a motel and began removing my sweat-soaked clothes in the porch of my room.

'Going far?' enquired a man who was staying next door. He had a shock of peroxide-blonde hair, arms covered in tattoos and spoke with a thick southern lilt.

Bryson Haire came from Franklin, Louisiana, 'about as far south as you can get!' His father left home when he was a child. His mother then spent most of his teenage years heavily addicted to Xanax. It was his grandparents who really brought him up.

'They taught me my morals. To shake hands and make eye contact. Present yourself. You never know who you might come across. And always do the best work, no matter how much you get paid.'

At age 18, desperate to make something of his life, he marched up to a group of long-haul truckers on the side of a road and convinced them to give him a job.

'I said, "Hey, you look like you're doing too much work for one person. You need a little ground hand or something?"' Bryson clearly had the gift of the gab. 'I said, "I'm 18 and I'm willing to work every day."'

They called his bluff. Gave him a job. And within three years, he had been promoted to working on the railroad. He now had his own company truck and travelled the country. Back home, he had a one-year-old daughter to support and was desperate to start his own business.

'I came from a place where everybody's mom and dad was a shit. In the school system it was a normal thing.'

According to the Institute for Family Studies, approximately 35 per cent of American adolescents live without one of their parents. Children from single-parent families are twice as likely to suffer from mental health and behavioural problems. They are also between 1.5 times and twice as likely to live in poverty. Bryson, however, was determined to buck the trend.

'I needed to make my way. Because where I'm from, you're either unemployed, on a shrimp boat, on a tugboat or you're offshore. But I don't like water that much. The end goal is to be an entrepreneur, to be in the business, not just be a part of it. To own a piece of it.'

Despite a very clear personal drive, Bryson believed that his fortunes: 'started with God … If you can handle hell on earth, then you can handle anything that is coming after this planet!'

Tattooed across his right forearm was a crucifix and the words: 'LOVE YOUR ENEMIES. DO GOOD TO THOSE WHO HATE YOU. BLESS THOSE WHO CURSE YOU. PRAY FOR THOSE WHO MISTREAT YOU.'

'For me, these tattoos were like a get back thing. I was like,

I'm going to get all these tattoos and I'm still going to be highly successful, just to prove people wrong.'

I confess to judging a book by its cover. When I'd stumbled in after a long day, I'd brushed Bryson off as someone to give a wide berth. The young man, however, buzzed with ambition and zeal. Sat before me was an American dream, personified. Before leaving to take a much-needed shower, I was curious to find out if he was optimistic for the future of America.

'I just feel like we're separated as a whole. Poverty is so high right now because of inflation. A lot of people are just lost. I bet you could ask 75 per cent of people my age what a Democrat or a Republican is and they don't know the answer. A lot of people my age go crazy over conspiracy theories. People would rather believe in aliens than believe in God.'

It was a hot night, still in the high twenties centigrade, and I enjoyed a beer and some food at the only place open: the Chubby Rhino Tavern. Inside, the town sheriff passed pleasantries with a few locals while he waited for two big bags of takeaway food. A buck-toothed man arrived to pick up a pizza, wearing a baseball cap inscribed with the words 'TRUMP: THE SEQUEL'. This sort of sight was commonplace now. Public displays of support for a genuine political player. Back in 2016, most of his devotees almost uttered his name under their breath, as though the chances of him achieving office were silly, unachievable. Now, though, these people appeared mobilised, confident. A billionaire from New York had resonated with rural America. Arguably because his election victory moved the focus away from Washington and its careerists, epitomised by the Clintons. Had the political outsider made the hinterlands and its people feel … seen?

In the space of just a few days, I had spotted half a dozen bright red MAGA caps and a handful of T-shirts emblazoned with slogans like 'GOD, GUNS AND TRUMP'. Not at political rallies. Just people out and about, filling up gas or buying groceries. And no one batted an eyelid.

I was well and truly in the Red Belt. Time to buckle up.

*

When I woke the next morning, a grapefruit sunrise cast colossal sheets of pink across Oshkosh. It was as though someone had left a red sock in the white wash overnight. I set out eastwards on old Highway 26. Back on the long straight road, accompanied by yet another three-mile-long Union Pacific train.

I generally enjoyed cycling the first hour on an empty stomach. It made me feel light and nimble, and it seemed like an achievement to get 10 or 20 miles done before breakfast. On this morning, though, my metabolism screamed for fuel as my stomach twisted itself in knots.

Thankfully, I found a small convenience store-diner in Lewellen – a tiny town of just 175 people – and gorged on a stack of pancakes, bacon and sausage patties, all soaked in lashings of maple syrup. Fox News blared out from a TV while a stuffed bobcat pondered a shelf of decoy plastic turkeys. I was only in there for 20 minutes but it was hard to get food into my mouth between conversations. Farmers urged me to eat plenty, to keep up my strength. A couple on a day trip from nearby North Platte offered advice on routes and restaurants. A father and daughter encouraged me to sample a local delicacy: Rocky Mountain oysters.

'Oysters?' I sneered. 'We're about as far from the sea as you can get!'

'OK, so they're not really oysters,' they laughed. 'They're bull's testicles, deep fried in butter.'

'Maybe,' I said, grimacing.

'Well, God bless you!'

Stuffed to the gullet, I gave my pancreas a few minutes to recalibrate while flicking through the local newspaper, *Garden County News* – a twice-weekly.

'You'll struggle to find any news in there!' said the elderly lady behind the cash register.

'It would seem like that.'

'Speeding tickets mostly.'

'They print them in the paper?'

'Oh yes, that's the main reason people read it. To be nosey.'

'Have you ever had one?' I asked, cheekily.

'Oh no, I'm too old!'

I spent the rest of the day flying southeast on a warm breeze. The verge had just been clipped and smelled of herbal tea. A delicious blend of mint, fennel and chamomile. With the continental divide now firmly behind me, I felt fit, like an Olympian. But a cyclist's legs can quickly become attuned to the terrain. When I did occasionally need to cross a small bridge or hillock, my quadriceps burned as though they were scaling the Rockies again.

Beyond the obvious flatness, the main aesthetic difference between Wyoming and Nebraska was the change from livestock to arable farming. Millions of acres of soyabeans and corn. The state ranked fifth and third for their production respectively. My journey through Montana and Wyoming had also been filled with regular wild animal encounters. So far in Nebraska, though, I had barely seen a horse, let alone a deer.

With the weather set fair, and the roads clean and straight, I was cashing in. Conveniently, there were also now small towns every 20 or 30 miles, perhaps the perfect distance for a cycle tour. I could rely upon finding food and water, without weighing myself down with unnecessary supplies.

My mind was, however, drifting home. Because Alana had just been for our first baby scan. On a blacktop road sticky with heat, she video called to tell me about the heartbeat, the spine, and the shape of the head. It was a beautiful moment. But a moment I had missed. Her awe was diluted by my absence. But we didn't dwell on it for too long, for fear of drifting into melancholy. Instead, we spent the last few minutes before she fell asleep joking about my haggard appearance.

'When did you last brush your teeth?' she asked. And I couldn't remember.

'Maybe two days ago?'

'Ewwwwwww!'

13

GOD, GUNS AND COUNTRY

I reached North Platte at rush hour, with 101 miles under my belt. A centurion – my first of the trip. It was time for a rest day, and after a quick beer and another Chinese meal – the only restaurant within walking distance – I allowed myself an evening of well-deserved calm.

A lie-in would have been useful, but once again my cheap motel was frequented by construction workers barging around as though they owned the place. You could set your watch to their movements. They arrived late, about 11pm – by the sounds of it from a bar – and restarted their vehicles roughly five and a half hours later. They then left half an hour after that. They were probably involved in the railways. Because just a few blocks away was Bailey Yard – the largest rail yard on earth. And after breakfast I paid my own visit. A pilgrimage, of sorts.

Spread across 2,850 acres, it is a site of epic industrial proportions. Two hundred tracks, totalling 315 miles, with 985 switches and 766 turnouts. All the Union Pacific trains that had accompanied me – and kept me awake – across the country had passed through this immense depot.

During the Second World War, 150 miles of military freight passed through the town each day. And over the course of 55 months, more than 6 million soldiers were given a morale boost by one of the biggest volunteer efforts in US history: the North Platte Canteen. In just one month in 1945, North Platte donated 40,161 cookies, 30,679 hard-boiled eggs and 6,547 doughnuts. The sight of females raised spirits considerably. 'Platform

Girls' handed out popcorn balls – some with their names and addresses on.

These days, an average of 139 trains and over 14,000 railroad cars arrive every day. From the top of the Golden Spike Tower – an eight-storey turret with an observation deck – Bailey Yard resembled a model train track. Dozens of vehicles, coming and going. Matchstick-sized men in high-vis jackets. Sparks flashing from a repair facility.

I had developed a strange affection for this sprawling network. Its steel tendrils fanned out across the country. It roared over state lines, through snowy mountains and thirsty deserts. This place represented industrial prowess. Continental expansionism. It stood for blue-collar ideals. But perhaps more than all of that combined, it was a bastion to American consumerism.

The heat rising, I retreated to Walmart. If Bailey Yard was the rickety old skeleton, then this was the country's beating heart. I pondered giant packs of breakfast cereal, industrial-sized tubs of peanut butter, 500 grams of dried marjoram, 164 nappies and a 75-inch TV. I stocked up on snacks for the days ahead: sports drinks, cashews, apples, pears, bananas, boxed salads. Enough fibre to fend off constipation and scurvy for another week. I also invested $11 in a travel cafetiere – a plastic French press that fitted into the bottle cage below my seat – and a kilogram bag of coffee.

But I admit that shopping in Walmart left me with a sense of guilt. I don't say that to signal virtue. I get it, money talks. But as a twee European, I am used to living in towns and villages where daily errands can be run on foot. You park your car or bicycle in one place and then walk to the butcher, the baker, the candlestick maker. The problem with many American towns, though, is the absurd acreage they cover and how utterly unpedestrianised they are. The epic size and sparseness of the country has allowed them to sprawl without restriction. Some supercentres resemble airports and boast parking lots of 1,200 spaces. But the dominance of a few convenient-to-reach (by car) edge-of-town brands has had a devastating impact on the small businesses operating within.

'People used to frequent downtowns all the time and now they just zoom right by them,' said Sarah Talbott, owner of the Flower

Market, an independent florist, who I met that afternoon in the recently regenerated Canteen District.

'[As a nation] we pushed to the mall thing in the 1970s and pulled our interest away from the downtown. But if your downtown dies, your community dies.'

With a $500,000 grant from the local chamber of commerce, North Platte's Downtown Association revived a few tired and neglected blocks with trees, flowers, benches and trash cans – 'to make it pretty and inviting'.

Surrounded by bouquets of lilies, peonies, roses and dahlias, Sarah's small-scale, bespoke product was the antithesis of big business. She was fighting an uphill battle but prided herself on having a greater human connection to North Platte's residents. In return, however, locals had to play their part.

'I just can't compete on price,' said Sarah. 'But I do think we can reach into a sense of nostalgia in people for wanting to hang on to the past a little bit. We can pull at the heart strings: come shop with us. If people don't support these businesses, then the same thing will happen as five years ago: 70 per cent of these stores will be empty.'

Sarah's efforts were admirable, but even on a warm midweek afternoon, the centre of North Platte felt extremely quiet. Old stores and hotels sat dusty and abandoned. In contrast, Walmart was heaving.

Without wishing to pick a fight with Goliath (and his lawyers), I would go so far as to suggest that the mega-successful department stores owe trillions of dollars in reparations to small-town America. Because their profits have come at an enormous cultural cost. Without footfall, the musicians and artists leave, too.

You could extrapolate further. When you prioritise just a few superstores and drive-thrus on the ring road, people walk less and drive more. Multiply these millions of journeys across thousands of towns and cities and not only do you have higher emissions and poorer air quality, but also billions of unspent calories.

The next morning, I continued southeast, escaping North Platte just after dawn but safely before rush hour. The sky was the colour of bruised plums. And when I crossed the North Platte River, tea-brown water whistled around little sandbanks. Every spring, these waterways welcome more than 400,000 migratory sandhill cranes. But not on this chilly autumn morning. A trickling silence and the unfamiliar echo of breeze.

After several days of convenient westerlies, the wind had shifted and was now blowing 20mph on the nose (and ears). I tried to ignore it, but when I passed an airfield, a bright orange windsock flew rigid – a warning of more sinister things to come. By the time I reached Brady, 22 miles east of North Platte, I felt physically and mentally beaten.

The convenience store doubled up as a coffee shop and a meeting point for the local community. On the table next to me sat six men, ranging in age from about 30 to 80. All were dressed in jeans, checked shirts and baseball caps, and voted Republican.

'We believe in GGC. God, guns and country,' said Bob Golter. Now retired, he had spent 37 years managing the local bank. 'I also want to say drill baby drill, we need to get back to energy independence.'

He was angered by President Joe Biden's 2021 decision to revoke a permit for the Keystone XL Pipeline, a 1,200-mile project that was expected to carry 830,000 barrels of Canadian crude oil to Nebraska every day. Opponents of the line celebrated its cancellation as a win for the transition to cleaner fuels. But the project remains a political hot potato. Vetoed by Barack Obama in 2015, resurrected by Donald Trump in 2019, then killed by Biden in 2021, what happens next is anyone's guess.

On the wall behind the cash register hung a hand-painted 1968 motorists' mileage chart detailing the distances between Brady, Nebraska, and towns and cities across the country.

SALT LAKE CITY: 714 miles
LOS ANGELES: 1,444 miles
NEW YORK CITY: 1,700 miles

There was also the curious addition of Da Nang, Vietnam: 12,652 miles. Several of Brady's young men had been drafted for the war, including 74-year-old Roger Wahlgren, who sat across the table from Bob supping coffee from an aluminium beaker. He spent two years in the army but didn't set foot in Southeast Asia. Nevertheless, simply being drafted made him a target.

'When I got out the service, the first thing I did was take my uniform off,' said Roger. 'People would call you a baby killer and spit in your face. So many liberals were opposed to the war and treated us like hell.'

'Have your feelings about that war changed?' I asked.

'Yeah. Definitely. When I went in, I thought I was fighting communism so we didn't have to fight it here. But then we walked out and probably left it worse off than when we went in there.'

It was a rare – but refreshing – admission of failure. Somehow, it didn't quite fit the American mould to hear someone speak so objectively. But perhaps that skill matures with age.

Their nation had always been divided to some extent, they conceded. Native American/European. North/South. Liberal/ conservative. Pro-Vietnam/anti-Vietnam. Right now was no different. And they appeared, very maturely, perfectly OK with that.

Proud Nebraskans, they cherished their fresh food, empty roads and wide-open spaces. They enjoyed being off the beaten track. 'Put it this way,' laughed Bob. 'If the world does a shit, you're going to want to be in rural Nebraska.'

They were also very happy to opine on subjects ranging from American foreign policy to social economics. And comfortable with me playing devil's advocate and challenging their right-of-centre views. It was, in many ways, good old fashioned offline conversation, which I struggled to imagine having with many people half their age.

But the road waits for no man. Especially one trying to cross the country on a bicycle. And after half a dozen handshakes, I rejoined the gusty outside world, buoyed – at least briefly – by their kind words and freedom of speech.

It grew into a tortuous day. Head down, unable to hear myself think, I made it to Gothenburg, a small town named by its first Swedish residents in the late nineteenth century. Cloaked in white smoke blown down by fresh wildfires in Canada, cylindrical concrete grain elevators resembled dystopian *Blade Runner*-like skyscrapers.

By mid-afternoon, the headwind was so strong that I could barely sit in the saddle. The sky turned black. My cheeks and panniers rattled. Cardboard boxes, plastic bottles and wooden crates flew across the road. Then came the hail. Penny-sized clusters of ice shot down from the heavens, rapping against my coat and helmet like frozen bullets. My ambitions of completing another 100-mile day would need to be revaluated, quickly. And with just 60 miles achieved in eight punishing hours, I stopped in Lexington – a dusty farm town – just as the 'storm' was upgraded to a tornado.

I took refuge in a downtown convenience store, across the street from a surprising sight: a mosque, a single-storey redbrick building built in the shadows of a few cone-shaped grain silos. Bright and silent, the room was at odds with the deafening darkness outside. The shelves were stacked with big boxes of Saudi Arabian dates, 20kg bags of Pakistani rice and boxes of Indian biscuits.

The Somali owner, Naji, sat behind an old computer screen and a leather-bound copy of the Quran. Not only was he the first person I'd seen wearing a thawb – an ankle-length robe – but he was also the first Muslim. In the most unlikely of places.

'There are around 1,500, mainly East Africans, living in Lexington,' he said. 'Somalia, Djibouti, Ethiopia. But also Kenya, Chad, Sudan. All of us came here for the job opportunities.'

Those opportunities were mainly in the nearby meat-packing plant, which – even amid the deluge – could be smelled from a mile away. It processed products for fast-food restaurants but also sold halal beef overseas. 'The liver goes mostly to Egypt,' said Naji.

After moving to Minneapolis, Minnesota, in 2006, Naji moved to Lexington. He was married with five children. 'They were all born here. America is all they've ever known.'

As a Black Muslim, living in a state that was 88 per cent white and 75 per cent Christian, had he ever experienced racism, I wondered, expecting him to reel off a litany of events.

'Minute, very small, tolerable. We haven't seen much Islamophobia.' There had, however, been some resistance to the building of the mosque. And as for the call to prayer: 'We've never asked for permission. We just have mics inside.'

As a Muslim, he was concerned about diminishing levels of

'morality' within society. Namely, a crumbling of the traditional family unit and issues surrounding LGBTQI. 'To me, I think it is very immoral, I think we are really going down in a bad direction.'

As an American citizen, however, he reconciled those concerns with the founding tenets of American freedom. 'Everyone is allowed to practise what they believe. As a Muslim, we are always required to be very optimistic. To me, I see my future very bright, prosperous and peaceful.'

It was a brief interlude, spent with an optimistic man who had travelled to America in pursuit of a better life for himself and his family. I wondered, though, what the white Christian population *really* thought about them being there. Surely resistance to the mosque was just the tip of the iceberg.

When I dragged myself back out into the storm, I made it as far as a nearby hardware store. The lady behind the cash register barely said a word. But as a lifelong Christian resident, she did hint at a simmering friction within the community: 'Maybe I'm wrong, but I feel like they [Lexington's migrant population] need to learn our language.'

It took me two more hours to travel less than a mile, cycling between fast-food restaurants and department stores. Every time I thought the storm had passed, a fork of lightning would strike nearby and scare me back under cover. This pattern repeated a handful of times, before a teenage store assistant bundled me into the back of a delivery van and deposited me outside a motel less than 500 feet down the road.

Roughly 50 miles to the south, a multivortex tornado – on the border with Kansas – ripped across the region, bringing hailstones the size of tennis balls. Observed from the safety of a motel room, the weather was tremendous – a spectator sport. My windowpanes quivered. A flood of oily water surged through the parking lot. Thunder and lightning cracked and fizzed over the bright neon signage of Burger King and McDonald's. With my clothes drying over the bath, I cosied up in bed and watched wall-to-wall local news coverage of radar images and windspeeds of more than 100mph.

For me, I admit, it was all rather exciting. But as I continued southeast the next morning, the destruction – even 50 miles away from the storm's epicentre – was obvious. Fences had been torn apart. A few cars had been ditched in laybys. Most notably, however, the farmland was saturated. A rain gauge on a rusty fencepost showed that nine centimetres had fallen overnight, pummelling fields of genetically modified corn, soyabeans, wheat and alfalfa to within 3.5 inches of their lives.

I stopped on an empty rural road for coffee and spotted a small lady, not much taller than five feet, walking my way. Dressed in an orange hoodie, jeans and gum boots, Dana Benson had worked the land for 42 years, having married into the farming life. She and her husband had a few hundred acres of crops, plus pasture for 'hogs and sheep'. Like many farmers, they waged a war against the elements. Often, there wasn't enough rain; sometimes, there was far too much. She believed humans were responsible for climate change 'to some extent'.

Modern farmers, she told me, played fast and loose with chemicals in an irresponsible bid to grow their profit margins. 'Herbicides, pesticides, fungicides,' said Dana. 'When farmers are spraying, you can smell the chemicals in the air. So don't tell me that doesn't have something to do with what's going on.'

As Dana and her husband reached retirement age, it was unclear who – if anyone – would take on the farm. Her six-year-old grandson was currently the most enthusiastic candidate: 'He'd be the sixth generation. He's still young, but ever since he could walk and talk, he's said, "I'm going to farm like my grandpa and work on tractors like my dad."'

She confessed, though, that farming got harder every year. 'All these young people now just want to spend money and buy things, but with interest rates going up and crop prices going down, I don't know what's going to happen.'

Dana told me that most local farmers were Trump-supporting Republicans, but she was undecided, calling him 'wishy-washy'. Instead, she chose to sit on her wind-damaged fence. 'We didn't get so much in debt just because of Biden; we've been in debt for years and years.'

She wished me well for the remainder of my journey, then returned to the farm to feed the chickens. I admired her graft and optimism; it would be an impossible job without it. But the history books paint a gloomy picture for the future. According to the US Department of Agriculture, there were 6.8 million farms spread across the country in 1935. Fast-forward to 2022, and just 2 million remained.

It felt oddly tragic that the legacy of all their ancestral hard work fell on the shoulders of a six-year-old boy. This wasn't an Old MacDonald nursery rhyme or a Playmobile farmyard. This was a lifetime's commitment to early starts and late finishes. Working from one unpredictable harvest to the next. And for what? A loyalty to the relatives that toiled before you? I could understand the instinct to leave something to the next generation. But there must be a fine line between blessing and burden.

I cycled through channels of rambling corn, their previously dried-out husks now dripping wet. After the rain, the warm road buzzed with bugs droning collectively like an air raid siren. A state trooper in aviator sunglasses drove past, flashed his hazards and then raised a singular finger from the wheel. That was it. The only human until lunchtime.

Cycling into the wind, progress across Nebraska felt like a giant game of snakes and ladders. The challenge was in deciding when to continue east and when to turn south. Mobile phone weather applications weren't to be trusted. So navigation was as primitive as holding a finger in the air or tossing a handful of grass into the wind.

Nevertheless, progress was made. Not as fast as a few days before but thankfully nowhere near as slowly as the previous night. And when I did finally encounter another person, a woman working at a removals company on the side of the road, she gave me a few words of encouragement: 'Don't worry, the food and coffee should get better the further south you go.' Followed by the now predictable farewell message: 'God bless you,' she said, with a broad smile and an enthusiastic wave.

It took ten hours to cycle 85 miles, but I made it to Hastings and went straight to the nearest pub: First Street Brewing Co. It didn't take long for the men at the bar to hear my accent and start a conversation.

'Are you independently wealthy?' asked a man with shoulder-length brown hair who was curious about my budget.

'No, I'm a journalist.'

'Oh, so you're broke!'

'I will be if no one buys this book.'

If the laughter wasn't enough to break the ice, then the exceptional craft ale certainly was. Battered as I was from the road, a pint of 7 per cent IPA went directly to my head (and legs).

Originally, from upstate New York, the barman, Adam Jacobs, had spent a decade studying around the country. He moved to Hastings when his English wife got a job teaching at a local school. Working at the heart of a busy bar gave him ample time to eavesdrop.

'We're Middle America, and all the trends that you see in the national news, those conversations are happening right here in this bar. But if you speak to someone for long enough, I don't think we are as divided as Twitter would make you think. For example, the idea of some people getting too rich and everyone else not getting a fair shake. You get that from both sides of the political spectrum.'

On a journey made up of random roadside encounters, my regular brewery visits nearly always guaranteed a sense of optimism. For Adam, these institutions were just as important as America's schools, libraries and churches.

'I think in some ways, ideas pass more freely here than they do in other places. A place like this can work as a meeting place for all groups. They are important points of cohesion, to remind us that we have more in common than we have that separate.'

As he was an American married to an Englishwoman, I was eager to ask how his perspectives on both countries might have changed.

'Quite frankly, the political milieu is trending in the same direction and tends to be getting crazier every minute. It's a shift to the right. I think we are seeing a polarisation in a geographic sense, as opposed to a class or race sense. It's a kind of coastal versus inner America divide.'

Four pints deep and contemplating a fifth, I swayed like a hiccupping sailor. Adam kindly offered up his couch, but he didn't finish for another few hours and had a two-year-old at home. On second thoughts, we decided to go our sperate ways. When I got up to leave, three drinkers in the corner, who had barely said a word, told Adam they were picking up my tab.

'You're cycling across the country! It's the least we can do.'

Just five minutes away, I found a rough motel with a droning fridge and a stained cream carpet and got into bed without even taking a shower or brushing my teeth.

Unsurprisingly, the next morning started with a pounding headache. Nevertheless, lemony sunshine kissed a greasy blacktop road abuzz with iridescent dragonflies. They had bodies as fat as index fingers and wings as wide as side plates. They skipped between my handlebars and the curious-looking shrubs in the verge. I stopped to take a closer look. Weed? Dope? Sweet Mary Jane? Not quite, but a close cousin: feral cannabis, with sticky buds and pointed green leaves.

Known locally as ditch weed, this hemp was cultivated industrially and used to help in the Second World War effort, making products like paper and rope. Thousands of rogue plants still line the Midwest's verges. But before the Snoop Doggs among you start planning a Nebraska road trip, take note: the tetrahydrocannabinol (THC) content is so negligible that you'd have to smoke a joint the size of a clarinet before getting anything close to the giggles.

The landscape was otherwise dull. Monotone. Predictable. Dreary. I feel guilty using such uninspiring vocabulary. As a travel writer I should be painting lush pictures. But much of southern Nebraska didn't exactly inspire awe but encouraged yawns. Feeling flat and unenergetic, I needed inspiration. So I stopped in a layby to throw on a classic American road-trip playlist, comprised mostly of Jackson Browne, The Eagles and Willie Nelson. The music provided an aural hit of vigour. I quickly went from Running on Empty, to Taking it Easy, On the Road Again. There did, however, exist an obvious juxtaposition between the often-verdant American landscapes immortalised in these mostly 1960s and 1970s tunes and what I now saw on the roadside. Agriculture, for hundreds of miles, across every bland horizon.

These tracts of battered, bleached, mostly GMO corn had little logos beside them detailing the chemicals keeping them alive. I listened to 'Big Yellow Taxi' (1970) by Joni Mitchell. More than half a century ago, she asked farmers to put away the DDT, preferring to have birds and bees even if that meant spots on her apples.

I thought back to Dana, the farmer I'd met the previous day, and the fragility of her land, lifestyle and legacy. For how long could this earth survive, I wondered. Pumped with chemicals, year after year. All eyes on next summer's yield, but barely a thought for the six-year-olds in 50 years.

I made progress east, then south, then east, then south again. Zigzagging along a vast grid system. The occasional truck rumbled past and sounded its horn. Hundreds of hairy caterpillars wriggled in the shoulder, resembling runaway Victorian moustaches. Roadside billboards belonged to churches and farms.

'SMILE. YOUR MOM CHOSE LIFE.'

'ABORTION. SHAMEFUL HUMAN SACRIFICE.'

'NEXT RIGHT: FREE RANGE EGGS.'

I made it to Shickley by lunchtime. Described on an entry sign as 'A Big Little Town', the village had a population of less than 350 but boasted a baseball field, a gym, a swimming pool, a library, a high school, a gas station and no fewer than four active churches. On the town website, there were more than 30 registered businesses. It reminded me of an abandoned *Truman Show*. A Warner Bros-style water tower loomed over its empty main street.

Inside the convenience store, I found owner Chris Schlegel describing the previous night's high school football match to a grizzly old farmer in mud-splattered jeans. 'It was ugly,' said Chris. The Bruning-Davenport/Shickley Eagles – a combined team of small local towns – had won 60–18 against Sacred Heart.

'We're not on the way to anywhere,' he told me. 'So, you're an oddity coming through here. We're very much a farming community. Agriculture is the backbone. It's what all the kids go into, in one way or another.'

The high school was, once again, a major source of identity. 'Town pride is often based on the success or failure of your team,' said Chris, who was optimistic for small-town America. He believed that the migration towards big cities had reached its peak and now people were returning for a slower and more rewarding pace of life.

'I have a hope for maintaining this kind of life. But it's busy. To sustain amenities in a small town you have to wear a lot of hats. I'm on two or three different boards.'

Chris described Shickley as having a somewhat homogenised culture: mostly conservative and Republican. Most people agreed on most things. The price of corn and beans, however, was the biggest topic of debate. That, and the desire to live self-sustainably, with a government that didn't 'try to micromanage every part of the world'.

Besides the high school, the church was a major community hub. Between 80 and 100 people attended Chris's church every Sunday, while the smaller ones welcomed 15 to 20.

'Is this the start of the Bible Belt?' I asked.

'I would say so, yeah. Historically, it's very Christian.'

Shickley didn't have any resident law enforcement. Instead, a county sheriff drove through once a day. A town ordinance also allowed golf carts and quadbikes to be driven on public roads without number plates. High school students could apply for driving permits. When two girls turned up in a pickup to buy cereal and orange juice, I was perplexed.

'That 11-year-old girl just drove here?'

'She's 14. In Nebraska, you can drive at 14, which is really convenient for farmers around here because kids can drive themselves to school.'

Just east of town, I turned southwards onto Highway 81, a road with a gravelly, potholed shoulder. The haggard surface left me wincing from saddle sores I didn't know existed. Cycling into a headwind, I dropped my shoulders, curved my spine and focused on the spinning front wheel. Switching from road to house music boosted my speed from 12mph to 14mph and provided a rush of endorphins akin to a late-night rave.

Hundreds of monarch butterflies swarmed over the road, but the prominent roadkill had now changed. No more mammals but snapping turtles – about the size of iPads, with sharp claws and beaks. Most had been crushed by passing cars or smashed and flipped by hawks, then gruesomely disembowelled via their soft underbellies. Most prominent, however, were the bullfrogs. After the rain, hundreds of squished green fatties now filled the road. Since being introduced to southeastern Nebraska by hungry French fur traders in the 1800s, they have multiplied in their millions. A single female can produce 20,000 eggs each summer. Some Midwesterners still scoop up hundreds a night, either by hand, line or net, and fry their chicken-drumstick-like rear legs in butter, then serve them with tartare sauce. The American novelist John Steinbeck had a soft spot for these noisy amphibians, too. In his 1945 novel *Cannery Row*, his central characters enjoy a whiskey-fuelled night hauling them into bags and making five cents a frog: 'There were frogs all right, thousands of them. Their voices beat the night, they boomed and barked and croaked and rattled. They sang to the stars, to the waning moon, to the waving grasses. They bellowed long songs and challenges.'

At surface level, Steinbeck's Depression-era stories speak of a mostly bleak American existence. They often concern the lives of working-class Middle Americans striving – physically, economically and culturally – to attain pastures green and new. Perhaps most notably in *Of Mice and Men* (1937) and *The Grapes of Wrath* (1939).

Seen in hindsight, though, these tales burst – at least in my eyes – with a somewhat dichotomous sense of togetherness. Families hunkering down in haystacks. Hard-up friends clubbing together to throw a party.

More than 50 years since his death, Steinbeck continues to sell more than 500,000 copies of his novels each year. Why? Probably because his work evokes nostalgia – even in the dustbowls – for an organic and idyllic America. A way of life which many of us continue to fetishise. Epitomised by the simple joy of slugging whiskey from the bottle and netting frogs by starlight.

14

SOUPY HEAT

With 100 miles on my cycle computer, I crossed the border into Kansas. 'We're off to see the wizard!' I sang. 'The wonderful Wizard of Oz!' I was ready for a celebratory beer and a hearty meal, so called it a day in Belleville, the first small town on the horizon.

But Belleville was dead. Deserted. The scene of a zombie apocalypse. It was 28 degrees centigrade at 5pm on a Saturday. And there was barely a tinman or scarecrow, let alone a human to speak of.

I cycled through a big green park: no one.

A town square ringed with flags: nothing.

Tennis courts, a bowling alley, movie theatre, swimming pool: nada.

Like every other town in the country, Belleville had a strapline to help separate it from the crowd: 'at the crossroads of America'.

The Road to Nowhere, more like.

Seventy miles north of Interstate 70 and 75 miles south of Interstate 80, Belleville looked as though it was suffering geographically. It had the amenities to serve 10,000 people but not enough people to serve the amenities. What it did have in abundance, though, was cats. I found half a dozen of the cute little critters huddled in the warm shade of a cottonwood tree.

Dinner was served in an edge-of-town Dairy Queen – which has, on balance, the best-quality Middle American fast food, with at least a few fresh lettuce leaves and some semblance of atmosphere. A cheerleading squad bundled out of a minibus and chowed down on cheeseburgers, onion rings and fried chicken, while a few local boys snatched sly glances from behind their ice-cream sundaes. Still hungry, I retreated to a grotty motel and ate instant noodles out of a paper cup.

According to the Kansas Health Foundation, more than 30 per cent of the state's counties are classed as 'food deserts' – regions described by the National Library of Medicine as 'neighbourhoods and communities that have limited access to affordable and nutritious foods'. This means a lack of grocery stores selling fresh fruit and vegetables. Instead, most small towns have just one convenience store and a gas station peddling heavily processed, beige ingredients, conveniently packaged into bread, batter or pastry.

Of the 76 counties across the US that don't have a single grocery store, almost half are found in the Midwest. This leaves mostly low-income, rural communities to survive on the long-shelf-life products found in dollar stores, an area of the US economy that – from what I'd seen – was far from struggling. Between 2017 and 2023, the number of dollar stores in America grew from 30,000 to 40,000. Not only does this make so many small towns look and feel the same, but it also paints a grim picture for American public health.

For 2,000 miles, I had been surviving on this crap. A small part of me was eagerly counting down the days to journey's end, just so I could eat real food again. Which is a cynical frame of mind to be in.

Most of us believe in the tenet of prevention being better than cure. But I couldn't help but wonder if America's private health insurance model had fostered an attitude of cure is better (or at least much easier) than prevention. Epitomised by the staggering number of pharmaceutical commercials on US television. Seemingly, there is a pill, powder or jab for almost every conceivable ailment. Most of which could be prevented by consuming fewer calories and doing more exercise.

I woke up early, just before dawn, to find a bright green praying mantis looking down at me from the ceiling. The day was forecast to hit the mid-thirties but the pumping headwind had dropped, thank goodness. There wasn't a cloud in the sky, just the night's last stars evaporating away. As I cycled south, on another long, straight road, the rising sun cast my oversized shadow against a never-ending horizon of corn.

Sunday morning, and Highway 81 was empty. Just the occasional long-haul trucker pulling enormous wind turbine blades or people making their way to church. With barely a bend ahead of me, I turned to the metronomic sounds of Kraftwerk, the German synth group and pioneers of modern dance music. Brilliantly repetitive, their beats had given me restless leg syndrome for two decades, particularly their 1983 hit 'Tour de France' – clicks and glitches with samples of spinning bicycle chains and heavy breathing. Performance-enhancing music at its very best.

I made it to Concordia for brunch. The first things I saw were the grain elevators, silos and water towers common to many Midwestern towns. Then the downtown streets were empty. But the highway running through offered a Subway, Dairy Queen, Arby's and McDonald's. All were rammed. The latter was packed with churchgoers in their Sunday best. Boomers in motorcycle leathers. Kansas City Chiefs football fans in red, white and yellow. A teenage baseball team, kitted out in blue pinstripe uniforms, caps and knee-high socks. McDonald's usually blared out nondescript muzak, but not here. On the radio, two Christian pastors conflated Old Testament scripture with the melodrama of office politics.

Sport, fast food and the bible all under one roof. Welcome to America. A handful of friendly people gave me God's blessings. Then, as I got up to leave, the radio station switched to the 1969 tune 'Aquarius/Let the Sunshine In' by the Fifth Dimension – an earworm that would accompany me all morning.

Let the sunshine in! Or, more accurately, the sunflowers. South of Concordia, fields of corn gave way to ten-square-mile blocks of them. Kansas, the Sunflower State, boasts a climate and soil perfect for their cultivation.

My spirits were high. Over halfway through my journey and going downhill, kind of. The state was made doubly enjoyable by the resplendent weather. By travelling 80–100 miles south each day, I was getting roughly 1.5 degrees of latitude closer to the equator. In late September, I was outrunning autumn, just.

By mid-afternoon, the black road was red hot. And as I bore down on Salina – a big town for Kansas, with a population of 46,000 – I cycled past the charred remains of a truck fire which had scorched the tinderbox verge with flames. A few miles on, I entered the aftermath of a massacre. Something bad had happened, perhaps just a few hours before. Five hundred feet of tarmac was covered in blood and animal flesh. An overturned livestock trailer, maybe. Or an entire herd of deer. Either way, it looked and smelled gruesome. Fresh offal on a barbecue.

As I wove through the sobering mess, my tyres sticky with blood, my own mortality returned to the fore. It was easy to be blasé about cycling across America. Eat, sleep, ride, repeat, and all that. But it was essential I kept my wits about me. My life, and the lives of the people – old and new – that I loved, depended on my safe return. For the rest of the afternoon, I cycled a little deeper in the shoulder, my shins whipping against the long grass, tiny seeds burrowing beneath their hairs.

I had planned to stay in Salina, but on a bicycle, the city left me feeling bewildered. Where was the downtown? The cycle lanes? The pedestrianised heart? Beats me. All I could find were department stores and drive-thru fast-food restaurants. Too big, too sporadic. So, I scanned a map for inspiration and pushed on another 25 miles.

The light at the end of the 95-mile-long tunnel was Lindsborg, A.K.A. Little Sweden, a town so chocolate-box it immediately lived up to its Scandi promise. Yellow and blue Nordic crosses flew beside star-spangled banners. Inside the supermarket, I found shelves packed with Icelandic chocolate bars and smoked liquorice fish. Lindsborg was settled by a group of Swedish immigrants from the Värmland province in 1869, and 30 per cent of the town's residents can still trace their heritage back to these original founders. It was clearly still a source of great pride. And a brilliant business opportunity. Giftshops sold Scandinavian trinkets. Restaurants served meatballs with creamy gravy. Bars and ice-cream parlours flavoured their cocktails and sundaes with lingonberries. Herds of carved Dala horses lined the redbrick high street. The town was – for want of a less vacuous phrase – instagrammable, epitomised by a British-style phone box painted in yet more Swedish yellow and blue. But, it being a Sunday, almost everything was closed. So I had to settle for a days-old sandwich on a bench.

When I checked into the Viking Motel, an immaculate spot

for a bargain price, the owner asked if I was in town to meet Jim Richardson.

'I'm not,' I replied. 'But I could be?'

Aged 76, Jim had travelled the world as a *National Geographic* photographer, reporting from the Arctic, Antarctic and more than 80 countries in between. He was clearly a local legend. I was handed his number and gave him a call. Miraculously, he wasn't in the Gobi, the Kalahari or hacking his way through the Darién Gap, but at home, just a few blocks away.

I had just enough time to shower before a grey-bearded and bespectacled man jumped out of a station wagon with a six-pack of icy beers. We then spent the next hour trading travellers' tales as thousands of starlings came in to roost on the trees and rooftops around us.

Born in Belleville, the deserted town where I'd spent the previous night, Jim wasn't surprised I'd found it empty. He could, however, remember a country before the interstate system was built. An era of mixed fortunes for rural America.

'Some towns far away, it basically sealed their fate,' said Jim. 'But then others got lucky and they have a totally different profile. Many of them have done well but they have done well at a price. Because you see that they developed services out by the interstate and it sucked everything out of downtown.'

Four miles from Interstate 135, Lindsborg felt like an anomaly. Close to a main thoroughfare, yet far enough away to retain a sense of uniqueness. The Swedish heritage story had been a big help. 'People here worked really hard on the tourist industry,' said Jim. 'The Swedish theme really got started in the 1960s. It helped create a sense of identity.'

Geographically, the town also found itself fortuitously positioned between 'two pretty dynamic job-generating towns' in the shape of Salina and McPherson, hubs for the pharmaceutical and fast-food industries.

Curiously, Jim likened rural, sparsely populated Kansas to the islands of Scotland, a part of the world for which he had a particular fondness.

'Kansas is a lot like Scotland, except they have more lighthouses and beaches. But when you get down to the level of small communities out here in the Great Plains and small communities on the isles of Scotland, you see lots of commonalities in terms of the kinds of problems and rewards.'

Jim's work on agricultural projects in the USA and the developing world had given him a unique perspective on the notion of American exceptionalism; the idea that the USA is morally, economically and industrially superior to the rest of the planet.

'I think there really is a profound theology in this country that America is the greatest country that ever existed, and for many people there's this idea that America is God's best vision. For many others, though, America is the tool of Satan. There's also this idea of freedom, that Americans have it and other places in the world don't. But the reality is that there are lots of countries around the world that, probably, have even more freedom. That's a hard nut to crack.'

We could have chatted all night, we were peas from the same pod. But I was exhausted and Jim had to drive across the country the next day to deliver a university lecture. So, we called it a night.

It was becoming hard to differentiate one day from another. But at least I had a new crop to look at the next morning: sorghum. Kansas produces more of the cereal than any other state in America – 169 million bushels, about 4.3 million tonnes. From the road, it looked like a hybrid of other plants: oversized wheat ears, with sugar-cane-like leaves, about the same height as maize.

I stopped at a gas station in McPherson. It was doing a roaring trade in 'Midwest breakfasts' – a mega slice of cheese and ground beef pizza, accompanied by a fountain soda. And all for $4.

'We're American, we like big things!' said the friendly man I got talking to outside. His V8, 6.7-litre pickup was the size of an army tank, three times longer than my bike and panniers. It sat idling as he personally worked through three Midwest breakfasts and a two-litre cup of 'coffee'. He was flabbergasted by my journey. So much so that he became a cheerleader, of sorts – the best agent I've ever had.

'Hey, dude, this guy's riding a frickin' bike across the country!' He told about three dozen people, grinning from ear to ear. Everyone was concerned for my safety. Most gave me God's blessings. Two were worried about my prostate. One tried to sell me a gun.

To the man, bicycles were silly toys that he messed about on as a child. It was incomprehensible to him that a grown-up might use one as a means of transport. We were aliens from different planets but became good friends in a very short time. And as I saddled up to hit the road, I built up the gumption to ask: 'Your pickup ... Do you really need a car that size?'

'Dude, this ain't big. They do one that's almost twice this size. When I get a new credit card, I'm going to get me that one next!'

Riding across the USA was such a peculiarity that I spent the next couple of hours being followed by a film crew from PBS Kansas. Their weekly show *Positively Kansas* aimed to 'encourage and inspire all of us to reach for the stars and make the world a better place'.

'What are you wearing?' the producer had asked on the phone. 'How will we know it's you?'

'Mate, I haven't seen a cyclist for 2,000 miles. I'm the only bloke out here.'

I put on my best broadcasting voice, wiped the grime from my brow and cycled a few extra miles up and down a dirt road until they had all the material required.

By early afternoon, it was 35 degrees in the shade. The black road must have been closer to 50 and radiated the sun's soupy heat back up at me. Cycling was the only way to create breeze. The landscape was mostly barren, copper brown and freshly ploughed. Quite boring, really. But the afternoon did throw up four firsts of note.

An armadillo, its hard shell popped open like a pistachio, gooey insides exposed to the birds and bugs. But an armadillo, no less. And an armour-plated mammal that inhabited the warm climates of the southeast.

Soon came the dust devils, two mini tornadoes about 20 feet wide and a few hundred feet tall. They swirled across an empty field and off down the vacant road. Then trees heavy with wild pawpaws, a squishy subtropical fruit with a green-yellow outer husk and a custardy centre. Tasting something like a banana-flavoured mango, they grow wild in America's warmer climes.

But what said the beginning of 'the South' more than any other sight? Cotton. As I made my approach to Wichita, the biggest city in Kansas, I saw hundreds of acres of the white fluffy stuff blowing on the prickly branches of knee-high green shrubs.

Midwestern Kansas produces less than 1 per cent of American cotton, but this number is growing thanks to climate change. Traditionally, the Cotton Belt ran through the southern states, but as summer and fall temperatures rise across the country, more northerly farmers are turning to the cash crop. After corn, soya, hay and wheat, cotton is the most profitable in the nation. I stopped on the roadside, stomped out into the middle of a field and picked a tuft. In my fingers I twirled the white fleecy substance, a commodity that had – perhaps more than any other – shaped America, its people, politics and prosperity (for some).

When Columbus discovered the 'New World' in 1492, he found cotton growing in the Bahamas, off the southeast coast of Florida. By 1616, European colonists were growing the crop along the James River in Virginia and by 1730 it was being spun by machines and turned into textiles. The owners of large cotton plantations became some of the wealthiest people in the world – achieved by exploiting enslaved Africans and their descendants. By 1850, 1.8 million slaves laboured in the United States' cotton fields. Unpaid and dehumanised, they toiled from dawn until dusk, under the inescapable terror of lashings, separation from their families, neck braces and leg irons.

Under southern law, slaves could not marry. However, some plantation owners allowed it as a means of fostering harmony and most likely boosting their profits. 'Masters' were also legally protected from using their slaves as sexual objects and many were the victims of rape.

It was the first time I had ever seen raw cotton in the flesh, let alone held it in my hands. A material so commonplace in our lives that we seldom consider its historical and cultural context, much in the same way we overlook the diamonds in our engagement rings or the lithium in our mobile phones. But as I stood in that scorching field, the sun beating down and searing my skin, it was impossible to escape the horrors of human greed and persecution.

By the time I reached Wichita at 4pm, the temperature had topped out at 37 degrees centigrade (in late September). When I took off my sunglasses and pulled back my long shirtsleeves, the backs of my hands were as red as cricket balls. Beneath my wedding ring I had a bright white hoop. My road-dusted shins were pink to the touch.

The city was busy but miraculously I found a cycle lane to follow, with a two-foot buffer between me and the traffic. My hosts for the night were partly to thank, because not only were they keen cyclists themselves, but advocates for a cycle-safe city.

I'd connected with Barry and Nancy via Warm Showers. Sweaty and dishevelled as I was, they welcomed me into their suburban home, handed me a fresh towel and pointed me towards the bathroom.

Married for 16 years, they were both on their second marriage and had bonded over their mutual love of bicycles. Once again, they were kind and warm-hearted hosts, adept at looking after weary cyclists. Within an hour of arriving, my clean clothes were drying, and I was two beers to the good and tucking into a huge plate of spaghetti bolognese with garlic bread and salad.

Born and raised in rural Kentucky, Barry's university studies were interrupted by the Vietnam War – a conflict he still wholeheartedly disagreed with: 'I felt like a political prisoner. It was so wrong, from start to finish. One of my best friends was killed.'

They were both proud of their country, its national parks, size and scale, but agreed there were state-by-state contradictions on laws and politics. For example, as left-leaning Democrats, they disliked how some parts of the USA were less tolerant of same-sex partnerships.

'There's so much "other" hate,' said Nancy. 'If you're not like me, there's something wrong with you. Being raised a Christian, I am appalled at fellow Christians hating people just because they don't love the person they think they should love. And that's wrong to me. That's not in the bible I read.'

Having grown up in rural California and later Kansas, Nancy believed that outside of America's big cities, there was still a lot of 'unchecked privilege' from people who 'had not gone very far out of their county. They're just very narrow-minded, not very understanding.'

After dinner, they took me for a drive around Wichita, a bustling and cosmopolitan-looking town built around the Arkansas River. They were passionate advocates for bicycles, exercise and pedestrianisation, and had co-founded Bike Walk Wichita (BWW). Based out of a 7,500-square-foot downtown headquarters, the non-profit refurbished donated bikes and then gave them to refugees, single mothers and homeless people. They also campaigned to make Wichita a safer place to travel, car-free.

'We gave a bike to a woman who was walking four miles to and from work every day and it changed her life,' said Barry, as we entered a building, quite literally, packed to the rafters with bicycles. Hundreds of them, in every shape and size.

'We've had people come to us and say they've lost 50 pounds (22.7kg) – "I'm not taking diabetes medication anymore." These bikes provide a sense of empowerment. We're building a community where we try to treat everyone with respect and dignity.'

People on low incomes could visit the facility, donate 15 hours of their time and then ride away on a bicycle with a lock, light and helmet. BWW also gave bicycles to felons released from jail and provided them with a place to volunteer and learn new skills.

'We teach people from zero,' said recycle shop manager Cody Custer, while he gave my bike the once over. 'People who know nothing about bikes. Everyone can be here.'

Cody believed these humble contraptions could change American society, one saddle and spoke at a time.

'Bikes are massive, historically speaking. When the suffragette movement was taking place, bicycles gave women the ability to go and protest. In modern times, it is a huge leveller, and in a city like Wichita it is life-changing.'

I slept like a log, in a spare bedroom full of world maps, bicycle trinkets and bumper stickers dedicated to Obama and Biden. One read: 'TOO POOR TO BE REPUBLICAN'. Another: 'CELEBRATE DIVERSITY'.

*

After a blueberry muffin and two cups of strong Guatemalan coffee, Barry and Nancy waved me off into another hot day.

A cycle path conveniently followed the banks of the Arkansas River. It was quiet and easy to cover ground, but housed hundreds of homeless people, who congregated under any bridge or flyover providing shade. The city was waking up, and so were they. I passed a couple of twenty-something men injecting into their bruised wrists, then a handful of women arguing over space in a tent. They were down on their luck, swept into the fringes, but at least most of them had bikes.

By midmorning, I'd reached the small town of Belle Plaine and stopped off in Dave's Diner for an omelette and a side of hash browns. Once again, it gave off a distinctly living-room ambiance. But with massive portions and a predictably friendly vibe, it was a good place to escape the sun and wind.

In the corner, a 60-inch TV jumped from one dubious commercial to another, advertising health insurance policies, medical lawsuit attorneys and dodgy-sounding pharmaceuticals. Incontinence pads, haemorrhoid creams and IV drips 'to improve hydration' – if only there was a readily available clear liquid that did the same job. Each was inevitably followed by extensive disclaimers, encouraging any human being with an ounce of common sense to categorically avoid said product. 'May cause blindness, bleeding from the rectum, cancer and heart failure.' All the good stuff, basically.

I left town feeling stuffed and optimistic, ready to make a dent in the day and – hopefully – reach Oklahoma by nightfall. Chubby catfish flipped and flapped in the greenish shallows of the Arkansas River. It was scorching hot again. A mirage whipped up from the road. But at least it was empty. I could cycle for hours without a care in the world. Or so I thought.

The first 30 minutes ticked by without a hitch. I didn't see a single vehicle. Then, I noticed a white pickup about half a mile behind me. With four bright panniers and the sun high in the sky, I was as visible as I'd ever be. Wrong.

Just as I started to wonder what had happened to the pickup, I looked over my left shoulder and saw a wingmirror flying towards the back of my head. I ducked just as the passenger-side door grazed my back pannier and thrust me off the road, down a slope, into a dusty gulley.

For ten seconds, I stared up at the blue sky, waiting to feel pain. I had grazed palms and a bashed shin, but thankfully nothing more sinister. About 50 feet away, a male driver stood next to the pickup.

'I'm sorry, Sir,' he shouted. 'I didn't see you.'

'What the fuck, man!' I screamed.

I picked up my bike and wheeled back to the road. In a state of hazy shock, I couldn't muster words.

'I thought I was over further, but I wasn't,' said the man, who was clearly shaken. 'I'm so sorry, Sir. Can I help you?'

There was nothing left to say. It was, however, the closest I had ever come to being killed on my bicycle.

I stood there, stewing over a conundrum that had accompanied my entire journey: cycle on busier, less attractive roads, with wider shoulders and rumble strips? Or ride the much quieter, prettier thoroughfares, often with no shoulders and motorists less switched on?

According to a study by the insurance company Compare the Market, American drivers are the seventh worst in the world, ranked behind only Thailand, Peru, Lebanon, India, Malaysia and Argentina. In 2021, 42,915 people were killed on American roads. By this point in my journey, I had already seen hundreds of people driving while texting – way beyond anything I'd witnessed elsewhere. I had also spotted several people driving with their left legs hanging out of their windows. Around 96 per cent of American cars have an automatic transmission. Had this ease of use bred a sense of comfort and complacency – a detachment between driver, vehicle and road?

If instinct hadn't told me to take a quick glance back at the road, then I would have been smacked in the head and probably killed instantly. As he drove off, I noticed that his pickup had a smashed right-side bumper. Not from collision with my soft panniers but with whatever unlucky thing he had hit last.

15

BETWEEN A DOG AND A FAST PLACE

Just before I crossed over the state line into Oklahoma, I bumped into a curious woman on the side of an otherwise empty rural road. From a distance, I had wondered if my eyes were deceiving me, a mirage – but no. In the unrelenting heat of a late summer afternoon, she was walking 'about 30 miles' between towns, without as much as a long shirt, let alone a hat.

'I got kicked out,' she told me. 'So I'm walking to Arkansas City. Where they should have a homeless shelter.'

It had been enough of a struggle on a bike moving at 13mph, but she was about twice my size, wore broken shoes and had short ginger hair. Her freckle-covered shoulders had turned purple with blistered sunburn. She didn't even have a bottle of water.

Concerned for her wellbeing, I donated a shirt to protect her shoulders and a T-shirt to tie around her head, Arabian headscarf style. She caked her arms and legs in factor 50 sun cream, downed the only bottle of Powerade I had left and took my last $9 in change.

'I'm sorry,' I said. 'I wish I could give you a ride but that's all I have.'

No older than 25, she had spent most of her life bouncing from one homeless shelter to another. She told me that the Covid-19 pandemic had, somewhat unexpectedly, offered a brief respite for people living on America's streets. It was, however, short-lived: 'In St Louis [Missouri], they had a programme but it didn't even last a year. Everyone got apartments but then they lost them. I was looking for a job but never found one.'

Talking to her for just five minutes, I could tell that she was clearly a bright young woman who had found herself in a potentially dangerous and vulnerable situation. Wichita, she told me, was too far to walk. If she could have got there, I would have directed her straight to BWW.

'If you're walking, not many people will stop for you,' she said, as she took off towards some bushes for shade. 'I've also seen loads of snakes today, so be careful.'

About ten miles east, I stopped in Arkansas City for water and mentioned my encounter to a male store worker. 'Oh, she was most likely just a druggie,' he replied, with zero sympathy. 'We get them coming through here.'

Shortly after, I crossed the border into Oklahoma – my seventh US state. Highway 77 ran south, adjacent to a semi-suburban road of single-storey clapboard homes surrounded by sit-down lawnmowers and rusting pickups. Quiet and treelined, it seemed like an ideal place to ride. Some houses were ringed by six-foot wire fences. Some, however, were not.

First, I heard a bark. Then, a crack of branches. Within three terrifying seconds, two salivating rottweilers were sprinting towards me, snapping at each heel. Should I stop and fight? Or try to outrun them? I hastily chose the latter and raced at over 20mph for more than 90 seconds before they mercifully gave up the chase.

Ashen with nerves, I resolved to call it a day at the first place I saw: a Native American-owned casino on the side of the highway. Clean, gaudy and cheap. It was high time for a rest day.

After a quick shower, I entered a vast casino floor. A thousand lights flashed to the beat of Bruce Springsteen. A thin halo of cigarette smoke floated over a sea of silver hair. It was 35 degrees centigrade outside but the hall must have been refrigerated to single figures. Teeth chattering, I half expected to find Antarctic explorers training with sleds and crampons.

As a guest paying $50 a night for a room, I was entitled to free food, drink and $30 betting credit. So, I sat next to a pensioner in a wheelchair, flagged down a waiter and haphazardly pressed a few buttons. I must have been the youngest player by 50 years. Some patrons parked oxygen tanks between their slot machines and ashtrays. Two paramedics beadily surveyed the crowd in a manner that suggested they worked on commission. The business model was clearly not designed for people like me, though. Because after half an hour, I cashed out $50 in credit and retreated to my room before I contracted bronchitis.

The next day, I did as little as possible. I washed my clothes in the bathtub, edited that week's YouTube video and savoured the air conditioning for as long as possible. The afternoon heat peaked at 40 degrees centigrade and showed no sign of letting up. Easterly winds were forecast for the foreseeable future.

Rest days were a blessing and a curse. I was now so accustomed to cycling 80 or 100 miles every day that when I didn't get that, I was filled with excess adrenaline. I tossed and turned throughout the night, playing out routes and counter-routes in my mind's eye. When my alarm sounded at 6.30am, I had only managed three hours' terrible sleep.

Nonetheless, I hit the road, desperate to have a good morning. The idea was to cycle for five hard hours, barely stopping. In theory, travelling 50 or 60 miles before midday. That way, if the heat became as powerful as the forecast predicted, I could call it quits with at least a reasonable return for the day.

It was the autumn solstice – exactly 12 hours of day and night – and I was on the road in time to see a pure orange sun fizz up from behind a railroad track just as a rusty freight train passed across the horizon. It was the sort of serendipity that Hollywood filmmakers would plan for months, stressing about the timings and details. This sunrise, however, was an ephemeral, fleeting moment. An audience of one. Or perhaps two.

Thirty seconds later, I passed a man waking up in a storm drain. He had long grey hair, a scraggly beard and had spent the night in a pile of old carpets.

'Are you OK, man?' I shouted.

'I'm cool dude, thank you.'

Of course, it is every person's prerogative to spend their money how they wish. But to think that just a few miles away, hundreds of people were mindlessly feeding $20 bills into blinking fruit machines left a slightly sour taste in the mouth.

I was, however, feeling chipper to be in Oklahoma. Bordering Texas to the south and Arkansas to the east, in my mind, and on the map, it marked the start of the final third of my adventure. My arrival also signalled an amusing – if not occasionally frustrating – new trend. I had reached a part of the United States where I could barely understand the English being spoken by the locals. While simultaneously, they could seldom understand me. When I reached Ponca City and ducked into a Starbucks for breakfast, this lingual impasse reached peak perplexity.

'Small Americano, please.'

The server looked puzzled.

'Black coffee? And a butter croissant, please.'

'One chocolate croissant!' she shouted, in a kind of Texan-Glaswegian drawl.

'No, a butter croissant.'

'Hey, Tamsin,' she yelled back to her manager, 'which are the better croissants?'

'Plain croissant. Normal croissant. Standard croissant. Please.'

'Can I take a name for the coffee?'

'Simon.'

'Samson.'

'Simon.'

'Simpson.'

'Simon.'

'Swanson.'

Five minutes later, I received a cheese sandwich and a cappuccino labelled 'Stephen'.

Southeast of Ponca City, I joined the shoulder of Highway 60, a 2,655-mile two-lane highway that runs diagonally between Arizona and the Atlantic Ocean. Route 60 might not have achieved the acclaim and fanfare of – arguably – the world's most famous road trip, Route 66. However, roughly halfway along its path, it passes through Oklahoma and, more specifically, Osage County: home of the Osage Indian Nation.

With a five-foot-wide shoulder to ride on, and a 30cm-wide rumble strip for 'safety', I cycled east into the Nation's green and blustery land. Across the horizon, 84 wind turbines chopped at the breeze. Controversially, they were erected on this sacred tallgrass prairie in 2014, but in December 2023, a federal judge ordered their removal. At the crux of the longest-running legal battle concerning wind energy in American history was a dispute over who owned the land the turbines sat on. The Osage Nation argued that the project violated their sovereignty and rights to its oil, natural gas and rocks.

The Osage Nation bought 1.5 million acres of Oklahoma from the federal government when they were driven out of their ancestral lands in Kansas in 1872. Less than two decades later, however, oil was discovered under their new home. By the 1920s, the Osage had become the richest people, per capita, on earth, worth around $400 million a year by modern standards. This black gold rush attracted chancers and buccaneers from around the country, assisted, in part, by a discriminatory US government policy that required Osage landowners to have a court-appointed 'guardian'. Intermarriage between white and Native American people was extremely rare in the United States. But not – suspiciously – in northern Oklahoma.

The years that followed became known as the 'Reign of Terror' – a spate of more than 60 unsolved murders. Deaths which, in many cases, resulted in Osage land rights going to white widowers. It took until 1925 for Congress to pass a law prohibiting non-Osage people from inheriting lands owned by those with Osage ancestry. Fast forward to 2011 and the US government awarded the Osage Nation a $380 million settlement.

If this potted history is ringing bells, it's because Oklahoma's biggest county provided the setting for *Killers of the Flower Moon: Oil, money and the birth of the FBI*. The *Sunday Times* bestselling book by David Grann was turned into a 2024 Oscar-nominated film by Martin Scorsese.

Osage lands remain both sacred and profitable. Unlike many Native American tribes and reservations that struggle economically, the Osage remains one of the richest, with a net value of more than $500 million. But the oil is drying up. Production in Osage County has declined significantly since the 1970s. Companies like Exxon and Chevron have left, and now just a slew of smaller operators is left to squeeze every last drop from the parched earth. Blessed with 2,300 square miles of mostly open prairies, solar and wind energy may well be a natural next step for the area. If monetised on the tribe's terms.

I wove beneath the swirling wind turbines, passing dozens of oil-sucking pumpjacks – some abandoned, some active. The heat and headwind combined to create the force of a giant hairdryer. It was so hot that a herd of black cows had sunk to the bottom of a roadside pond, just their eyes and ears poked out above the mirror-like surface. They resembled water buffalo bathing in a sultry Indian lake.

With the wind in my face, it was impossible to determine just how burned I was getting. But by the time I reached the outskirts of Pawhuska, headquarters of the Osage Nation, my skin looked and felt like beef jerky. And it must have smelled like it, too. Because having not seen a dog all day, I was now the source of great canine intrigue. At first there was a little Maltese, yapping from behind an ornamental garden pumpjack. Then came a pair of German shepherds, barking at the full length of their chains. A final scare came from a mangy looking farm dog, leaping maniacally around the back of a battered pickup.

Pawhuska's redbrick downtown was a welcome relief, but it throbbed with heat. Every last patch of shade was commandeered by panting tourists, most of whom had travelled from far and wide to visit a bijoux department store and a handful of equally gentrified businesses. The town boasted an olive oil tasting bar, Oklahoma's second oldest performing arts centre – the Constantine Theatre – and an ice-cream parlour that served up sundaes covered in whipped cream and glacé cherries.

It was far too hot for sightseeing, so naturally I took refuge in the nearest pub. Beside me sat 41-year-old Ryan Schutz. Born to a Texan father and an Osage mother, he had grown up between two cultures.

'I didn't understand what it meant [to be Osage] until I was older because I thought I wasn't Osage enough,' said Ryan. 'But that's not how it works. You're either Osage or you're not. Whether your 97 per cent white and 3 per cent Osage, you're still in the tribe. All we have left are 22,000 people in a tribe that has been broken off and splintered from day one.'

With shoulder-length black-grey hair and a big bushy beard, Ryan had recently retired from the United States Coast Guard, completing 100,000 miles at sea.

'Eleven years, 28 days,' he said, proudly. 'Lifesaving, not life taking.'

Now living in Pawhuska, he was eager to learn the Osage language and pass tribal values down to his young son. He also insisted on buying my drinks.

'Come here, get fed and in the morning, we'll send you on your way with more food. That's the Osage way. If someone comes to you for help, you say yes.'

As Ryan was a veteran of the United States Armed Forces, I was curious to find out how his Native American roots had shaped his sense of American patriotism.

'I feel like America is in an era of accountability. Everybody should be equal but we're not. You can't be Black and go for a run. You're white – you get to cycle on the road. But if your skin was darker, you would have been harassed all the way from Seattle.'

Ryan believed that films like *Killers of the Flower Moon* are part of a long-overdue desire to redress racism in America: 'For centuries, we've been murdering people that weren't white, but now we have people onboard having these conversations. That's new. Sure, in the 1960s, we had the Civil Rights Movement, and people thought that we had achieved equality. But we didn't and we're still fighting for it. Only white people think we achieved it in the 1960s.'

For less than $100, I bagged the best hotel room – not just in town, but of my entire trip. The top of an art deco-style, five-storey triangular building. Cool and quiet. I slept soundly, then took off early the next morning, desperate to avoid the heat.

By 6.30am, it was already a sticky 20 degrees centigrade. With my lights flashing, I cycled into an epic, turmeric-coloured dawn. Behind me, the harvest moon shimmered like a polished pound coin.

Before hitting the open road, I stopped at the gas station and stocked up with six bottles of Powerade and four litres of water.

Wrapped in a plastic bag filled with ice, a morning's liquids weighed a hefty 10kg.

'Hey, dude, where you headed?' asked a man in high-vis.

'Miami.'

'Miami, Oklahoma? Dude, that's like a hundred miles!'

'No Miami ... Miami. As in: Florida.'

Rendered speechless, he shook his head, jumped into a van, then wound down the window.

'Be careful out there, man. This is a fucking wild country!'

I was used to brushing this sort of statement off as hyperbole. But the deeper I progressed into eastern Oklahoma, the more I got the heebie-jeebies. Most homes along the highway were ringed by tall wire fences. Some brandished 'BEWARE OF THE DOG' signposts. But it was the houses with torn curtains and overturned trashcans that scared me the most. Nearly always surrounded by dozens of random objects of varying shapes and sizes, unleashed beasts lurked in their shadows. Owning a ferocious guard dog seemed to be as much of an American birthright as owning a V8 pickup. One moment, I'd be cycling along in my own little world. The next, all hell would break loose and I'd need to cycle at breakneck speed to avoid the jaws of a razor-toothed pit bull.

But despite the looming fear of having my femurs gnawed like butchers' bones, the landscapes were changing again. The Oklahoma in my mind's eye was an arid dustbowl, as depicted so vividly in John Steinbeck's *The Grapes of Wrath*. North of Oklahoma's second-largest city, Tulsa, though, the land was lush and unexpectedly fertile. The earth rolled gently in 40-foot waves, about an 8.5 on the Douglas Sea Scale.

For the first few hours, autumn caught up with me. Golden leaves swirled across the road. Mile-wide microclimates sucked in clouds of cool white mist. Occasionally, I'd pass a patch of fresh mushrooms, their stalks glistening with dew. All had eye-catching shapes that only Mother Nature could sculpt. Some looked like 99 Flake ice creams. Others resembled delicate yellow flowers. The edible ones had fantastical names: shaggy mane, wood ears, milky caps and sulphur shelves. But they were all best kept at a bike's length. A hungry idiot could mix up an oyster with a mock oyster.

It was a mixed morning. I was cycling quiet, treelined roads, yet stuck in an unshakeable state of mutt-induced anxiety, with a canister of bear spray fixed permanently in my sweaty palm. Nevertheless, by the time I reached Skiatook at noon, the heat had risen to such an extent that the mad dogs had given up and only an Englishman remained.

In the convenience store, I spotted a brilliantly passive-aggressive sign sellotaped to the counter. It read: 'DUE TO HIGH TEMPERATURES WE WILL NOT BE ACCEPTING MONEY OUT OF YOUR BRA!!!'

'Is this for real?' I asked.

'You have no idea,' replied the clerk, with a roll of her tired eyes.

From Skiatook, I joined the Osage Prairie Trail, a 16-mile bike path shaded by trees. When you could find them, these thoroughfares were a godsend. But cycling infrastructure was few and far between, and, away from main roads patrolled by police cars, these clandestine corners attracted America's most desperate and marginalised people. I found a man smoking crack, or maybe meth, in the meagre shadows of a derelict gas works. Gaunt and fitful, he wore an embarrassed expression, but continued to suck at the glassy smoke through a broken pen and a shattered smile. A few miles further on, I passed a woman, probably about 40, pushing a shopping trolley piled high with plastic bags and dirty clothes. Clearly in a state of psychological distress, she yelled 'Fuck!' at the top of her voice, as tears ran over her cheeks. Then, two shirtless teenagers ran out from a tent in the sticky undergrowth and shrieked in my direction. 'Hey, man! Come here, we want to talk to you!' But I kept on going.

All these people were Black. African American. And living in poverty.

Until now, probably around 95 per cent of the people I'd met, or seen at a distance, had been white or Hispanic. My only significant encounter with a Black person had been right at the start of my journey in Seattle. The man I bought dinner, who believed he was the son of the Christian minister and political activist Martin Luther King Jr. This lack of diverse voices – from a racial sense, at least – had been playing on my mind. Had I somehow ignored a major racial group? Perhaps as a subconscious response to my own inherent white privilege? Or had they just not existed where I was?

The premise of this book was to meet people at random. Let the world come to me. And while I had seen people of colour on my journey, they were greatly outnumbered by white Americans. Sure, I could have marched up to a random Black person at a gas station and said: 'Hey! You're Black. Tell me about life in America.' But this might have risked creating a contrived and artificial narrative. I hadn't done this to anyone else.

In the space of a few days, though, while I was still not technically in 'the South', the racial makeup of the region had visibly changed. According to the Pew Research Center, an estimated 47.9 million people self-identify as Black in the United States, making up 14.4 per cent of the country's total population. In the South, however, 56 per cent of people were Black, compared to just 10 per cent in the West.

Historically, this makes sense. Millions of enslaved Black Africans were transported across the Atlantic Ocean and forced to work on plantations, most of which existed in the southern states. When slavery was abolished in 1865, many of these people stayed in their new 'homes'.

Fast forward 160 years, and a striking disparity still exists within American society. According to the National Alliance to End Homelessness, 37 per cent of all homeless Americans are African American – despite forming less than 15 per cent of the American population. 'From slavery to segregation,' its website reads, 'African Americans have been systemically denied rights and socioeconomic opportunities.'

The National Registry of Exonerations found that Black people are roughly 7.5 times more likely to be wrongfully convicted of murder in the US than white people. Meanwhile, research conducted by the Centers for Disease Control and Prevention revealed that Black women are three times more likely to die while giving birth, in comparison to white women.

According to the United States Census Bureau, Black median

household income trails other races significantly: $40,258 in contrast to $68,145 (white) and $81,331 (Asian).

Out West, it had been easy to overlook these hard truths. I hadn't seen them in the flesh. But now, as I entered Tulsa, the scene of the 1921 Tulsa Race Massacre – these issues came rushing to the fore.

I made it to the city's Greenwood District, also known as Black Wall Street. In 1921, it was one of the wealthiest African American communities in the United States. Over several decades, it had grown into a thriving and self-sustaining business district, where a single dollar was believed to circulate 'between 36 and 100 times'.

On 31 May, however, the *Tulsa Tribune* newspaper reported that a Black man named Dick Rowland had attempted to rape a white woman, Sarah Page. This sparked two days of unprecedented racial violence, which would become known as the Tulsa Race Massacre. Instead of waiting for the findings of a police investigation, hundreds of armed white men looted and burned Greenwood – 35 city blocks were set on fire, 300 people died, 800 were injured and 9,000 left homeless. The white men argued that they were defending female virtue. For Black residents, however, the destruction of their successful neighbourhood was born out of jealousy and racism.

Dozens of businesses were razed to the ground. And as I rode around Greenwood, I found plaques dedicated to feed stores, barbershops and cigar shops – many of which were destroyed and never reopened. Significantly, the predominantly Black neighbourhood also lost its newspaper, the *Tulsa Star*, a staunchly democratic African American publication. In its place, the *Oklahoma Eagle* was born. For more than a century, it has served as an advocate for the African American community and its nationwide struggle for human rights, civic equality and judicial reform.

'We write about a section of American society that normally isn't written about,' said the *Eagle*'s 84-year-old publisher, Jim Goodwin. Who at just an hour's notice welcomed me into his office at the newspaper's headquarters.

'Black folks are people, just like any other, and we want to read about ourselves. The ups and downs of our community. In the white press – because of racism – we aren't important. This neighbourhood was destroyed but it had the resilience to come back.'

A few hundred feet from the newspaper, at the top of East Archer Street, was the spaghetti-like confluence of Interstates 244 and 444. Jim and the *Eagle* were campaigning to have the road removed. Until now, I had seen how the absence of interstate highways could negatively affect the fortunes of small American towns. Here, though, the proximity of the road was inhibiting the development of a predominantly Black neighbourhood. By rerouting its course by just a mile, Jim believed a further 40 acres of land could be freed up for business and residential use.

'Is that highway a symbol of racism?' I asked Jim.

'Yes. No question about it. And it didn't just happen to Oklahoma. It happened all over the country. In Oakland, New York, Chicago. The railroad tracks used to separate us from white folks, so this [the highway] is just that in modern day. Ironically, this road is called the Martin Luther King Expressway, and it is a symbol of division rather than unity.'

Jim's wood-panelled office was the archetypal setting of an old-school newspaper editor. Transcriptions piled high. Old editions stacked behind a grand mahogany desk. A Lord's Prayer dangled proudly from the wall beside a photo of Jim and President Joe Biden. Below that, another, with the boxer and activist Muhammad Ali.

'There seems to be some feeling that the Black man is replacing the white man,' said Jim. 'But as Black Americans, we want "life, liberty and the pursuit of happiness" – we believe that all men are created equal. As a newspaper, we strive to write about all people – no matter their colour – who are similarly situated or challenged. But the call for treating people as people is an ongoing job that's plagued this country.'

Jim wished me well on the remainder of my journey and I headed back out into an afternoon heavy with heat; the air so dense you could practically ladle it with a spoon. The expressway roared with acrid traffic. In the shade beneath its steel girders, a Black man slept deeply on a mattress.

That night, Tulsa's brewpubs buzzed with chatter. A candlelit concert played out on nearby Guthrie Green, named after Woodrow 'Woody' Guthrie, the American folk legend and son of Oklahoma. As promised, the food was getting better: half a fried chicken with fries and coleslaw. Not the healthiest choice but cooked to perfection and served on a metal tray lined with greaseproof paper. I was, however, struck with a big thwack of homesickness. On the table next to me a couple sat cooing over a weeks-old baby. Alone, and contemplating the next chapter in my life, I found it hard not to stare. Bleary-eyed but radiant, they looked about as exhausted as I felt.

Rather than propping up a nearby bar, I spent the evening flicking through more confusing, yet utterly addictive, American television. There was *Miss USA*, a pageant that expertly coalesced sequins and vapidity into such a hypnotic format I found it painful to watch but impossible to look away. A bit like staring directly at a solar eclipse.

I turned over to the Trinity Broadcasting Network (TBN). If ever there was a doubt about the mixing of Christian and Republican values, then look no further. I caught the end of *Huckabee*. The former governor of Arkansas Mike Huckabee has his own – hugely successful – show, which blends to-the-camera, mostly Democrat-bashing monologues with interviews with country singers and conservative politicians. For the British reader: think GB News, just with brighter smiles and the production values of Hollywood.

16

HITCHHIKERS MAY BE ESCAPING INMATES

I left Tulsa at 6.30am – it always made sense to escape big cities at the crack of dawn – and followed a bike path heading southeast along the northern banks of the Arkansas River. For me it was morning, but for many others it was still night. There must have been 200 people sleeping homeless nearby. Some behind trash cans, some in the curvaceous branches of oak trees.

By 7am, there was a strange collision of worlds: the drunks and drug users that had been up for days, staggering about with bottles in their hands, and the fitness freaks sporting shiny trainers and smartwatches, running 5K before breaking their intermittent fasts.

At one point, I took a wrong turn and ended up under a bridge. I looked behind me and a muscular man with a baseball bat in one hand and a can of beer in the other stood less than ten feet away. I had been in situations like this before. Assuming him to be a threat could create a situation out of nothing but to do nothing might risk being robbed or injured.

'Good morning,' I said.

'Good morning,' he said back.

That was it. He dropped a shoulder and let me continue on my way.

After about 20 miles of cycling past sporadic properties, some with dogs, some without, a curiosity caught my eye: a good old-fashioned garage sale. A century's worth of novelty plates, Christmas decorations, old umbrellas and plastic ducks was laid out on trestle tables. A time capsule of tat.

I got chatting to the owner, a remarkably sprightly 91-year-old lady named Natalie. She had graduated from the local high school in 1950, then started a family in post-war America, an economic boom time for the nation. Her husband built the very house where we stood, buying the land for just $8 an acre. The couple had enjoyed a simple and self-sufficient life, earning money 'from crop to crop' and selling off fields as needed. Natalie believed that modern America was a 'throwaway world' and that the secret to her longevity lay in a clean and organic diet.

'Never smoked, never drank, and ate food with no additives. We'd can vegetables in summer and kill a hog for pork in fall. We would can the sausage, too. Preserve stuff, so we could live. We didn't have a car but we thought we were rich!'

God had looked after her, too. Her father and brother had been Christian ministers.

'We grew up in church and lived by the good book. But so many people today don't know what that is. We've lost a generation. People don't live by the Ten Commandments anymore.'

'As an American Christian,' I asked, 'do you agree than all American citizens should be able to practise whatever religion they like?'

'Yes. Yes. I don't think it's right but yes. I don't condemn them.'

And what of the future? For Natalie, the country was better off under a 'God-fearing and conservative' government. Even the modern Republican Party was 'far too liberal' for her tastes. And as for Trump? 'A good businessman, but his personality and language: not good.'

We chuckled over the similarities between her garage and that of my parents, who had decluttered theirs but re-cluttered mine. I liked the look of Natalie's 1960s aluminium blancmange mould – it would have made a fantastic reflective sunhat – but I continued my journey empty-handed.

The eastern frontier of Oklahoma reminded me of England in a heatwave. Big grassy meadows were studded with grand oak trees – the sort you'd find in the grounds of sprawling National Trust properties, just without the sixteenth-century mansions.

Just outside Haskell I passed a big green sign pointing towards a correctional centre. Below it, a yellow notice warned:

'HITCHHIKERS MAY BE ESCAPING INMATES'. Then, a few miles after that, I cycled over the squidgy remains of a large snake. A copperhead? Possibly a cottonmouth. Maybe even a rattlesnake. My biggest worry, however, was still dogs. I made the alarming discovery that I'd lost my bear spray at the precise moment I needed it the most. On the far side of a flimsy farm fence, two German shepherds sprinted behind me, loping in unison like African cheetahs. They followed for half a mile, but eventually gave up the chase. Unarmed and feeling extremely vulnerable, I stopped at the next roadside coppice and fashioned a baseball-bat-sized club out of a fallen branch.

I am a dog lover. These beautiful, warm-hearted animals have made my life richer since I was a boy. But my trip through the Midwest was leaving me with PTSD. Almost every property had at least one dog. Some had half a dozen and hardly any were chained. Were these dogs for protection, I wondered. Was the threat fact or fiction? Because to me, this was a safe and rural region. Once again, I found it hard to understand why anyone would need to live behind a six-foot fence with CCTV cameras, 'NO TRESSPASSING' signs and a pack of prowling beasts. America was becoming more populous with every mile I inched eastward. Ironically, however, I felt more alone.

Later that afternoon, I met a man on the side of a rural gravel track dragging a pickaxe. Dressed in denim dungarees and a straw hat, chewing tobacco, he put the wind up me even further. Besides all the semi-domesticated guard dogs, eastern Oklahoma was apparently infamous for its semi-wild dogs, released by farmers and deer hunters who were known to 'starve and beat' the animals to 'make them extra vicious'.

'They get the mange. Some um got the rabies,' he told me. One dog had attacked his young nephew, so he 'put a bullet between its eyes'.

Even more alarming was the story of a cyclist that had been chased up a nearby tree.

'It took chunks out his legs. Took me six shots [to kill it] with a pistol. He [the cyclist] had to go to the hospital to get fixed up. We had to cut the dog's head off to be tested for rabies and it sure did.'

Unless treated quickly, there is no cure for rabies and is fatal in 99 per cent of cases.

He was worried about my route towards Muskogee. Highway 62 had an unreliable shoulder. Yet the winding quiet road I was currently on could throw up plenty of surprises, too.

'I know there's a lady a few miles down. She's got about 30 dogs. They'll probably just chase ya. But I'd be more worried about the people. In about four miles, you be careful. I got six druggies up there.'

Sure enough, I hit the 30 dogs. But I tried a slightly new, seemingly counterintuitive, tactic. Rather than build up speed as I approached them, I slowed down. So, rather than inciting their predatory canine instinct – like greyhounds chasing a hare – the sight of a slow-moving human on two wheels left them more baffled than boisterous.

I wish the same could be said for the 'druggies'' dogs. Because rather than letting me saunter past, they went berserk. Two Staffie-like mongrels, one with a missing back leg, caught me off guard and in the wrong gear. I had no choice but to jump off the bike and use it as a shield.

'Help! Help! Help!' I screamed. As the dogs took turns at testing my defences, I kicked out at their bared teeth.

After about 90 terrifying seconds, a skeletal man walked slowly from a shadowed house. He had sunken eyes, jaundiced skin and blotchy sores across his emaciated face. A filthy toddler cried in his withered arms.

'They won't hurt ya,' he whispered unconvincingly. But he managed to hold on to them just long enough to give me a head start.

By the time I reached Muskogee – a decent-sized town of almost 40,000 people – I was a nervous wreck again and desperate for a beer. Thankfully, I found a brewery and some friendly folk, but after that, I retreated to a motel and contemplated my next move. For the first time in 3,000 miles, I felt on edge and unsafe.

Oklahoma is America's tenth poorest state. While Muskogee, according to the online finance website 24/7 Wall St, is its poorest city, with a poverty rate of almost 25 per cent. All I can say is that my motel was decrepit, the worst of the whole trip. And as I entered, five stern-faced men in white vests drove slowly past, then parked a few doors down. For the remainder of the evening, visitors came and went.

I had to rely upon another gas station for dinner: instant noodles, a microwave burrito and a can of sweet green peas, to keep me regular. It was an otherwise uneventful evening spent in a filthy room flicking through a newspaper I'd picked up in the lobby: *Jailbirds*, a monthly publication filled with the mugshots of recently arrested criminals.

One of the salacious headlines read: 'COLLATERAL DAMAGE. A MUSKOGEE MAN WHO COLLATERALLY KILLED A TODDLER DURING A GANG HIT JOB WILL NOT SEE THE OUTSIDE OF A FEDERAL PRISON AGAIN UNTIL HIS 56TH BIRTHDAY. FIND OUT MORE ON PAGE 17.'

I double locked the bedroom door and pushed my bike, panniers and bedside cabinets against it.

The next day became a head-down push to Arkansas. Seventy miles of hot grey road, fringed by long green grass and just a few occasional trees. I stopped for breakfast in Warner and made a beeline for the frigid refuge of a fast-food restaurant. Once again, there was no other choice. Burgers and fries for breakfast, lunch and dinner.

As I entered, a shattered window caught my eye.

'Some dude shot it,' said an old man passing in the opposite direction.

'Why?'

'Who knows, but I hope you've got a gun.'

This was becoming a running theme. When I stopped to chat with a man in nearby Vian doing garden chores in overalls and thick latex gloves, he looked at the stick strapped to my front pannier and laughed.

'If I were you, I'd swap that twig for a pistol.'

Aged 60, James Watson recognised my accent and immediately asked what part of 'Queen's country' I was from. To my surprise, he had worked in Hull and Newcastle – as well as Russia, Bolivia,

Saudi Arabia, Pakistan and Mauritius – selling cyclotrons: machines that use electromagnetic fields to diagnose cancer.

'A lot of people bash America, but I've seen how great we have it here,' said James, as he threw logs into the back of a quadbike trailer. 'There are some ugly Americans and they don't know how the real world works, including a lot of politicians.'

In America, he told me, there was a sense of entitlement – especially among generations Y and X. Young people had been given too much by their parents, distorting their appreciation of wealth, value and success.

'It's not their fault. It's just how they've been raised. Their parents want them to have a better life, so they give them everything. And this generation coming up thinks they should be living in 5,000-square-foot homes with swimming pools, and they don't want to work for it.'

In 2023, the average American credit card debt was $5,733 – more than any other country on earth, totalling $1.13 trillion. This had left 56 million Americans in credit card debt for more than a year. To live within one's means seemed almost … un-American.

'America is a nation of consumers,' said James. 'We get everything shipped in. It's all about "me culture" – how much money can I make, how much stuff can I acquire. It's very sad.'

I enjoyed ten minutes in the shade of James's whitewashed home, and as a parting gift he upgraded my anti-dog stick to something more substantial – a freshly cut branch, now resembling a cricket bat.

For the rest of the afternoon, I cycled on the side of a semi-rural road, passing through occasional little towns along the way. Each one had a welcome sign proudly listing its minor celebs and accolades. Like Roland: 'WELCOME TO ROLAND, HOME OF CASSIE JO RUTHERFORD. MISS RODEO OKLAHOMA 1996. HOME OF NORRIS (MR COOL) WILLIAMS. WORLD CHAMPION PROFESSIONAL KICKBOXER AND MARTIAL ARTS HALL OF FAME INDUCTEE. HOME OF RYAN NOLAN. WORLD DUCK CALLING CHAMPION 2008.

I crossed the border – marked by the Arkansas River – and entered Fort Smith, gateway to my eighth state: Arkansas –

pronounced Ar-kan-saw. Drenched in sweat, I ducked straight into the nearest bar and downed a pint of zingy IPA.

'You're a journalist?' yelled one of two men wearing shorts and bucket hats swaying at the bar. They were about to leave and downing martinis 'for the road'. Curious but volatile, they were smashed. They were probably the drunkest people I had ever encountered who were still capable of sitting on bar stools without falling off.

'You don't have to talk to me.'

'I don't give a fuck!' slurred one.

'Hey, I'll give you a quote,' said the other. 'Arkansas is like 30 years behind everywhere else. Hillbillies and inbreds!'

Speaking at top volume, with zero inhibitions, they were looking to antagonise their fellow patrons. They were also keen to remind everyone that they were 'from California, not Arkansas'.

I managed to 'chat' with them for about 20 minutes, but with their gobbledygook making little sense, I retreated to a table for dinner. When I left half an hour later, I watched them get up from their stools, stumble to a car and drive off.

My very first encounter in Arkansas had provided food for thought. Because their use of the words 'hillbillies and inbreds' felt loaded. Something like ignorant Britons describing Irish or Romani Travellers as 'pikeys'.

The Collins Dictionary defines 'hillbilly' as 'usually derogatory. An unsophisticated person, especially from the mountainous areas in the southeastern US.'

American cinema has dined out on this cliché for decades. Notably in the 1972 film *Deliverance*, directed by John Boorman, starring Jon Voight and Burt Reynolds. The film depicts banjo-playing 'inbreds' and raping mountain men. Even if you haven't seen it you're probably still familiar with the infamous quote: 'What's the matter, boy? I bet you can squeal. I bet you can squeal like a pig. Let's squeal. Squeal now. Squeal.'

It would have been easy for me to enter Arkansas and regurgitate more of these lazy stereotypes. But these buffoons had provided a wakeup call. And as I began my journey into an often-misunderstood region, I yearned for more of the random and authentic. In whatever weird and wonderful shape that might be.

I found a motel and got some rest, then rolled out early the next morning. Fort Smith was surprisingly well-to-do. Perhaps I'd already jumped to my own lazy conclusions. I cycled down wide, treelined boulevards, past mansion-like homes surrounded by white picket fences. A sheriff's shiny car sat next to a lush green lawn, its hubcaps glistening like polished trophies. On the bonnet, read the words 'honor and integrity' – next to chunky black bars used to protect the chassis in a car chase.

Beyond the suburbs, though, the city was not just a nightmare to traverse on a bicycle, it was – in fact – impossible to leave. For more than two hours I tried to escape. Every road southeast snarled with traffic. No bike paths. Not an inch of shoulder.

'I just need to get out!' I said to a man stood outside his house. Who couldn't offer any hope, or a ride, but did give me some unsolicited advice.

'Are you headed to Memphis?' (The second-biggest city in Tennessee, 300 miles east.)

'Maybe.'

'Well, make sure you're not out after dark.'

'How come?'

'Not with skin that colour.'

I eventually convinced an electrician with a van to drop me a mile outside Fort Smith. He didn't say much but without him I might still be standing on the side of that busy road, wondering what to do next. Once again, I was left to rue America's lack of cycling infrastructure. And by 'infrastructure' I mean a cohesive network that links one bike lane to another. Not just a few trendy painted lines in a 'bike-friendly' downtown.

With a little bit of help I made it to Highway 22, a quiet and rolling road with a reasonable shoulder that could take me all the way to Russellville – 80 miles to the east. Each small town had plenty of abandoned buildings – commercial properties that were once hardware stores, diners or doughnut shops, and wooden houses, former family homes, strangled by trees and vines.

After the sprawling barrenness of the Great and agricultural Plains, Arkansas felt lush and subtropical. The grassy verges teemed with bugs and gnats and were specked with sweet-scented yellow wildflowers. Trees, trees and more trees: mostly pine and fir. And snakes, too. I thought nothing of the discarded black motorbike tyre about ten feet from my front wheel. Until it moved. A fat black serpent, most likely a rat snake or a southern black racer.

Thirty miles into my day, I stopped at a gas station in the tiny town of Caulksville – population 155 – and tucked into the only 'fresh' food available: a deep-fried meat pie. Or, perhaps more fittingly: a greasy gristle pasty.

'Where the heck are you going?' asked a man in a torn checked shirt, jeans and a baseball cap who pulled into the forecourt in a battered white pickup hauling heavy machinery.

Twenty-four-year-old cattle farmer Garrett was from Subiaco, about 13 miles further east. Friendly and forthright, he was another one of those no-nonsense Americans who dropped soundbites like cluster bombs.

'We are American. We love to talk. It's a great country. You can say what you want and do what you want.'

He must have been twice my size. Wide and stocky with a big bushy beard, he reminded me of *The Dandy*'s Desperate Dan, raised on a diet of T-bone steak and buttermilk. He believed that American farmers – the small ones, especially – were taxed too heavily.

'I wish the government would look after us more; we're just trying to feed the world. Soon I might not be able to make enough profit just to do my daily job. So I'll have to sell out to a bigger farm.'

This was a sentiment I'd heard across the country. Small-scale, multi-generational farmers feeling squeezed by taxes and dwindling profit margins to such an extent that their land was barely profitable anymore.

Garrett worked from dawn until dusk. He believed strongly that money taxed in each Arkansas county should be spent locally rather than being syphoned off at state level: 'It should stay here and take care of us, not somebody else. It's like me buying you new tyres when I need new tyres.'

He raised 200 head of cattle a year, 'all hormone- and steroid-free'.

'I hope it wasn't that meat pie I just ate. Because it was awful!'

'We are some obese fat asses in this country. Most people think that hamburger meat is just something made in the back of the grocery store.'

And what of the correlation between cattle, methane and climate change?

Garrett was sceptical: 'Put it this way: I want you to sit in your garage at night, with a cow, and see if you die. And then I want you to sit in the garage with this truck, with the door shut, and see if you die.'

According to the International Trade Administration, an agency of the United States Department of Commerce, Arkansas welcomed a meagre 31,000 overseas visitors in 2022, giving the state just a 0.1 per cent market share. Compare that to Florida (29.8) and California (18.6), and by entering 'The Natural State' I now found myself even more off the beaten track than in the so-called Wild West. Imagine my surprise, then, at the sight of Subiaco Abbey, a Benedictine monastery of epic proportions founded in 1878 in the Arkansas River Valley.

I had seldom seen a building quite so at odds with its surroundings – in the world, let alone in the United States, where so much of the country's architecture looks the same. Grand and arresting, its dense sandstone walls were arranged around a square medieval-style cloister and a 125-foot-high bell tower. Built in a Romanesque Revival style from curvaceous brick columns and terracotta-hued roofs, it was home to 34 monks.

I cycled into its grounds for a closer look, expecting to be asked to leave. But no – one of the monks, Brother Damien, drove past in a golf buggy and took me under his wing. Dressed in shorts, a T-shirt and gardening gloves, he had been tending to the roses.

While outside the grounds sweltered, the abbey's interiors provided cool, dark respite. Bright sun pierced through stained-glass windows and refracted a kaleidoscope of colour across a few dozen pews and a cold marble floor. From the top of the building, we took in the true scale of our green and muggy surroundings: the abbey boasted tennis courts, a swimming pool, flower gardens and a baseball field. The monks also bred black Angus cattle, brewed their own beer and produced hot sauce from habanero chillis imported from Belize.

Brother Damien had been raised a Catholic by his parents but, by his own admission, never really was one. After graduating from college in Wisconsin, he spent 20 years as a ski instructor in Colorado. But as time went on, he found himself drifting into dark worlds.

'I had got involved in womanising, drugs, drinking and pornography,' he told me. 'And I loved to fight. I was also into ghost hunting, all this occult stuff, trying to contact spirits from the other side. And during this one episode, I was in a basement on a ghost hunt and ended up contacting a daemon disguised as a little girl.'

Brother Damien made a habit of provoking these spirits. Spirits that would go on to attack him.

'I felt so emboldened, that I was such a good ghost hunter, and that this tough guy attitude was what you needed to be safe from daemons. I challenged all of them.'

One day, however, he woke up to a voice. A voice he believed was God.

'I heard this voice and it said "don't pick a fight" – I got a warning, but I disregarded it. The next time I antagonised a spirit, my world came crashing down. I went from a strong, confident guy one second, to a quivering puddle on the ground the next. This daemon destroyed me in the snap of a finger.'

This experience that 'destroyed' him at first later helped shape the rest of his life.

'I found out from God that He allowed this to happen to break me down so that He could build me back up as the person He meant for me to be. That unbelievable agony ultimately became the best moment of my life.'

In the months and years that followed, he returned to Catholicism and now lives as Brother Damien Cafaro, OSB, in Subiaco Abbey, where he has been for 13 years. He and his fellow monks live by the 1,500-year-old Benedictine Tradition, praying seven times a day.

'God had spoken to me many times but the message that left the biggest imprint was: "Enjoy life!" God was telling me that there are two paths people take in "enjoying" life: doing whatever you want whenever you want, which is how I lived for forty years. Or, enjoying life with God and for God. Take it from me, there is no comparison.'

Sometimes, it was easy to see this bike ride as a grind to the finish line, but I had to remind myself to enjoy every moment. To 'enjoy life'. One day soon it would be over and become but a memory. And, as days go, it had been a glorious one. Dog- and headwind-free. Plus, a handful of chance brief meetings that I couldn't have dreamed up if I'd tried.

But life has a habit of sobering up the cocky. I saw my first cyclist for about 3,000 miles, a svelte pensioner in tight Lycra who kindly offered to fill my water bottles with ice. He didn't say much, other than to offer a sombre warning.

'We've had two people killed in our cycling group in only the last year. Make sure you stay in the shoulder. And even that I can't guarantee will keep you safe.'

I arrived in Russellville in late afternoon, sunburned and desperate for bed and board. But first, there was the small but not insignificant task of crossing the Arkansas River – again. Just like my day had begun, the road into town was heaving with rush-hour traffic. The bridge had a slim shoulder but it was filled with the oversized right-side wheels of pickups and lorries. So, after just hearing about two local cyclists losing their lives, I confess to playing a trump card I'd been saving until now: received pronunciation.

'I'm terribly sorry,' I asked an old-ish couple filling up their SUV in a nearby gas station. 'But might I be able to trouble you for a lift across the bridge?'

The trick was to sound like an aristocrat from *Downton Abbey*, without accidently drifting into *Oliver Twist*.

'You see, I'm cycling across the USA, and I don't want to end up flat, like a pint of British ale.'

Before I could say *'Midsomer Murders'*, the seats were down and I'd been bundled into the back. It only took 90 seconds to get across but it might have saved my life. And with another decent day behind me, I took their recommendation for dinner: Fat Daddy's Bar-B-Que. Which turned out to be the best meal I've ever had in America.

Friendly and unpretentious, their food sang: beef brisket and pork ribs, glazed in barbecue sauce and smoked for eight hours at just 70 centigrade. People throw around the words 'melt in your mouth' all too often, but this meat was exceptional and served with sides of onion rings, coleslaw, cornbread and pickled jalapeños. OK, it wasn't 'healthy' per se, but it was clearly made with love and passion. Better still, the manager was so impressed with my undertaking that it was all free. She even gave me a Fat Daddy's T-shirt – which immediately became the only clean item of clothing in my possession.

I found a motel for the night and rolled out early the next morning. A stone's throw away, a gas station flickered in the muggy gloom of dawn. As I walked through the door to fill up with water for the day ahead, a Black man with no shoes and an amputated left arm stood beside a shopping cart stuffed with blankets.

'Excuse me, Sir,' he said. 'Can you spare a few dollars so that I can get some breakfast?'

Forty-three-year-old Charlie was originally from Pine Bluff, a city 120 miles southeast with a crime rate four times the national average. He had left in an effort to stay clean from drugs and had just spent the night sleeping in a tent.

'I'm just trying to make a new life,' he told me. 'I've been clean for ten days now.'

He lost his arm in 2009, as a result of being heavily addicted to sleeping pills. He had passed out and cut the circulation off, killing it from the elbow down.

'I laid on it for, like, three or four hours.'

I didn't want our conversation to be a trigger for his trauma, but at the same time he seemed chronically lonely and perhaps also clinically depressed. Even in the seconds before he spoke to me, I had watched half a dozen people walk past him as though he was a ghost. I handed over some snacks and all the dollars I had and encouraged him to stay clean for another ten days. And then ten after that. And that.

But the odds were stacked against him. According to America's National Institute on Drug Abuse, relapse rates while in recovery range between 40 and 60 per cent. What made things even more challenging for Charlie was that he was attempting to do it alone. In a new city. Without a home. Nevertheless, even in his darkest hour, he seemed to possess an uncompromisingly American attitude towards betterment. He was eager to work, go to school and become an artist.

'I want to teach people how to draw. I love art, it's my passion. I have a drawing; do you want to see it?'

And with that, he grabbed a sketchpad from his cart and flicked to a pencil drawing of a duck sitting on a rippling pond.

'Life begins now,' I said. 'You've been through some hard shit and only you can change that future for yourself.'

'Thank you, Sir. I needed to hear that.'

I spent the next hour in a state of quiet reflection, hugging the shoulder of US Highway 64, a single-lane road that ran parallel with Interstate 40. How could Charlie even begin to start again? How could he muster hope and grit in the face of such hardship? In a tent, with just one arm? Were my words encouraging or, ultimately, hollow? For a country that – at least traditionally – prided itself on the idea of an American dream, the theory of upward mobility and economic success, people like Charlie seemed trapped. Forgotten. Alone.

I thought back to Tacoma and the Tiny Housing Village built for homeless people. But significantly, I thought of Dianne's words: 'The true success of any society is surely how it looks after those most in need.' From what I'd seen on my journey, though, that 'success' is few and far between. And for all the pickups on lease and debt-filled credit cards, there were humans with nothing. The greatest country on earth? At times, I struggled to see it.

At some point in midmorning, I had my scariest dog encounter yet. Two Great Danes and an American pit bull must have picked up my scent long before I heard them coming. I might as well have been dragging a bag of bones, shouting, 'Here, doggy, doggy!' because they were on me like a shot, saliva dripping from their baying mouths. Still without a fresh canister of bear spray, all I could do was cycle at full tilt and hope to outrun them. After about 20 seconds, I looked down at my cycle computer: 28mph. Unsustainable for anything more than about 30 seconds, but thankfully they gave in.

If one of those dogs had planted its jaws into my ankle, then I would have slammed to the floor and been mauled by all three of them. What made that prospect even more terrifying was that these dogs had been entirely left to their own devices. Their owners were either at work, baking cookies or nodding out on heroin. There was no one to call them off if they sank their teeth into my jugular or femoral artery.

I was a jangling bag of nerves. Haunted by the sound of vrooming cars and howling dogs, every semi-rural route ahead of me looked bleak. It was a miracle I hadn't been attacked, but with my mental and physical energy starting to wane, it was only a matter of time before I lost concentration or took a wrong turn.

At the end of my tether, I marched into a nearby police station and demanded to know my legal rights should I end up bludgeoning a dog to death in self-defence. My secondary fear was accidently killing one but then enraging an unhinged and gun-toting owner.

'If a dog comes at me, what rights do I have to defend myself?'

It was a question that left the receptionist stumped, but after conferring for ten minutes with a few officers in the back room, she returned. If I was on a public road, then I could defend myself 'by any means necessary' in the same way I could against a human.

'How am I meant to do that?' I asked.

In silence, she made a gun shape with her right hand and pulled the trigger.

For the rest of the day, I contemplated the bonkers possibility of purchasing a firearm. Even if I could legally buy one as an overseas tourist, where on earth would I keep it? Could I travel with it between states with different laws? And what would I do with it at the end? Perhaps even more pertinent: did I have it in me to aim a gun at a dog and kill it?

By the time I made it to Little Rock, Arkansas' biggest city, I had talked myself out of it. However, I had settled on a novel new weapon for my growing armoury: Coca-Cola in a glass bottle. The previous day, one had fallen from my pannier and exploded loudly on the asphalt. From now on, I would carry one at arm's length, like a hand grenade.

17

A SHOULDER TO
RIDE ON

A much-needed rest day coincided perfectly with a whole day of rain. A deluge so intense that it served to wash away the last of the summer's mugginess and welcome in fall. For most of the morning, I pottered around my motel room, catching up on chores: editing for YouTube, cleaning out manky water bottles, charging gadgets and doing laundry. And by 'laundry', I mean swirling dirty clothes around a scalding hot bath and then leaving them to dry on the shower rail.

Thank goodness for Tori Rogers, tourism manager for Little Rock, because without her enthusiasm for my madcap project, I would have never have had the motivation to venture out in the rain. It was only her second day in the job but she gave me a full tour of the city. We visited the Clinton Presidential Center, which included replicas of the White House cabinet room and Oval Office. William (Bill) Jefferson Clinton served as governor of Arkansas from 1979 to 1981 and then again between 1983 and 1992, before becoming America's forty-second president in 1993.

Since 1968, the state has voted Republican in ten of thirteen elections, voting twice for Democrat Clinton in 1992 and 1996, and once for Jimmy Carter in 1976. Otherwise, Arkansas is a solidly red state. In 2020, Donald Trump defeated Joe Biden by almost 28 points.

Tori also took me to see the Arkansas State Capitol building. Designed in neo-classical style and built from Arkansas granite, it is a replica of the US Capitol in Washington D.C., albeit three quarters of the size. And then to see Little Rock Central High

School. In 1954, the United States Supreme Court ruled that racially segregated schools were illegal, marking the beginning of the end of segregation in the USA. Until then, so-called Jim Crow Laws in the South had forbidden African Americans from attending the same schools as white children.

In 1957, Little Rock Central High School opened to its first Black students, 'the Little Rock Nine', to the anger of many in the white community. At first, they were denied entry by a belligerent mob and the state's National Guard, under the orders of Arkansas governor Orval Faubus. It took 16 days for a federal judge to remove the National Guard, but several more days for the Black students to begin 'normal' lessons – when President Dwight Eisenhower sent in the US Army.

On the inside, the students' learning was far from normal and they were harassed by many of the white students. Nevertheless, despite an atmosphere of immense animosity and danger, the following spring, Ernest Green became the first African American to graduate from the school. To this day, the Little Rock Nine remain iconic figures in the ongoing battle for American racial equality.

Little Rock was, by far, the biggest town on my route for the next few hundred miles, so I splashed out on a fresh canister of bear spray, snacks for the days ahead and a new back tyre. After 3,000 miles, it was time to replace the Schwalbe Marathon Plus, which had transformed from a barely bendable ring of reinforced rubber into a flimsy hoop not much thicker than a balloon.

Tori and I finished our day with a big ol' plate of barbecue – an American culinary powerhouse that I could now get fully behind – and a delicious pint of craft beer.

I had dried out and carefully repacked my panniers. My journey towards the Mississippi Delta felt like the start of the final quarter. But the weather gods had other ideas, and when I opened my curtains the next morning, torrential rain lashed against the windowpanes. The only saving grace was that the wind had shifted and gusted as a tailwind. If I could just get through the day in one piece, then cool, sunny weather was forecast for the foreseeable future. It therefore became another 'head down, crack on' sort of morning, and by the time I reached Lonoke – a town of about 4,000 – I was so wet that I might as well have just put on my bath-soaked clothes rather than bothering to dry them.

Thankfully, I was given a warm welcome, just when I needed it the most, by artist Terri Taylor, who owned a delightful little cafe-cum-gallery, The Cozy Nook. With high ceilings and walls covered in community-made art, the room pulsated with the scent of freshly baked breads, cookies and cakes. Customers came and went. By the time I'd finished my first cup of (proper) coffee, I had already exchanged pleasantries with a farmer, a nurse and a police officer.

'Lonoke is probably the most supportive community I've ever lived in,' said Terri, as she kneaded a fluffy ball of dough. 'Everybody is down to earth and real, and I love that.'

The church and Christianity provided a 'support network' to the farming community. Hope and prayers, she told me, were important to securing a good harvest. Terri described herself as: 'A-political. I don't play that game. I just make sure everything I do has a positive impact. Everybody has a right to see and experience art. To me, art was my segue into quality of life. Fun stuff helps build community. Public and green spaces are hugely important.'

Terri's food and art clearly brought people closer together. They created a sense of uniqueness and identity in a country that can, so often, look and feel the same. She'd had a dream and then worked her socks off to achieve it. Sure, it was a business, but The Cozy Nook was born out of a sense of altruism. A desire to enrich people's lives. A tasty and colourful protest against American monoculture. What advice might she give to other small towns, I wondered.

'You need to have optimism and creativity,' said Terri, brushing flour off her face with a forearm. 'People thought I was crazy putting an art gallery in a small town but now we've become a destination. Don't fixate on what was done before, or elsewhere. Small towns need to find their own stories and pivot to the needs of their community. And don't be afraid to risk it all to make something happen.'

I was too early for the chicken and dumplings simmering on the hob, but right on time for breakfast: biscuits with sausage gravy.

Through my unaccustomed British eyes, the meal resembled suet dumplings covered in a creamy white sauce and flecked with chunks of sausage meat. I confess to finding the textures somewhat bizarre for my palate, but as winter warmers go, it filled my empty tummy with more than just calories. Terri's optimism gave me the energy to hit the road again.

She waved me off into the grotty day and urged me to give farm vehicles the widest possible berth. It was the start of the rice harvest and some of the trucks used to transport the crop had been sat unmaintained for over a year.

'Stay away from their tyres, give them a good distance and stay conscious,' she said, before handing me a bag of warm cookies.

When the rain finally abated, a hot sun burned through and steamed the flat and puddled land, locking in humidity like a chef's cloche. Arkansas produces more rice than any other US state – 40 per cent of national yield – mostly long- and medium-grain varieties. The state is also the epicentre of American warm water aquaculture, rearing more bait fish than anywhere else, alongside pet goldfish and crustaceans. I cycled past pond after pond labelled 'striped bass' and 'Chinese carp'. Dozens of white egrets waded through the shallows, waiting for an easy meal. All this moisture and rice created the strange sense of pedalling beside the paddy fields of Southeast Asia.

Nevertheless, I was now well and truly in the heart of America's Bible Belt. It was becoming hard to speak to anyone without the conversation drifting into verse and scripture. Outside a gas station in Hazen, a small farming town surrounded by prairie, I got chatting to an elderly couple who had benevolently bought someone else their gas.

'That was incredibly kind,' I said.

'God's will,' said the man, who put an arm around me, then asked: 'What church do you belonged to?'

I hesitated for a few seconds. 'Personally, I don't believe in God. I'm an atheist.'

'Oh my!' yelped his wife, who raised a hand to her mouth in shock.

For the next five minutes, they reeled off half a dozen pastors I should watch on YouTube, interspersed with quotes from the Bible. They were lovely people. Kind-hearted and amiable. But while I could accept their decision to believe in a deity, they could not accept my decision to not.

'You live in, probably, the most Christian place on earth,' I said. 'Therefore, if your parents were Christian and everyone you know is Christian, how do you know there is any alternative?'

Unsure how to respond, they recited the Old Testament at me.

I was at risk of getting into a full-blown theological debate with two octogenarians, which probably wouldn't have been a good look. So, I smiled and wished them a lovely day.

'We'll pray for you,' said the woman. And I have no doubt that they did.

What was I meant to do in these situations, I wondered. Should I lie and pretend to be something I wasn't? Or be polite-ish and just tell the truth? This played on my mind for the rest of the afternoon as I rode through a flat, sodden and greenish land down to Clarendon and checked into the only motel.

'Give me those wet clothes,' said the 81-year-old owner. 'You'll catch cold.' And by the time I'd taken a shower, she'd already dried, folded and left them on a plastic chair outside my room.

Before dinner, I headed back to reception for a chat. I stood on the sidewalk but she spoke to me from behind a reinforced metal grate resembling prison bars. She believed that America had descended into a state of lawlessness. A country where people could commit crimes, without repercussions. And while she didn't disagree with gun ownership per se, she feared: 'Young kids with guns, they're killing people!'

'Is that why you've got these metal bars?' I asked.

'This was here when we came, but yeah. A couple times I've been real glad it was on there. Mad people!'

The summer of 2023, she told me, had probably been the hottest she'd ever known.

'Our water bill was over a hundred dollars this month. Because we had to water the plants. Not even the lawn! The heat this summer was relentless, every day. Over 90 degrees.'

'You're 81, you've seen some of the hottest summers on record, do you believe that humans are responsible for that?'

'No, not really. What they're [the government] trying to do is play God, but what they're really doing is spending too much money. All this "green" stuff they're talking about. We can't do anything about the weather. That's God's area, you know.'

The next morning was bright but crisp, and I made speedy progress towards the border with Mississippi. I had now spoken to dozens of people about climate change and no other issue had left me feeling quite so confused. As a tourist, I was very happy to keep America's idiosyncrasies at arm's length. Gun ownership, politics, pop culture, trans fats, whatever. In the grand scheme of things, none of my business. But until Americans – and its leaders – can agree that climate change is even a thing, then how can they take the next steps to do something about it? Likewise, if tens of millions of citizens in the most powerful country on earth believe that climate change is an act of God – and not down to human behaviour in any shape or form – then what chance do the rest of us have?

There is perhaps no better place from which to contemplate one's navel, or the futility of human survival on a warming planet, than the comfort of a bicycle. But before I could become too introspective, the world threw me yet another four-legged curveball.

About 500 feet ahead of me, there must have been 20 dogs angrily pacing around a large kennel. Hypervigilant, I pulled my headphones out of my ears and watched intently. The position of the dogs was doubly troublesome because any loose beast would be running at me, rather than chasing from behind. Moreover, they were on my side of the road.

So, at 250 feet, I stealthily crossed over, giving myself two lanes of asphalt between me and them. I thought invisible thoughts. But at 200 feet, BOOM. Every kennelled dog saw me and went berserk, like football hooligans in a scrap.

All bark and no bite. Apart from one.

Loose and wild-eyed, a big dog with a mangey grey coat had broken free from its shackles.

150 feet: Yep, it is definitely coming at me.

100 feet: This is not a drill.

50 feet: The dog is nearing the road.

40 feet: I reach down for my glass bottle of Coca-Cola.

30 feet. Give it a vigorous shake.

20 feet. Don't fuck this up.

Three decades of very mediocre cricket had been building up to this pre-emptive strike. And – if I say so myself – it couldn't have gone much better. Just as the beast was about to pounce, I threw the bottle between us, creating an almighty, fizzing explosion. The dog had never seen or heard anything like it. It was caught so off-guard that it instantly recoiled and ran straight back to the kennel from where it came. Better still, apart from a bruising of its canine ego, the animal was left totally unharmed. Not even a glass splinter in its paw.

I rolled into Marvell in late morning feeling as though I had brushed a giant monkey (dog) off my back. And before doing anything else, I stocked up on two more glass bottles of Coca-Cola and a bottle of extra-spicy hot sauce. For if the shit really hit the fan.

There was no diner to speak of. Just dollar stores and a couple of gas stations serving crispy grey matter formed into slightly different shapes. I was hungry but I didn't fancy riding the rest of the day fuelled on chicken and chips dripping in oil. So I settled on trail mix and a sports drink and enjoyed a rest on the dusty kerb.

After a couple of minutes, a man jumped out of a pickup and was immediately fascinated by my bike. Over the years, I've developed an intuition. There are the people who are trying to rob you and then there are others just interested in a chat. And this was very much the latter. African American, he wore red tracksuit bottoms, blue sneakers, a white vest and a black headscarf. When he spoke, half a dozen gold teeth glimmered in the late morning sun.

'You're going to Miami!' he screamed when I told him my story. 'You know what, bro, that is something I've always wanted to do.'

'You should do it, man.'

'Man, I'm a felon. I can't do shit like that.'

He had just served a five-year prison sentence for possession of drugs and was now on probation.

'There's a whole big system in this country, they just lock you up. I was locked up with guys who were doing 30 years for being caught with $300 of cocaine. What sort of a life is that? I'm just trying to stay clean now. But I don't have many options.'

I can't corroborate the details of the man's crime or sentence. To me, it sounded harsh. But don't forget that the United States has more people incarcerated than any other country on earth: 1.8 million people in jail, plus a further 2.9 million on probation and over 800,000 on parole.

Thoughtful and eloquent, the man had a unique but familiar story to tell. One that would resonate with millions of families around the country.

'Can you not run for mayor?' I asked, somewhat naively. 'Get your story out there.'

He shrugged his shoulders. 'I'm a felon. It's illegal.'

Under Arkansas state law, the man wasn't even allowed to vote until he had served his probation term.

'We live in a country where if you don't have a college degree people think you're an idiot. But I've met lots of people that went to college, and they don't know nothing about this country.'

In 2020, 92 per cent of single-race Black, non-Hispanic voters cast a vote for Democrat Joe Biden, while only 8 per cent backed Republican Donald Trump. This man, however, was disillusioned. Democrat or Republican, he felt burned by the system.

'Black people are programmed to vote Democrat,' he told me. 'But it ain't that simple anymore. It's like someone pissing down your back and telling you it's raining.'

It's impossible to know the specific details of the man's case. I only spoke to him for a few minutes. But when we looked each other in the eyes – from one human to another – we were both just men trying to make our way in life. However, while I was free to take off on this joyride across the country, he seemed trapped in a cycle that was hard to escape. Living in a rural town with few employers and with a conviction to his name, his options were limited.

I spent the rest of the day cycling towards the Mississippi River – the border with the state of Mississippi. With sweet potato farms on one side and cotton fields on the other, the road was so quiet that I indulged in a musical treat: the Mississippi Delta blues. We all know that travelling with a smartphone can negatively transport us to a digital otherworld when we should really be living in the present. But on this balmy fall afternoon, with fluffy clouds hanging in the hard blue sky, the sounds of Muddy Waters, Robert Johnson and Charlie Patton carried me along on a wave of good vibes.

Characterised by mostly solo singers with harmonicas and guitars, sliding glass bottles and knives along their fingerboards, Delta blues was born out of the field hollers and work chants of the Black south. Mississippi's roving musicians eventually migrated north, spawning the Chicago blues. In the early twentieth century, it was one of the first musical styles to be pressed on vinyl, or – more accurately – the 78-rpm records used by gramophones.

The genre went on to heavily influence rock and roll. The Muddy Waters track 'Rollin' Stone' sold 80,000 copies and would inspire the band name The Rolling Stones, Bob Dylan's song 'Like a Rolling Stone', and even *Rolling Stone* magazine.

I reached the river in mid-afternoon. America's second-longest waterway flows north to south for 2,350 miles from Minnesota to the Gulf of Mexico. Besides being a major recreational hub for boaters, canoeists, hunters and anglers, approximately 175 million tons of freight travels up and down its murky – or indeed, muddy – waters each year. Without the Mississippi River, the geopolitical superpower we know today may never have come to be. In his 2015 *Sunday Times* bestseller *Prisoners of Geography*, Tim Marshall writes that the river, in addition to its Pacific and Atlantic coasts, gave the United States an unassailable advantage over its rivals, as the river's multitude of tributaries 'were the natural conduit for ever-increasing trade, leading to a great port and all using waterborne craft which was, and is, many times cheaper than road travel'.

In a normal year, the river serves as a superhighway for the region's farmers. Around 60 per cent of all American grain exports are moved by barge to the 'great port' New Orleans. But 2023 was no normal year. Satellite photos taken by NASA's Earth Observatory showed that excessive summer heat had left the mighty Mississippi looking mighty parched.

'It's all an added expense,' said a farmer – white, male, early forties – who picked me up next to Helena Bridge, a 1.5-mile-long cantilever bridge that carries Route 49 across the river, narrowing to one lane in either direction. I couldn't have crossed without him.

'When it's as low as it is now, we can't ship our grain out. So we're having to pay to store the crops. We'll either have to wait or drive it out, which will mean more money. This is the lowest it's ever been.' He wouldn't, however, call it 'climate change', just 'lack of rain'.

Perhaps his biggest problem, though, was finding staff. 'Everybody around here just wants to sit on the front porch and draw a cheque,' he said. Instead, he employed temporary agricultural workers from Romania. 'If it weren't for them, I wouldn't be farming half the land I do. I love them, they turn up every morning eager to work.'

As I'd heard elsewhere, he felt hamstrung by taxes and policies made in Washington: 'I wouldn't pin it on either party, they're both corrupt. In the past, Democrats have been more favourable to farming, but that can change at any time.'

Deep in conversation, we continued talking in a layby. Totally unfiltered, the man was a firecracker. 'The politically correct crap is what winds me up. That just drives me insane. Everybody is waving this racist flag and that's a bunch of bullshit. Right now, we're in Mississippi and the Blacks are more racist than the whites are. That's a freaking fact.'

'OK, do you have examples?'

'They're robbing and beating up old people, and all that white people are doing is trying to make a living for themselves. In all these little Delta towns the Blacks have taken over and ran it into the dirt.'

The man had a lot to say on race. Beyond what I feel comfortable transcribing onto this page. When not farming, he stayed mostly at home and hardly ever visited nearby towns. They were, in his words: 'Filled with Black people causing corruption and destruction.'

'You got a gun?' he asked, when I jumped out.

'No.'

'Well, I'd make sure you stay in tonight. It's the high school homecoming and last year six people got shot!'

And with that, I was back on the side of the lonely highway, cycling towards Clarksdale: 'Birthplace of the Blues'.

I agreed to keep a low profile after dark, but before that enjoyed a stroll around town, perusing music-themed murals, fusty record stores and blues clubs ablaze with neon. For the first time on my trip, it felt as though I had landed in a tourist hub, epitomised by the legendary blues club Ground Zero, owned by Morgan Freeman. The actor was born in Memphis, Tennessee, but grew up in Mississippi. A truly toe-tapping, head-bouncing joint, it was rammed with locals and visitors alike.

I watched a band, ate pulled pork, then peach cobbler, and made light work of three pints. But skulked off to bed at 9pm. Every hotel room in Clarksdale was filled, thanks to a nearby music festival. So, for the first time in almost two decades, I found myself sharing a six-man hostel dormitory.

Unsurprisingly, I slept terribly. Half-cut festivalgoers came and went throughout the night. And when the room was finally at full capacity, each bunk occupant snored raucously, like rusty pistons in a combustion engine.

By 6am, I was drinking coffee downstairs, preparing to hit the road. But not before I could meet Anthony, a 62-year-old maths and science teacher. He'd gone to school in Clarksdale but now lived in Chicago, and had returned for the weekend to attend a school reunion.

At first, we bonded over English football; he was up early to watch his beloved Liverpool FC. Then, he told me about growing up in 1960s Clarksdale – a racially segregated town. As a seven-year-old Black boy, he was ignored by his white teachers – 'For three days, I'll never forget it, just totally ignored.'

A few years later, his parents took him out of the public school and moved him to a Black-only agricultural school.

'You were given the choice. Be put in the city high school, and know that there is segregation and discrimination, or there's a separate high school for you guys, if you want to go.'

How much had America changed in the subsequent half a century, I wondered. I told him about the farmer I had met less than 24 hours before. A white landowner who believed that racism barely existed.

'Institutional, racist slavery was real. What can I tell you? Racism is real. No matter where you are. This country was created by bad elements who came here with bad intentions, and they have exponentially increased over decades and centuries. Racism, crime, murder, mayhem. How does it get better? It's inbred, from the time the babies come out the womb. In some people's eyes, I am still a slave.'

As a Black male educator, Anthony's ambitions went well beyond what he could teach from a textbook. Young African American men, he told me, needed positive role models. What advice, therefore, would he give to the man I'd met the day before who had recently been released from jail?

'If you're so inclined as to believe a label put upon you, then it's the only label you'll ever know. If he's living in small-town Arkansas, then the first thing he should do is change his surroundings. If you don't change the surroundings, and the characters, then you're going to encounter them again.'

As I saddled-up and pushed out into Clarksdale's chilly downtown, Anthony had a few final words for me; his tried and tested technique for dealing with my arch nemeses: 'If a dog comes at you, don't try to outrun it. Give it your weakest hand and then try to grab it with your strong arm. After that, you've got to worry about all that tetanus and rabies stuff. But hopefully it won't come to that.'

I joined a service road that intersected a handful of electricity substations. A flock of rubicund birds – red cardinals – clung to a spaghetti-like tangle of copper wires, millions of volts fizzing through their tiny feathered bodies. My original plan had been to go to Granada, a town about the same size as Clarksdale, roughly 70 miles to the southeast. But with the wind blowing directly from the north before shifting to a westerly the next day, it made more sense to zig south now, before zagging east tomorrow.

As the crow flew, I would have already made it from Seattle to Miami by now: 2,730 miles. But once again, it felt like I was sailing. Tacking in one direction, then jibing in the other, using (or avoiding) the wind as efficiently as possible.

Most of my route, however, was semi-rural, passing through one small town (village) after another. These were the worst places for dogs because their owners were more inclined to let them run free. At one point in midmorning, I had three chasing me down a bumpy path beside a railroad track. Thank goodness they gave up after about half a mile because I soon ran into a thicket of impenetrable undergrowth. A dead end.

Unable to turn back, I had no choice but to trudge across recently ploughed, and rained-on, fields – the soil gloopy like melted chocolate. For an hour, I pushed my bike, its tyres growing heavier, terrified that I'd run into another pack of dogs and have no way to escape. I eventually staggered into a cotton field and found a surprisingly chipper farmer tending to his crop. From a layby, Crump Britt watched a pair of combine-like vehicles suck up clouds of white fluff.

'They cost about a million dollars apiece,' he told me. 'And they can only do one thing: pick cotton. At least a combine is versatile and can cut corn, beans, oats, anything. But that thing right there is the most expensive piece of John Deere equipment they make.'

After four and a half months' growth, Crump was eager to harvest the crop before any more rain.

'If it rains you've got to let it dry so it can fluff back out, because you cannot pick cotton wet. If it's too heavy, it gets mouldy and can even catch fire.'

The raw lint would now be separated from its seeds and formed into 480-pound (220-kilogram) bales – enough to make 250 bedsheets or 1,200 T-shirts. Cotton's value, however, fluctuated throughout the year.

'It can go from 70 cents to a dollar per pound,' said Crump. 'But I still don't think there's any reason for us to buy cotton. I think we should keep it in America. You know: "Made in America". But we're up against India and China. They buy a lot of cotton from us, but then we also buy cotton from them.'

What about staff, I asked. Had he struggled to find workers, like the grain farmer I'd met the previous day?

'South Africans,' he told me, waving to the two men driving up and down the field. 'I employ six of them and they're all 19 or 20. But 98 per cent of our labour is local. The problem, though, is that they're all over 60. The younger generation round here does not want to work.'

As a parting gift, Crump picked a sprig of cotton and tucked it into the buckle of my pannier. We shook hands and I hit the road. All was quiet ahead. But about 20 minutes later he caught up with me in his pickup – beeping his horn and flashing his lights, as two glossy-coated Labradors wobbled their heads and tongues out the window.

'Hey, Simon!' he shouted. 'Do you like cheeseburgers?'

'Hey, Crump! I wondered who the hell that was! Yeah, I love cheeseburgers!'

Another 20 minutes later, I found him stood in a layby holding a cheeseburger, fries and a bottle of Powerade.

'You stay safe out here, Simon. And if you can help it, don't go anywhere near Greenwood!'

As I watched him disappear into the distance, I stuffed my cheeks with grease. On a trip punctuated by decent burgers, this one – completely unexpected – was the best. There was, however, no way of avoiding Greenwood, purportedly one of the most dangerous cities in Mississippi. And to get to the other side I had to negotiate a dodgy neighbourhood.

First, I passed three men stood beside a beaten-up saloon. Shirts off, they all had black pistols peeking out from the waistbands of their baggy jeans. Then, when I stopped at a convenience store to fill up with water, the Yemeni shopkeeper told me not to linger.

'Have you heard of Yemen?' He asked.

'Socotra?' I said, proudly. To be fair, this was my area of expertise.

'Oh nice! *Inshallah*, my friend.'

'*Inshallah!*'

I stood outside for a few minutes and attracted the attention of a passing police car containing two ... thickset officers.

'What are you training for?' they asked.

'I'm training for this. Cycling across America.'

'You for real? What do you eat?'

'Whatever I can get my hands on at gas stations, basically.'

They laughed and looked at each other, as though their principal diet was also 'road food'.

'Sorry, but did I do something wrong?'

'No, we were just worried about you. Keep on going, yeah.'

I pushed on south, on a road entirely bereft of a paved shoulder. Instead of sealed asphalt, Mississippi had grass or gravel instead, kryptonite to the long-distance cyclist. Juddering along, I was lucky if I could maintain 10mph.

I made it to Winona just before dusk, feeling as though my spine had been compressed by a few inches.

Food. Bath. Bed. Sleep. Dust myself down and go again.

18

SPEED WEED

Without my bicycle and its chubby red panniers, I would have never met half the people. Unlike anything else on America's roads, I was a curio that drew people (and dogs) in, rather than repelled them away.

In the small town of Eupora I took a break in a fast-food restaurant and got talking to a lively, thin, bearded man in his late seventies. Dressed in a pink vest, torn jeans and a leather belt – supporting three 10-inch hunting knives – he was eager to sell me a weapon, drugs or his beaten-up bicycle. Curiously, everything for sale had an astronomical price attached.

'That ring,' he said, pointing at his right hand. 'That one is $17,000. And that one, maybe $7,000.'

'$17,000? For that ring?' It looked like something out of a McDonald's Happy Meal.

'You offer me a thousand. As you're from England, maybe I'll let it go.'

The man had English–Irish heritage, and was proud of it, too. His parents had met during the Second World War.

'I know people all over England. Hey, do you know Aunt Rita?'

'I can't say I do, no. Sorry.'

'Those British girls make my heart go tweedled dee.'

Apparently, he owned great swathes of local land worth millions. And the key to his spritely longevity? 'I make love two or three times a night.'

Sat at my table, with sharp blades on his waist, he made me feel uneasy. Nearby customers stuffed food into their mouths in double-quick time, happy for me to take the heat. When I occasionally glanced away from him, I caught the clerk giving us the side eyes.

Leaning in, his pupils dilated, he said: 'Hey do you want some weed?'

'I'm fine, thank you.'

'It's speed weed. You'll do 50 miles an hour!'

'I'm not so sure. If I smoked weed right now, I doubt I'd get very far.'

'Hawaiian Gold. Purple Kush. Green Guy. Black Gunge. I'll give you some, man.'

'I'm fine, thank you.'

I made it back out to my bike, followed by the man. Acclimatised to the restaurant's air conditioning, I felt the midday sun sear my shrunken skin.

'Hey, do you want to buy my bike?' He asked. 'This bike is worth $88,000.'

'That bike?'

'Yeah!'

'I don't think I can afford it but thanks for the offer.'

He leant in and whispered again: 'Hey, you want a girl? I can get you a girl.'

'I'm fine, thanks. I'm married.'

'They're nice, not meth heads, either.'

'I appreciate the offer, but I'm fine, thank you.'

'You got a gun? I wouldn't do what you're doing without a gun. You give me ten minutes and I can get you a gun.'

'I'm good.'

And with that, I dragged myself away, back to the grassy shoulder.

Ten seconds later, the man was shouting and running after me.

'Hey, Simon! I want you to have this.'

I was expecting him to pass me a bag of weed or maybe a weapon. He handed me a small bottle of water instead.

The roadside was lush and pretty. But cycling without a shoulder became an immense drag. My back, and backside, felt every bump and bobble. All I could do was persevere. One foot in front of another, over and over again. Headphones in, music on, progress was slow but sure.

But then, in the sleepy heat of early afternoon: POP. A

three-inch staple had punctured my back tyre: in one side, out the other. You couldn't get a cleaner piercing at a tattoo parlour.

I paced around the shoulder, searching for a solution. This was beyond a puncture, it was a full-blown laceration. On closer inspection, my new tyre – the one with just a few hundred miles to its name – was already as thin as the one it replaced.

'Please stop, somebody please stop,' I whispered to the oncoming traffic. But they didn't. Not even a flash of headlights. I might as well have been holding a chainsaw dripping in blood.

It took me almost an hour to bodge it back together. Mostly with the thick silver electrical tape I had carried across the nation. The tyre was beyond proper repair but at least I could limp on. And as for the enormous staple that had stopped me in my tracks? It was so impressive that I threw it in my pannier as a souvenir. In America, even the punctures were supersized.

For the next few hours, I hobbled towards the outskirts of Columbus. Food, beer and rest were almost at my fingertips, just across a concrete flyover. But as the sun started to set, the road narrowed. Without a shoulder, and with cars rushing into the city at 70mph, I would be riding in the danger zone – slowly.

OK, I thought, I'll ride back. Impossible.

With two deep ditches, an intersection between the lanes and no shoulder to return on, I was stuck, good and proper. Think of a fish swimming down a bottleneck, the space getting narrower, until it can no longer move forward or back. This was me.

I waved maniacally at passing cars. Nothing.

I dialled 911 into my phone, then stopped myself.

Was this really an emergency? Would I be reprimanded for wasting police time? Would that be a better fate than being stranded on the side of a highway all night? A police cell would save on accommodation, I thought. Every cloud.

Desperate for answers, I found faint hope on Google Maps: a tiny strand of manmade something or other running through a forest, about a mile to the south. So, rather than cycling forward or back, I diverted entirely off piste into a sticky, prickly, cobwebbed woodland, hauling my bike and panniers over fallen trees.

Don't step on a snake.

Don't break your leg.

Don't fall into a gulley.

By the time they find your body, you'll be a withered, sundried husk.

These are the silly things that went through my head as I waded through no man's land.

Finally, I emerged onto a sealed asphalt walkway, with twigs in my hair and blood streaming down my legs. Feeling like David Livingstone without a machete, I had tamed the impenetrable woodlands of eastern Mississippi. Hurrah! But then my sense of adventure was sobered suddenly when a woman in yoga pants and flipflops wandered past walking a Bichon Frisé.

Nevertheless, adventure is relative and I celebrated with a big bottle of beer dunked in an ice bucket on the sunny porch of a motel. Three doors down, a strung-out-looking couple were having some sort of altercation with six police officers.

On my schlep through the woods, I'd exchanged my big stick for something even bigger and better: a three-foot-long, three-inch-wide length of aluminium pole.

'I know it looks like a weapon,' I said to one of the policemen. 'But it's not for humans, just dogs.'

'Yep, that'll do it,' he responded nonchalantly, before dragging the man out in handcuffs.

Everything was shut apart from a Mexican corner shop, which was doing a roaring trade with mostly male Hispanic construction workers stocking up on black beans, tostadas and avocados. Exploring a labyrinth of pinatas and dried chillies, I feared dinner would consist of a packet of crisps and a chocolate bar. But then I noticed the men were paying for something extra and taking handwritten receipts to the back of the building. There, two old Mexican ladies worked feverishly, pressing fresh tacos and wrapping fat burritos. I had stumbled across the Holy Grail, so spent the next hour chatting Spanglish to exhausted Guatemalans as we ate taco soups, fried fish, enchiladas and guacamole as good as anything I'd ever eaten in Central America. I ate until my pores oozed cilantro, lime and habanero.

*

The next morning, I exchanged the busy highway for a meandering country road that snaked across the border into Alabama – my penultimate state – and into a hilly and densely forested landscape that caught me off guard.

Stupendous in its infinite greenness, these were woodlands to rival the Pacific Northwest. Millions of oaks and pines, warmed by the first sparks of dawn, yet simultaneously cooled by the opening salvo of fall. If I could have bottled up any morning of my trip, then this was it. I would glug it down on my deathbed.

Buttery light. No cars. No dogs. Rolling hills. A road so clean and smooth it might have been laid just the night before. Every few miles I stopped to breathe in the silence. I could practically hear every falling leaf landing on moss. Chipmunks scampered between lichen-covered trunks. High above the canopy, three soaring raptors looked down from the heavens. In the blue abyss beyond them, the outline of a bleary moon, its contours just visible, like a deflated football sunk to the bottom of a swimming pool.

At one point, a dozen white-tailed deer skipped nose to tail across the road ahead of me. Alabama has one of the highest deer populations in the country – 1.75 million, approximately 34 per square mile.

I was consumed by such a state of bliss that I cycled for an hour in the wrong direction, adding another 20 miles to an already 70-mile day. Back west, this would have left me fuming, but not here. This was a glorious micro ride within a mighty one. And anyway, without my mistake, I would have never ended up in Carrollton, chatting to the friendly employees at a diner in the town square, overlooking Pickens County courthouse. They were initially flummoxed by my accent, but soon I was the talk of the town. Within ten minutes, a reporter from the local paper arrived looking to interview 'Salmon Packer'.

But I spent most of my time chatting to 25-year-old employee Zach Johnson. When he wasn't serving customers, he served as a youth pastor in a nearby Baptist church.

'Mississippi and Alabama are always the butt of the joke,' he said. 'We're always depicted as dumb. Elsewhere in America, our accent sticks out. It's also definitely perceived that people from Alabama have a lot of racist tendencies.'

'Is there any truth in that?'

'I would say that if it [racism] was alive in any mass quantities in the US then it would be right here. Some people would have you believe that it's still like Jim Crow levels of hate and violence. I haven't personally witnessed that. But I'm also white.'

In his lifetime, Zach had seen Alabama become more culturally progressive, just at a much slower rate than in places like California and New York. His work as a youth pastor involved teaching teenagers how to incorporate God and the Bible into their – sometimes troubled – lives.

'Broken homes,' said Zach. 'Divorce rates are crazy. And drugs. Always getting younger and younger. Kids are getting their hands on all kinds of drugs. Mostly meth and pills. I try to be a positive voice in their lives.'

In nearby Aliceville, a small town ten miles to the south, two shootings had taken place less than a fortnight before, resulting in the death of a 30-year-old man.

'I hate to say it,' said Zach. 'But it happens everywhere. Is it [gun crime] really not a thing in England?'

'No.'

'It's a Wild West. I stick out like a sore thumb because I'm not a big gun person.'

Before I hit the road, Zach and his fellow employees welcomed me into the kitchen for a selfie. They were up there with the kindest and most hospitable people I'd met so far. I felt comfortable asking them difficult questions, while they seemed to revel in responding to them. So, what next for America?

'We are so divided,' said Zach. 'More than we have ever been before. Hate now drives us apart. Right off the bat, you have to choose a side, left or right. There's no room for middle ground. And you lose friends and family over that. The political debates have become a clown show, it's just yelling and no intellectual conversation. It's been driven into religion as well.'

I could sense what he was getting at. But could tell this was a subject that made him feel uncomfortable.

'A lot of people say you can't be Christian and Democrat, but I want to be on the record as a Christian. If you are mixing your political party with your belief, that is wrong. I love my church, I depend on those people, and they care for me and love me, but if they were to find out that maybe I voted a certain way, I would be concerned for how that might play out.'

Over the course of half an hour, I watched dozens of people come and go. Almost everyone entered with the phrase 'How ya'll doing?' then left with a 'See ya'll soon.' Words so infectiously jovial and unpretentious that I too departed with a 'thanks ya'll', much to the restaurant's amusement.

For the rest of the afternoon, I floated southeast on a wave of goodwill. I'd heard of 'good ol' Southern hospitality' but had brushed it off as tourist board tosh. Not only was it remarkable what an English accent could achieve, but overall, Americans nearly always gave as good as they got. If you wore your heart on your sleeve, then so did they.

Cycling under a hot afternoon sun, I tried to place my morning into a British context. But concluded, rather sadly, that if some random American cyclist talking like Colonel Sanders rocked up unannounced in my local pub and started asking questions about race, religion and politics, then it probably wouldn't take long for the words 'fuck' and 'off' to be uttered.

I reached Tuscaloosa – Alabama's fifth-largest city, with a population of over 100,000 – and checked into a hotel overlooking the Black Warrior River. Home to the University of Alabama and its 40,000 students, seldom had I found anywhere quite so alive. And today wasn't even game day. When the college football team were in action, the city's population doubled thanks to 'the Crimson Tide' – their vociferous, cherry-red-wearing fanbase.

The college is one of the most successful in American sports history and dozens of its athletes have progressed to the NFL. It would, however, be remiss of me not to mention one of their most famous, albeit fictitious, players: one Forrest Gump. The 1994 film about an Alabama man growing up in twentieth-century America was made on a budget of $55 million but grossed an enormous $678 million at the box office. It also scooped six

Academy Awards, including best picture and best actor for Tom Hanks.

'People from Alabama affectionally call themselves Gumps,' said Jimmy Hart, a friend of a friend, who kindly offered to take me out for dinner. As we drove through town, at least 50 per cent of people wore crimson. I must have spotted half a dozen stores selling merchandise. And as for the Crimson Tide's home: Bryant–Denny Stadium is the eighth biggest in the USA, with a capacity of 100,077 – that's 25,767 seats more than Manchester United's Old Trafford, 10,077 more than Wembley Stadium and 87,577 more than the three-sided scrapheap where my beloved Oxford United ply their trade.

When he wasn't working for the local tourist office, Jimmy was a barbecue devotee, and – knowing I probably only had an hour of decent chat in me before I started slurring my words – took me to a Tuscaloosa culinary institution: Dreamland Bar-B-Que. Until this evening, I had merely dabbled. But Jimmy insisted we order one of everything, roll up our sleeves and chow down until our cheeks ached.

'The term "barbecue" confuses people because they think of a grill,' said Jimmy. 'But for it to be authentic "barbecue" it needs to be smoked over wood or charcoal. The general rule is "low and slow" – it might be all day, or multiple days.'

Different states barbecue in different ways. The temperature, the glaze, the chosen animal. In Kansas, where Jimmy grew up, they 'pretty much barbecue anything with meat on it'. In North and South Carolina, however, the meat is almost exclusively pork. In Texas, meanwhile, it is nearly always beef.

Since opening its doors in 1958, Dreamland Bar-B-Que has welcomed US presidents and celebs to its spit-and-sawdust surroundings. Neon signs bounced electric light across old licence plates, Crimson Tide football flags and big rolls of tissue paper – for mopping up sauce-covered hands and lips. This was clearly more than 'just' food. Barbecue, for many, is a religion. It speaks to the core of Southern values.

'In the 1800s, the good cuts of meat went to the fancy people, but the rest of us were left with the brisket and the rump, so we had to figure out how to make it delicious. Growing up, you knew that some of the best food was in some of the sketchiest neighbourhoods, because they're pits that have been burning for a hundred years.'

I had been seeing these 'pits' throughout rural Arkansas, Mississippi and Alabama – black cylinders that served as ovens. Often, the sweet and smoky scent of slow-cooked red meats wafted from backyards to the road. Perhaps this helped explain why the dogs were so crazed. Barbecue, Jimmy told me, was an egalitarian American tradition: 'Big portions, paper plates, sauce on your clothes. You can get the cheapest cuts of meat from the market and still have excellent barbecue.'

We had a 'full slab' of pork ribs, glazed in a vinegary BBQ sauce and smoked over hickory woodchips. Then shared half a chicken, a smoked link sausage and half a dozen slices of white bread. There were sides, too, in little polystyrene cups: coleslaw, baked beans, potato salad and mac 'n' cheese. Which, despite being slathered in butter, mayonnaise and cream, was a bona fide 'vegetable' in Jimmy's eyes. And who was I to protest? Hearty, umami and unpretentious, this food warmed my soul. There was even enough left for breakfast.

As we got up to leave, I spotted a bumper sticker with the words: 'SWEET HOME ALABAMA' – homage to the 1974 Lynyrd Skynyrd song and a phrase recognised globally.

'What does that slogan *really* mean?' I asked Jimmy.

'For a person from Alabama to not greet you with kindness, openness and a giving spirit is just a complete betrayal to who they are. For "native Southerners" and "real Southerners" they would put that hospitality above all else [politics].' Jimmy paused for a second. 'What happens when you leave the room,' he laughed, 'might be a completely different story.'

I slept like a baby. Albeit a half-cut baby with meat sweats. In the morning, I waited for the local bike shop to open. Begrudgingly, I had to spend another $80 on a new back tyre. Because with approximately a Land's End to John o' Groats left to cycle (874 miles) I couldn't risk getting to Key West on my current one, which was held together with electrical tape. The delay allowed me to catch up with all the admin I neglected while riding and put me perfectly on course for a midmorning pitstop in Tuscaloosa's steamy outskirts.

An issue had been playing on my mind: drugs. Since touching down in Seattle, I had encountered dozens of people clearly struggling with addiction. And while my enduring memories of cycling across the USA will be of long roads, big conversations and even bigger portion sizes, I'll also remember it for coming face to face with America's substance abusers surviving on the fringes of the largest economy in the world. To get a better understanding, I decided to visit a treatment centre, and, after some advance emailing, counsellors Jennifer McDanal and Karen Gresham kindly agreed to meet me.

'There probably isn't any family in America that could say they haven't been affected by substance abuse,' said Karen, as we entered her bright, strip-lit office. She described the challenge facing them as 'astronomical'.

America's drug problem, they told me, diverted in two, slightly different, directions. On one hand, there were the mostly alcohol, cocaine and heroin users that have existed in the USA for half a century or more. President Richard Nixon inaugurated this particular 'War on Drugs' in 1971. But then came the 'opioid crisis' – a much newer, doctor-led over-prescription of pain medications like oxycodone, which had contributed to an enormous increase in opioid-related deaths. According to the Centres for Disease Control and Prevention, 645,000 Americans lost their lives between 1999 and 2021.

'If you said you were in pain, they [doctors] gave you something for it, a narcotic. It got a little out of hand and then we hear the words "opioid crisis", and the bottom line is that care providers had been prescribing narcotics carte blanche.'

Not only did Karen work directly with Tuscaloosa's drug users but she was also in recovery herself. She was prescribed Lortab (a mixture of hydrocodone and paracetamol) for an ankle injury when she was 19. This began a 15-year addiction.

'Not only does it kill your pain but it also increases the

neuroreceptors that give you pleasure. It makes you feel good. Wow! I can now run on this leg, but I feel good about it, too.'

Approximately 90 per cent of Karen and Jennifer's patients became addicted to opioids as teenagers while in recovery from sports injuries. Until the early 2010s, most of them could get their pills on repeat prescriptions. But then, America woke up. Pressure mounted on doctors and prescriptions declined dramatically. So, what happened to the millions of people left clucking for a drug that was now much harder to get?

'By that point, it was too late and too significant,' said Jennifer. 'Mothers, fathers, nurses, lawyers. I've even seen a doctor. That led to people addicted to these substances needing to find the narcotic somewhere else. Heroin was cheap and now we also have the fentanyl issue.'

Approximately 100 times stronger than morphine and 50 times more potent than heroin, fentanyl is a synthetic opioid that is made both pharmaceutically and illegally. Added to street drugs like heroin and cocaine, users can very easily overdose. The substance is linked to more than 150 deaths in the USA every day.

The challenge facing Karen and Jennifer was undeniably 'astronomical', but before I hit the road and continued my journey south, I wanted to know what gave them hope. What motivated them to keep going in the face of such personal, familial and cultural damage?

'Seeing someone hold down a job,' said Karen. 'Or seeing them buy a truck with money they've saved. Money they would have spent on drugs.'

'Or having a baby,' said Jennifer. 'For years, I had a patient that had tried to get pregnant but that didn't happen until she got clean, and that was amazing.'

It was an upbeat note on which to end a somewhat chastening conversation. But as I cycled south on a country road – just as quiet and as beautiful as the day before – my mind drifted, first to Seattle and then to the countless people I'd seen along the way.

Was the man who overdosed in the bus stop still I alive, I wondered.

Where was the guy with the shattered smile outside Tulsa?

Or the filthy toddler in those withered arms?

Was Charlie, the amputee, still clean?

Karen and Jennifer's patients were the lucky ones. But for each of them, there were thousands more unable to find, or afford, the healthcare required for their recovery.

I spent the rest of the day scratching off miles in blocks of ten before stopping for a few minutes to scoff a cereal bar or wander into the woods for a wee. Under the dappled shade of the forest canopy, I managed to avoid the intense heat of an Alabama afternoon. Moreover, with a brand-new tyre and the wind pumping cleanly from the north, I could average 16mph without breaking too much of a sweat.

The route was so quiet that I whiled away a few meditative hours with my headphones in, watching big golden leaves float slowly to the road and collect in the verge.

Naturally, I started with Lynyrd Skynyrd and 'Sweet Home Alabama', before drifting down a Spotify wormhole that called in at Neil Young, Bob Dylan and Sam Cooke. The algorithm progressed to Prince, followed by Bob Marley. Laid-back and easy-going, the Jamaican's smooth and soulful tones did, however, become the discordant soundtrack of an unexpected brush with snapping jaws. One moment, I was bobbing up and down listening to the bouncy intro of 'Three Little Birds', the next, I noticed a stocky German shepherd-type sprinting alongside me.

There was no time to remove my earphones, so bizarrely, everything played out while Bob was telling me not to worry ...

'Fuck off, you bastard dog! Get the fuck away from me!' I roared, reaching for my bear spray.

... And that everything was going to be alright ...

'No! No! Back! Back!' I yelled deeply, kicking out with the hardened heel of my cycling shoe.

Safety catch off. Can at arm's length. I steadied my finger, and ... The dog listened to its instinct and curled away, like a fighter jet at Mach 5.

Thankfully, the rest of the afternoon was spent dogless, but I killed the music just in case. And when I finally reached the outskirts of Selma, my nerves had been replaced by excitement. Because in the centre of town, stood beside the Edmund Pettus Bridge, I found my wife, Alana. Twice as wide as the last time I'd seen her.

'I feel like a bowling ball,' she said.

'You look radiant!'

'Piss off. I know you're lying. What's for dinner?'

19

FREE MEAT

Alana's return created a sense of my trip coming full circle. Or squiggly line. However we chose to look at it, this was the beginning of the end. For this adventure, at least. But the prelude to the next chapter of our lives.

At dinner that night she presented me with the first ultrasound scan of our child. I hadn't wanted to see the image via a grainy WhatsApp message and had held off so I could hold it in my fingers. A real thing. These moments only happen once and I wanted to experience it with my wife, rather than on the side of a road, alone.

'Long legs,' said Alana.

'Good for cycling?'

'Maybe ...'

'Perhaps we could all cycle around the world when they're 18?' I asked.

'You two can but I'll follow in a van. Make the sandwiches.'

'Deal,' I said, as we shook hands over plates of barbecued meat, and I ordered a celebratory pint.

I fell asleep with my head on Alana's tummy, listening out for swishes and wriggles. But most likely indigestion.

The next day, Alana rested in our apartment in downtown Selma. She was exhausted from the jetlag. And, in all honesty, wasn't particularly enamoured with schlepping back across the Atlantic just to check in with her itinerant husband. But, to quote my mother-in-law, Ruth: 'You knew what you were signing up for.' And the world always looked a little brighter when we were together.

With my family close and sleeping soundly, I explored Selma, a city synonymous with the Civil Rights Movement. In March

1965, it was at the centre of an African American campaign to increase voter registration led by Martin Luther King. Despite the Fifteenth Amendment, ratified in 1870, prohibiting states from denying male citizens the right to vote – based on their 'race, colour or previous condition of servitude' – in the South, in particular, discriminatory practices were used to prevent African Americans from voting. Black people attempting to vote were often told they didn't have the necessary level of literacy required, that they possessed incorrect documentation or had got the polling date wrong. Some election officials asked Black voters to recite the entire US Constitution by heart, which, unsurprisingly, most found impossible.

On Sunday 7 March, a peaceful protest of around 600 people marched onto the Edmund Pettus Bridge, named after Senator Edmund Pettus, a former leader of the Alabama Ku Klux Klan. In what would become known as Bloody Sunday, the protestors were attacked by state troopers with truncheons, whips and tear gas. More than 50 people were hospitalised. Images of the assault were broadcast around the United States. Notably, the American Broadcasting Company (ABC) broke from its transmission to show the events unfolding.

Over the next two days, demonstrations were held in a further 80 US cities. With outrage growing across the country, President Lyndon B. Johnson introduced voting rights legislation on 15 March, identifying Bloody Sunday as a turning point in American history. His address to a joint session of Congress was interrupted more than 40 times by applauding politicians. He said:

'What happened in Selma is part of a far larger movement which reaches into every section and state of America. It is the effort of American Negroes to secure for themselves the full blessings of American life. Their cause must be our cause too. Because it is not just Negroes, but really it is all of us, who must overcome the crippling legacy of bigotry and injustice. And we shall overcome.'

On 21 March, Martin Luther King led thousands of marchers out of Selma, across the Edmund Pettus Bridge and towards Montgomery, Alabama's state capital. They were chaperoned by more than 1,800 National Guardsmen, 2,000 soldiers and FBI agents who protected them on their five-day journey. On arrival, King addressed the crowd:

'I know you are asking today, "How long will it take? How long will prejudice blind the visions of men, darken their understanding, and drive bright-eyed wisdom from her sacred throne?" How long? Not long, because no lie can live forever. How long? Not long, because the arc of the moral universe is long, but it bends toward justice.'

A few blocks from the Edmund Pettus Bridge, I met Jo Anne Bland – a civil rights activist and former director of the National Voting Rights Museum – in a cafe that was once off limits to Black people. 'We weren't allowed in,' she said, pointing at a small hole in the wall. 'We had to order from the window.'

Born in 1952 in a racially segregated Alabama, Jo Anne remembered having to walk to school while the white kids took the bus. 'They would pass us walking in the rain and shout nasty things. We also didn't get new books. The white schools would use them for four years then give them to us.'

By the age of eight, she was attending civil rights meetings with her grandmother, who encouraged her to recognise the discrimination around her. 'She said to me, "Look in there, in that diner. Coloured children can't sit at the counter. When we get our freedom, you can do that too.'

A year later, Jo Anne attended her first freedom and voters' rights meeting, led by Martin Luther King. She was taught the principles of non-violent protest. Which, in Selma, didn't come easy.

'It's not a normal reflex for a child, you know. If you hit me, I'll hit you back. As I got older, though, I learned that fighting back would be useless because they had so many more weapons.'

By the time she was 11 years old, Bland had been arrested 13 times. On Bloody Sunday, she watched friends and family being beaten by police and state troopers.

'Before we could turn and run, I heard gunshots and screams coming from the front. It was too late; they came in from the front and back and they were just beating people; old, young, Black, white, it didn't matter. People everywhere, bleeding, not moving. It seemed to last an eternity. And even if you could outrun those on foot, you couldn't outrun the horses. People were being trampled; bones were being broken.'

Six decades on, and with a lifetime of activism in the interim, what legacy did that day leave, I asked.

'I don't understand how Selma isn't Mecca,' replied Jo Anne. 'After the history that happened here, we should be booming.'

But it wasn't. A beacon of Black equality is now one of the poorest cities in the United States, with a poverty rate of almost 40 per cent. As Selma became 'more Black', Jo Anne witnessed 'white flight' – a phrase defined by the Collins English Dictionary as 'the departure of white residents from areas where people of other ethnic groups are settling'.

Selma's population has been in steady decline, down a third from its peak in the 1960s, and by 13 per cent between 2010 and 2020. On my approach, I had cycled past several industrial parks and factories, seemingly doing well. Downtown Selma, however, was probably the most deserted city I'd seen – mostly boarded-up shopfronts. A ghost town.

A few doors down, I met Selma's mayor, James Perkins Jr, at City Hall. In 2000, he became the city's first African American mayor, serving a first term until 2008 and then again from 2020. Born in 1953 – a year after Jo Anne – he too grew up under Jim Crow Laws in a segregated city.

'If I was approaching a white woman,' said James, 'I would have to look to the ground and not look her in the eye. I can still remember the last [Ku Klux] Klan parades coming through my neighbourhood burning crosses. My grandmother would rush us into the house and hide us under the bed.'

By the age of 12, he was attending the same rallies and marches as Jo Anne. 'As teenagers, when they came through, we threw bricks at their cars. That was the last time a Klan rally came through Selma.'

In Tulsa, I had been told how the interstate highway system marginalised Black people by cutting through their neighbourhoods. Selma, however, was about as far away from one as you can get in Alabama. In Mayor Perkins' eyes, its absence was an even greater example of institutionalised racism: 'Eighty-five percent of economic development in this nation takes place within five miles of an interstate exchange. You eliminate the highway system from a region and you significantly reduce the possibility for economic development. It was systematically done. And it still hasn't been fixed.'

However, Mayor Perkins believed that modern Selma had an opportunity to become a world-renowned tourism destination. The city was '20 years ahead of the rest of the country' on the issue of race relations. He described it as 'a blue island' in a sea of red.

'Selma is prepared to become the Camp David, the Mecca of racial reconciliation in this world. This is where people can come and have a safe place to have that conversation. What we did inspired protest in places like South Africa and Tiananmen Square.'

As is so often the case, though, progress boiled down to money. To achieve his dream, huge investments would need to be made into the city's infrastructure, for tourists and locals alike. Hope, however, had blown in from an unlikely source. Downtown Selma was ravaged by a tornado on 12 January 2023, destroying 40 per cent of residential properties and killing seven people across Alabama. In tragedy, an opportunity developed. Because with the nation's TV news cameras pointing his way, Mayor Perkins managed to fast-forward his fundraising process.

'January 12 comes along and puts Selma's name back on the radar. I had been going to Washington to try to get in to see President Biden, but then he had to come to Selma to see me. And he publicly committed to help Selma.'

That commitment was $100 million – money now being syphoned into housing, economic development and infrastructure. Already, it was being used to replace lead pipes, resurface streets and fix roads. The long-term goal, however, was for Selma to become a logistics hub – using the money as an investment for future prosperity, rather than a one-time handout.

I spent an hour with Mayor Perkins; we could have nattered for many more. And as a parting gift, he awarded me the key to the city of Selma. An actual gold key in a felt box. We posed for photos and handshakes behind his mahogany desk. Dressed in a smart blue suit, starched white shirt and shined leather shoes, he was the picture of diplomacy. I, on the other hand, wore flipflops, my only pair of trousers and a sports shirt covered in stains. Nevertheless, it was a proud moment.

It rained so hard that night that our apartment trembled. So, rather than going out, Alana and I relished the simple joy of cooking our own food and watching trashy TV. It was spending protracted periods alone that made me appreciate just how exciting the mundane could be.

The next morning, I cycled across the Edmund Pettus Bridge and out into the damp wilds of rural Alabama – a swampy, forested realm, now at the unrelenting mercy of autumn. Normally, I hated this time of year. Browning leaves and shortened days sent a shiver down my spine. This year, however, felt different. Because in a period of seasonal decline, we were bringing new life into this world. Not only had Alana sent me off with three freshly made sandwiches, but I also had the photo of my son or daughter in my breast pocket, keeping me company.

The trees were ablaze with reds and golds. Squirrels bounced from branch to branch. Occasionally, a deer skipped in the soft mud beside me, before clip-clopping off down the hard road, its mucky hooves stamping the blacktop with halfmoons.

About 40 miles in, I almost jumped out of my skin when a turkey vulture, about the size of a small ostrich, jumped out from a branch at head height and clipped the top of my helmet. This was a rainforest, alive. Not turned over to intensive agriculture, like vast swathes behind me, but a lush, subtropical ecosystem throbbing with life. It was so resplendent, in fact, that I couldn't shift a song from my lips: 'Zip-a-Dee-Doo-Dah', from Walt Disney's *Song of the South*, released in 1946. I remembered being plonked in front of this VHS as a restless toddler, and now its jovial, bouncy melodies had sprung to my mind's ear, as butterflies, bees and birds fluttered around me.

I only saw a handful of mammals all day. Hardly any humans and only a couple of dopey dogs. So, I whizzed along the empty road and reached Luverne in time for an early dinner. The town's claim to fame: home of the world's largest peanut boil. Go figure.

Not only ravenous but also becoming something of a barbecue bore, I tore through a slab of ribs while extolling the virtues of 'low and slow' with the gusto of a half-cut Keith Floyd.

'You know that meal we had on our first date?' said Alana.

'Yeah,' I replied, slurping meat from the bone, my hands caked in sticky sauce, strands of napkin hanging from my mucky cheeks.

'Well, I think if it had been barbecue, then we would have never got married.'

While we waited for the antacids to kick in, we drove around town looking for action. Smoky pubs were now totally off limits but the local high school was lit up like a flame and surrounded by cars. It was hard to know what we were about to walk into. A parents' evening? A musical recital? An AA meeting? Instead, we found the girls' volleyball team taking on Straughn – '42 miles south', explained a grandmother dressed in a replica jersey. 'Who ya'll cheering for?'

'Whoever you are,' I replied.

She chuckled, then offered us a boiled peanut.

For $6 each we could watch a sport we barely understood in the company of friendly strangers, most of whom munched giant pickles wrapped in tinfoil. An American flag dangled above us next to a big sign: 'HOME OF THE TIGERS'. Between every play, the home side threw their hands into a pile and yelled: 'One, two, three, Tigers!'

All the whooping and fist pumping looked tiring enough, but the girls also managed to fling themselves around a shiny court, their sneakers screeching like chalk on a blackboard. After about 45 minutes, we were dizzy from the commotion and left with settled stomachs and a dozen of God's blessings.

The next morning, I set off early. Very early. Alana was still fast asleep, but I wanted to put in a proper shift and push south. Ideally, cycling at least 120 miles and across the border into Florida while a cold front blew in from the north.

The volleyball fans had told me how lucky I was to hit their very short fall, an autumn that only lasts a few weeks, before 'bark crack'

– a local term used to describe the first cold snap of winter, which causes subtropical tree trunks to split. For now, though, southern Alabama was caught in a brief temperature limbo. Outside, the mercury hovered at roughly 18 degrees centigrade, while inside all the gas stations and convenience stores, thermostats were still programmed to summer. Dashing inside to grab supplies required a hat and gloves just to ward off frostbite.

I rode through little villages filled with more white-painted clapboard homes. Some had caved-in roofs but others were manicured, with picket fences and delicate flower gardens. I exchanged pleasantries with men scooping leaves from gutters and an old lady on a swing chair in a see-through nightie.

I amused myself with a game of bingo. Because nearly every property – irrespective of social strata – displayed the holy trinity of American garden ornaments.

1   A ride-on lawnmower. Bingo! (One point. It may or may not have moved for decades. Two points for those with exposed rusted engines. And three points for each additional lawnmower thereafter.)

2   A flag. Bingo! (One point for the star-spangled banner. Two points for the crimson cross of Alabama. Three points for the University of Alabama. Four points for a flag instructing a politician of any party to 'fuck off'.)

3   A car big enough to transport a men's rugby team. Bingo! (100 points for anyone seen carrying a passenger.)

I barely stopped all morning, pushing south, mile after mile. After the rain, the cool, humid air reminded me of moist teabags. I was reaching the southern edge of Alabama's black belt, a region characterised by its dark fertile soil. The road curved, swept and dipped. I heard mooing cows long before I saw them. Then bleating goats. In the gloomy half-light of the swamp, their pained, humanlike voices echoed spookily, like sailors screaming in a storm.

I went two hours without seeing anyone, but then noticed a figure standing in the long grass on the verge.

'Are you OK?' I asked, as I neared a balding man in jeans, gum boots and a sleeveless checked shirt. Muscular and bronzed, he looked more Venice Beach than Deep South.

'Deer,' he whispered, his narrowed eyes scanning the trees.

Apparently, a woman had hit one on her commute to work.

'Free meat if we can find it.'

While he waited for his friend to arrive with dogs, the 60-year-old told me how much his home had changed. 'There used to be stores all through here,' he said, placing a long strand of grass between his teeth. 'You could get gas, soda and a moon pie. But the big malls killed all that.'

He could remember the very road we stood on being dirt. 'If it rained, you didn't travel. Or you'd get stuck in the mud.'

Over the past half a century, he had watched the surrounding farms get sold off. This had ruined the sense of community. 'You don't know your neighbour no more, cut and dry.'

He was, however, proud of Alabama and cherished his rural lifestyle.

'I don't like to go nowhere else. I just like to stay right here. Nobody is in a hurry.'

He had seen a decline in American living standards – particularly under the stewardship of Joe Biden and the Democrats.

'The border, the economy. Everything is doubling in price. It's just killing people. I don't like where we're going, it's just sad. Hope? It's a very dim light. They're spending our money on everyone but us.'

'You mean places like Ukraine?' I asked. According to the Congressional Research Service, the US committed more than $47 billion to the war effort between 2014 and 2023.

'I'd stop it immediately,' he replied. 'My goodness, man. There's got to be a stopping point.'

The arrival of a pickup and three erratic dogs was my cue to leave. Knowing my luck, they'd ignore the deer and turn on me instead. So, we shook hands and I made a break for it. As I cycled off down the greasy road, barks ricocheted against the trees.

20

SNOWBIRDS

Somewhere around Chattahoochee, Alana dropped a pin on WhatsApp and ordered me to call it a day. I'd hit a mean tally of 130 miles in a single sitting, although also slightly counterproductive, because once I'd showered, downed two cans of beer and eaten a burrito, I could barely stand, let alone talk.

After almost nine weeks and more than 3,500 miles in the saddle, I had entered my eleventh and final state. The town sits on the southern banks of Lake Seminole and the Chattahoochee River, the meandering border between Alabama, Georgia and Florida. It is, apparently, quite pretty, but I wouldn't know. Instead, I spent eight hours dead to the world while Alana tossed and turned, wired from two cups of sweetened iced tea. It would be fair to say we were on slightly different trips.

By crossing into northwest Florida, we had also gained an hour and were now just five hours behind GMT. I had cycled through a total of four time zones since leaving the West Coast. But this meant we were up at the crack of dawn itching to hit the road. Or, more accurately, I was. Bumbling around the room like the proverbial bull in a china shop, just as my wife was finally drifting off to sleep.

Adrenaline is a cruel mistress and strange things happen when you cycle day after day after day. Within the space of ten hours, I went from feeling chronically exhausted, as though I might fall asleep and never wake up, to clucking for movement. I had every intention of tapering off in a few days' time, but for now, the road was calling.

Instead of cycling along the highway, I set off down back roads that cut through sprawling forests, made up of mostly tall, straight, longleaf pines, but also curly branched southern live oaks, found mostly in grassy, savannah-like openings bathed in sunshine. There is no other tree that says 'the South' quite so profoundly. In Harper Lee's 1960 novel *To Kill a Mockingbird* – a story set in small-town Alabama about a Black man wrongly accused of rape – this iconic tree becomes a symbol of community strength and morality. Native to the United States, they can live a thousand years and have been credited for saving countless lives. When hurricanes rolled through, locals would strap themselves to these 'storm trees' and pray to their Almighty God. Moreover, they provided shade, shelter and a place to worship for enslaved African Americans toiling on plantations. In the late 1700s, the US Navy recognised the tree's immense strength and used its curved branches for the hulls of their ships. The world's oldest still-floating vessel, the USS *Constitution*, got its nickname 'Old Ironsides' thanks to the wood that made it. Enemy cannonballs bounced off its solid flanks.

But beyond all that, they are simply, and profoundly, beautiful. Like giant bonsai trees. With their desiccated curves draped in Spanish moss – a flowering plant that is, curiously, neither Spanish, nor moss – they emit a mystical quality. Something George R. R. Martin, of *Game of Thrones* fame, might dream up.

Perfect weather, perfect scenery – it was a quiet and thoughtful morning. But as I had come to understand, perfection is only ever short-lived. And as I rounded Tallahassee International Airport, American and United passenger jets roaring into land, I noticed a strange clicking sound, followed by the familiar and sobering squeal of a bicycle rim grating on tarmac.

Somehow, a three-inch nail had pierced my back tyre, leaving me no option but to retreat into the middle of busy roadworks for a fix. I had managed to cycle 3,000 miles across America on a single back tyre, but this one and the one before it had both lasted just a few hundred. It seemed like only yesterday that I'd forked out $80 in Tuscaloosa for a new one and I was loath to buy yet another. American-made tyres just don't cut the mustard. They cost twice as much as European brands but wear ten times as fast.

I flipped my bike onto a big concrete bollard and removed not one, but both wheels. I then patched the inside of the broken tyre with a few lengths of trusty duct tape, but instead of returning it to the back rim, put it on the front wheel instead. In its place, my German-made Schwalbe Marathon Plus front tyre, which was still raring to go.

After 45 minutes of tinkering, I was ready to hit the road. Or not. During my pitstop, a tiny, unique bolt, not much bigger than a fingernail, which held my derailleur to the frame had lost its thread. Without it, I would be condemned to cycling the rest of my journey in one agonising gear. The solution? A cable tie. And once I'd zipped the gadget tightly to the frame, you couldn't tell the difference.

So, there I was, nearing the end of an epic adventure across the USA, riding a bicycle that cost circa £5,000, held together by a length of tape and a strand of plastic probably costing less than five cents combined. If I'm honest, though, I enjoyed the irony. It spoke to my inner egalitarian adventurer. Because a £5,000 bicycle is still just a bicycle. And if you're reaching this point in the book and planning your own madcap journey, don't think you need heaps of cash. Just go with the best thing you can afford at the time. When I cycled across the USA in 2016, I did it on a budget of less than £1,000, on a £500 city bike with a borrowed tent and festival sleeping bag. Don't get sucked into thinking you need every mod con. To borrow Nike's famous tagline: Just Do It. The more you save, plan, pack, route and reroute will be time spent not doing it.

Case in point: in 2016 I spent several days cycling with two German students who were riding across the USA on their grandmothers' rusted bicycles dating from the 1950s, with big soft saddles, baskets, bells and pink frames. 'This is all we had, so we thought, let's just go!' they said, as we camped on the side of an Ohio road.

Since entering the world of self-anointed 'adventurers' and 'explorers' chasing commercial partnerships with bike, tech and clothing brands, I always keep those words with me. Adventure is about your state of mind and your desire to live life to its fullest. Not the value of your cagoule.

With a tailwind building by the hour, I joined the Tallahassee-St. Marks Historic Railroad State Trail, a delightfully asphalted former train track which once carried cotton from the Cotton Belt to ships destined for England's textile mills. Hands down the best cycle path I'd travelled on since the Olympic Discovery Trail in Washington, it provided 16 miles of shaded, car-free bliss. It spat me out at St Marks, an unpretentious little town on the banks of the Wakulla River, a stone's throw from the Gulf of Mexico.

Alana met me for lunch – an exceptional softshell crab baguette – at a riverside cafe surrounded by several decades-worth of oyster shells and signs warning: 'PLEASE DON'T FEED THE ALLIGATORS'. There was also guidance on what to do in the event of a hurricane. One notice read: 'HURRICANE EVACUATION PLAN: 1. GRAB A BEER. 2. RUN LIKE HELL'.

Most of the surrounding houses had been built on stilts between 20 and 30 feet high to mitigate the risks from storm surge. Officially, it was still hurricane season but the laid-back clientele seemed unfazed.

Surrounded by mangroves, fishing boats and palm trees, I was finally in the land of T-shirts and flipflops. Alongside 'California' there is perhaps no other place name that evokes a sense of the American good life like 'Florida'. In my mind's eye, the state was synonymous with bronzed sixpacks and big boobs. None of which I'd spotted yet. On the women, at least.

Nevertheless, something had been bugging me ever since I'd crossed the border, but I'd reserved judgement until now. Obviously, Florida looked totally unlike anything I'd seen. But it felt different, too. Notably, my bike and panniers no longer turned heads. Which is, of course, an entirely satisfactory Floridian prerogative. My bicycle and ego didn't need to be stroked daily to achieve a good night's sleep. All I'm saying is that the atmosphere was somewhat … anticlimactic. Despite my best intentions, the only people I spoke to that day were:

1   My wife.
2   A man in a grocery store selling weed ($35 for an eighth of an ounce).
3   The owner of a gas station who grunted at me from behind a smartphone.

Please don't @ me on social media. All I'm saying is that the handful of random people I ran into were noticeably standoffish. I might have just caught them on a bad day. Or year.

Later that afternoon, I built up the courage to ask a fellow 'cyclist'. A man, riding a gasoline-powered bicycle, in America's flattest state, dressed in full Lycra so tight it was impossible not to stare at the outline of his medium-sized penis.

'Are people from Florida known for being rude?' I asked, averting my eyes.

'Rude?'

'Yeah, like, a bit ... off.'

'I'd say the people you've met are probably Northerners,' he sneered. 'The Snowbirds. Not proper Floridians.'

About a million Americans and Canadians migrate to the Sunshine State every fall to see out the northern hemisphere's colder months, increasing the population by around 5 per cent. In 2019, this flock of mostly pension-aged out-of-towners boosted the economy by $95 billion and helped support 1.6 million jobs. Nevertheless, the tone of this 'native Floridian' implied that he had little time for them, or me. He then 'cycled' off in a cloud of black smoke.

Unlike the flyover states, Florida welcomed 8.3 million international tourists in 2023. Even in its northern reaches, still 200 miles from the amusement parks of Orlando, my English accent was no longer a curiosity. In fact, around 400,000 British expats live permanently or temporarily in the state. That very evening, when I switched on the TV in the small town of Perry, the first commercial I heard was for a car dealership owned by a Scouser.

I laid awake that night feeling stuck in a strange dichotomy. For two months, I had craved Florida, its sunshine and sea breeze. But now I had arrived, I longed for Middle America, its friendly folk and open plains. Was I being needy, I wondered. Desperate for attention? Or was I was starting to close down a little bit, too? Transitioning, subconsciously, from the extrovert required to ride this ride to the introvert who would soon need to sit alone in a room and write this book.

*

The next morning, I resolved to find a second wind. 'What will be, will be,' I whispered to myself, as I set off into a muggy, bright dawn.

On the ride out of Perry I passed the aftermath of Hurricane Idalia, the category-3 twister that had torn through northern Florida seven weeks before, uprooting thousands of trees and homes. The clean-up would last months and cost billions of dollars.

In Cross City, a temporary federal emergency management agency/state disaster recovery centre had taken over a redbrick store. I watched residents come and go. They held insurance documents in their hands and hopes of assistance in the hearts. Some houses had been destroyed beyond repair. Local motels offered discounted rates, some as cheap as $25 a night.

The verge was piled high with debris: hundreds of tonnes of dead foliage and tall stacks of mangled corrugated iron. I found three young men on quadbikes with trash cans attached to their front bumpers. Each had an extendable claw.

'What are you doing?' I asked.

'Picking up trash.'

'On quadbikes?'

'Yes, Sir. It's a good day for it too. It can get hella hot!'

Three agile men using gasoline-powered machines to drive a few feet between discarded fast-food cartons, using tools that saved them straining a vertebra. Efficiency, maybe. But a scene that felt as American as the Rocky Mountains.

At the end of a mostly dull and uneventful morning, cycling along a straight grey highway, I reached Chiefland and sat on a bench outside the Walmart. For ten minutes, people came and went. It was my very own Forrest Gump moment. But instead of a box of chocolates I had a boxed salad and an apple.

'You're going to need more than that!' screeched a 78-year-old white woman with a purple rinse who sat down beside me last. She spent a few minutes extolling the virtues of cats but then went on to tell me about her life. She'd grown up in Alabama but later moved south to Florida.

'I grew up in a very racist family, which was just typical. That's just how it was,' she said. From a young age, this created friction between her and her parents. One of her earliest memories was of being chastised publicly for politely addressing an elderly Black man.

'My mother made it very clear to me that you don't say "yes, Sir" to Black people. When I finally turned 18 and went to college, I got heavily involved in the Civil Rights Movement.'

The more we spoke, the more she opened up, in a candid and unfiltered way that felt – once again – unequivocally American.

'I was open to being different to them because they abused me. Sexually. Part of me could identify with the abused outcast because that's what I was.'

I was wary of asking further questions. There is a duty of care, a fine line between uncovering 'a story' and potentially triggering memories that have been buried or supressed for one's own psychological protection. But the lady went on. The abuse she suffered as a child had altered her hopes and ambitions for the future.

'There are after-effects to child sexual abuse and they are very long term, like depression or PTSD. I couldn't go and be a teacher and work in a classroom, and I spent most of my working life alone, not around too many people.'

Before we went our separate ways, she told me that America was more divided than she'd ever known. But after immense childhood trauma, she saw hope.

'America is divided. But I try to take a balanced view. And while there's still a lot of racism, there's still been a lot of progress. I live at a poverty level but I now live a very happy life after putting myself back together.'

From Chiefland, I began a diversion east, towards north-central Florida. Maybe I'd eaten too much or not enough. Perhaps the sun was killing me with its fierce rays, but the patch of concrete unfurling ahead failed to inspire. How many car body shops can one road sustain, I wondered, as I morosely and stubbornly plodded on.

My pregnant wife had flown 4,000 miles to see me and was enjoying a leisurely lunch 40 miles behind. Yet I still felt compelled to see this thing through. Were we living the dream? Or enduring my addiction?

Thankfully, we were not far from friendly and enthusiastic faces. Alice and Geoff, the skiing couple who had given me a place to stay in Wallace, Idaho, lived half the year on the outskirts of Gainesville and had kindly offered us their spare room for the night. I arrived in palm-shaded suburbia just before Alana and they welcomed us in like old friends.

Ollie, their border collie, immediately set about restoring my faith in dogs. First, by rushing in for a hug and licking my dusty legs. And then by chasing golf balls chipped from one side of the garden to the other. It was a back and forth that could have lasted all night, but Alice and Geoff were keen to show us around.

'This is the blue [Democrat] oasis of Florida,' said Alice a little later, as we cruised around the campus of the University of Florida (UF), the college where she spent 34 years teaching audiology. 'People in university towns are taught to question things.'

Surrounded by grand buildings and live oak trees draped in Spanish moss, the pristine campus was a source of great pride. Students sat in little study groups wearing UF sweaters, reading chunky textbooks on lush green lawns. A girls' running group jogged past, followed by the boating shoes and wide eyes of the preppy boys in chinos and blazers. 'He's not even shaving yet!' laughed Geoff.

Gainesville was thriving. The antithesis of many towns I'd seen. The university employs roughly 20,000 people and has a student body of approximately 60,000 students.

'The university is the lifeblood,' said Alice, when we parked beside a downtown lake surrounded by yet more bookish young adults and sunbathing ten-foot alligators.

Refreshingly, every patch of grass hadn't been mown to within an inch of its life. On our short walk, we passed wildflower gardens, vegetable plots, banana and orange trees. There were bat houses, too, providing refuge to roughly 500,000 of the tiny winged mammals, capable of eating their bodyweight in moths, beetles and mosquitoes each night.

In opposition to the Florida governor Ron DeSantis' climate change denialism, the UF student body passed a ground-breaking 'green new deal' in early 2024 calling for campus-wide changes to help tackle the climate crisis. This included a ban on research funding from the fossil fuels industry and cutting down on carbon emissions.

Alice and Geoff took us to the Grove Street farmers' market, a short drive from the campus, for spicy organic veggie tacos and craft beer. It was a delightfully balmy night; bluebirds twittered in the branches of pine and cypress trees, while teenagers in baggy jeans whirred around an adjacent skatepark.

It was here that I met Joe Courter, editor of the *Gainesville Iguana*, a left-leaning free newspaper that has been published in the city since 1986. Grey-bearded and bespectacled, Joe's cap read: 'ABORTION IS HEALTHCARE'. A badge clipped to his brown woollen sweater read: 'END THE ILLEGAL OCCUPATION OF PALESTINE'. On the cover of his latest issue was a 1950s-style comic strip depicting two women speaking on the phone and the words: 'I hope some big strong men can pass some laws on how we use our uteruses ... Said no woman ever.'

'Gainesville is one of the most progressive cities you'll find,' said Joe. 'And that's by virtue of being a university town. We've always been around feminist issues, environmental issues and gay rights. We don't have a specific agenda but we are pro-peace, pro-environment and pro-social justice.'

Printing roughly 5,000 copies eight times a year, the *Gainesville Iguana* uses mostly advocates and campaigners to write op-eds, rather than a team of reporters. They distribute to subscribers all over the country, including prisoners – some of whom were on death row.

'This one guy wrote to me and said, "It comes into our cell block and one paper gets read by 26 different people." It's amazing to think that those people are also getting the information.'

Throughout my journey across the United States, I had been both fascinated and horrified by the news media. Polemical and one-sided, it was commonplace to see news anchors ranting into the camera unchallenged. It was no wonder that so many people believed the country was 'more divided than ever'. A person could simply turn on a news channel and have all their ideas, biases and prejudices – right or left – reinforced.

'The most dreadful example of the deterioration in news was of Donald Trump in 2016,' said Joe. 'TV stations would keep their cameras on an empty mic for an hour, waiting for Trump to speak. He was good for ratings, good for the stations' bottom line, and that's what it comes down to.'

The quick-fire format of the modern TV news programme had, in Joe's opinion, changed the way people not only thought but also conversed in wider society.

'The news in this country is argumentative rather than substantial. Just talking heads talking at one another. My mother-in-law consumes a lot of MSNBC and CNN, and it can be really hard to have a discussion with her. Because if you differ, it's like a challenge, as opposed to a discussion. People have been turned off talking to their friends or neighbours because they don't want to descend into an argument.'

Later that evening, Alice echoed Joe's thoughts, almost word for word. 'You can really tick people off,' she told me, as I stuffed my panniers with freshy laundered clothes. 'You can't have a conversation anymore. And I really regret that.'

The next morning, Alice, Geoff and Ollie hugged and licked us goodbye. I was sad to be leaving so soon again but we promised to return one day, the three of us (at least), for a more leisurely vacation, either in Florida or Idaho.

Laid-back, generous and hospitable, the couple epitomised everything I loved about travelling in the USA. They buzzed off meeting new people – Britons, especially. 'Oh, I just love Paul Hollywood,' said Alice just before I hit the road. 'That baking show, in the tent. I just love it. Spotted dick, jam roly-poly, it's all just so awesome.'

Buoyed by their kindness and a tailwind, I flew away from Gainesville into a surprisingly lush and fertile land, divided into pristine, picket-fenced paddocks occupied by posh ponies with braids and ribbons. Trademarked 'the Horse Capital of the World', Ocala/Marion County produced its first Kentucky Derby winner, Needles, in 1956, and is now home to more than 35,000 thoroughbreds living on 195,000 acres of prime real estate. According to the Marion County Chamber & Economic Partnership, the equine industry is worth $2.62 billion to the local economy.

It was easily the wealthiest neighbourhood I'd passed through in America. Ostentatious homes sat on vast lots, shaded by live oaks and scanned by an extensive network of CCTV cameras. I passed men in cowboy hats and blue jeans throwing branches into smoky bonfires. Then fit, horsey types, in jodhpurs and gilets, meticulously scrutinising the anuses of their shiny steeds, like jewellers inspecting diamonds.

If my morning was characterised by people keeping expensive animals alive, then the afternoon was mostly about making cheap ones dead. The road south was lined with billboards advertising pest control services. Unsurprisingly, Florida's moist, warm climate is ideal for bugs and critters. Thousands of contractors promise the removal of termites, roaches, bedbugs and ants, plus bigger invaders, like rats, mice and alligators.

Around 1.25 million of the giant reptiles reside in Florida's swamps and waterways. Some become 'nuisance alligators' when they end up in gardens and swimming pools. According to the Florida Fish and Wildlife Conservation Commission, more than 450 alligator attacks were recorded between 1948 and 2022, 30 of which proved fatal. Just three weeks before my arrival in the state, the body of a 41-year-old homeless woman was found in the jaws of a 13-foot alligator, which was later 'humanely killed' by the authorities.

I made it to Inverness – a small town named by a homesick Scot in the late nineteenth century – in mid-afternoon to find Alana waiting for me in a coffeeshop. Somehow, we had already reached the Last Supper, again. And regardless of however many times we'd done it before, the anxiety of our imminent separation left us holding back tears until bedtime.

'Who knows,' I said, as we lay in bed, forcing ourselves to sleep. 'This whole travel thing might be over for me now. When the baby comes, I just might not have the hunger for it anymore.'

'Maybe,' she replied, holding back the urge to sob and scream.

'For the foreseeable future, anyway, this is it. The three of us. None of this crazy stuff, I promise.'

It was hard to know how true that promise might be. There was always the call of the wild echoing in the back of my mind. An affliction. A disease. I had been this way for 20 years, unable to stay grounded for more than a few weeks before dreaming up the next mad idea.

But with a baby on the way, that lifestyle would need to change. I would need to change.

21

DEEPER SOUTH

The next morning, we hugged until our eyes and arms ached, then Alana diverted southwest to Tampa International Airport, while I set off southeast on my big push to the finish line. The road was loud and scary again. As souped-up pickups roared past, my head shrugged instinctively, like a turtle flinching into its shell. The stench of traffic now stung my nose. A squeak in my front wheel annoyed me just a little bit more than usual. Alone again, I was a Road Man once more, wandering the murky depths of Florida, and my mind.

It took a few hours for the fog to lift and to appreciate just how far I'd come. Almost 4,000 miles. Under my own steam. And now with a tailwind keeping me company. I had to remind myself to appreciate every last minute. Family life beckoned, in whatever shape or form. This was a privilege, after all. Not a thing to be rushed and ticked off, but savoured for what it really was: a once-in-a-lifetime experience.

About 40 miles into the day, my bottles were bone dry. So I pulled into a parking lot and made a beeline for the nearest bar. Inside, half a dozen stubbled men stared silently into their bottles of beer. Before I could even reach the smoky countertop, the barman was ushering me out the door.

'Can I help you?' he said.

'I was wondering if I could have some water, please?'

'Water?'

'Yeah. Please can you fill up my bottles?'

'No.'

'No?'

'There's a tap around the back, you can use that.'

I had, unbeknown to me, attempted to walk into a members-only veterans' bar. And, without wishing to pick a fight with America's armed forces, been met with the most unfriendly atmosphere I'd experienced anywhere in the country. It didn't seem like a place to linger or protest, so I kept going, along a busy road with no shoulder. Not long later, a man overtook me with a leg hanging out the driver's-side window, staring down at his smartphone.

'What the fuck!' I screamed, before taking refuge in a residential sideroad.

This coincided with a man taking out the trash.

'Hey, dude,' he said. 'Where you headed?'

After a few formalities, the man became convinced I was a professional ice hockey player.

'No, sorry to disappoint,' I said.

'Are you sure?'

'Yes.'

He rushed inside for a minute, then returned with a few cans of cold soda. Faced with his piercing blue-eyed stare and two barking dogs trapped in the garage, I was eager to keep moving. But his heart was in the right place.

'Let me see what else I can find you inside,' he said. 'Wait here.'

He returned two minutes later with a flick knife in his hand. Its eight-inch, razor-sharp blade glinted in the hot sun.

'I want you to have this,' he said, before demonstrating the best way to use it, with a hard flick of the wrist, so that the blade springs out in front of you, towards an assailant.

'I really think you need this, man.'

'Are you sure?'

'Yeah, man, be safe out here.'

Within a couple of miles, I was negotiating the industrialised outskirts of Lakeland, bisecting a stifling concrete world of workshops, packaging and logistics depots. Unavoidable and grimy after the pristine equine world further north, this felt like the nerve centre of Floridian commerce. Forklifts beeped. Lorries grunted. Men in high-vis jackets, shorts and steel-toecap boots lobbed boxes in and out of refrigerated vans.

I was moving along in my own little world when a man waved me down outside a factory.

'Where are you going? Where have you come from?' he asked.

Alan Bell, it quickly transpired, was the manager of a facility that distributed hundreds of thousands of sandwiches and boxed salads to supermarkets and convenience stores across the state. He had a grey goatee and short, combed-back hair. And was desperate to fill my panniers with calories.

'Lakeland has changed a lot in just five or six years,' said Alan, as we walked into his deliciously frigid stores. 'It has boomed. A lot of people coming from the "liberal states" – California, New York, places where they're taxed to death and have so much government regulation.'

Lakeland is one of America's fastest-growing cities. In August 2023, Mayor Bill Mutz said: 'This is a city that is 260,000 today and will be 500,000 by 2035.' Amazon have their southeast distribution hub there.

Pro-Trump, pro-industry, Republican Alan thought highly of Florida's governor Ron DeSantis. 'He's conservative and about letting people run their own lives. The way he handled Covid and the natural disasters we've had, I think he's been very good overall.'

Alan's biggest problem, however, was finding staff.

'It has changed in the past 15 years or so. The work ethic, unfortunately, for the younger generation is not like it should be. And I hate to say that as an American, but it's the truth.'

This sentiment had followed me across the nation. On farms, mostly, but now in a factory. Alan worried this feeling of apathy had also led to a disengagement from politics.

'The younger generation, I don't think they know what's going on. They're not in tune and are often off in "Facebook Land" or listening to music, not paying attention to what's going on around them. There's too much distraction.'

Alan kindly offered me the grounds of the factory to camp in overnight, but I was eager to make progress south. And with a handful of sandwiches and salads to keep me going, he waved me off with a few final words: 'America is less divided than the left says it is. When Trump was in office, we were doing good, but now we're not. The two biggest issues for me are, number one: the border [with Mexico], and number two: inflation. Things just cost too much. As a company, we can't keep up with it.'

Lakeland was a tale of two cities. In the industrialised northern outskirts, I passed young women in short skirts soliciting old men in cars and people living in tents. Then, after half an hour of zigzagging through a sweltering downtown – which, for 'Florida's fastest-growing city', was dead – I made it to the southern suburbs, where topless hunks exercised for fun. Pristine emerald lawns encircled bright white mansions, most with Barbicide-blue swimming pools. Tanned old ladies played tennis in fluorescent visors.

Rather than take on Lakeland's rush hour the next morning, I continued south, to the much smaller town of Bartow, where I collapsed into the air-conditioned local brewery. With a day's sweat freezing to my skin, one pint became two, then two pints became three.

It's hard to imagine Florida, or indeed the United States, without air conditioning. According to the US Energy Information Administration, almost 90 per cent of American homes rely upon 'AC'. The father of the ice machine, John Gorrie – Daddy Cool, if you will – is held in such high esteem that his statue stands beside that of civil rights activist Rosa Parks in the US Capitol.

First patented by Gorrie in 1851 to blow cold air across patients suffering from malaria and yellow fever, the technology moved to commercial and public spaces in the 1920s. Infamously, it almost ruined the 1926 grand opening of the Florida Theatre in St Petersburg. According to the historian Raymond Arsenault: 'the proud management had the temperature down so low that ladies in evening dresses almost froze!'

Air conditioning finally reached homes in the 1950s and correlated with a post-war population boom. In 1950, Florida's population stood at roughly 2.8 million. By 2023, that figure had increased to almost 22 million.

When the heat and humidity dropped, I enjoyed a half-cut ride across town, then ducked into a fried chicken joint busy with locals. Crispy, savoury and succulent, this was chicken fried with love and spices, not just grey matter blanched in oil.

Warm and buzzing, I was given a free soda, and then offered a few words of advice.

'Dude, be careful around here,' said the 18-year-old man behind the counter. 'Do you know where you're going?'

'I think so. There's a motel just down there, yeah?'

'Yeah. Just don't go wandering around.'

'A bad neighbourhood?'

'We used to have a big meth problem and it's still pretty bad.'

'OK, man. Thanks.'

'Have a blessed one, dude.'

The motel was ropey, to say the least. Set around a years-empty swimming pool, an online booking platform described it as 'passable' with a 5.2 rating, which was … generous. As I checked in, a man remonstrated with the owners, trying to negotiate an hourly rate while simultaneously talking to a woman on speaker phone.

When I entered my room, a few cockroaches scurried into the shadows. The shower was cold, the bedsheets stained, the TV defunct. A driver would have turned straight around and demanded a refund, but I was tired, stuffed with fried chicken and slightly pissed. So I barricaded myself in and tried to sleep.

All sorts of commotion went on outside throughout the night, and I must have woken up half a dozen times to the sound of voices and police sirens. Who knows, I may have also swallowed a cockroach or two. But as soon as dawn broke, I loaded up on coffee and set forth into a cool morning – chilly enough for a hat and gloves.

I was determined to complete one final big day. And for the next five hours, I followed a mostly empty road through orange groves heavy with bulbous fruit. Thousands of citrusy acres, rambling across every blue horizon. Alongside California, Texas and Arizona, Florida produces the bulk of American oranges. Originally from Asia, they were brought to the 'New World' by the Spanish in the early 1500s. Five hundred years later, and the industry is worth roughly $7 billion to Florida's economy.

The nation's myriad crops had coloured my way for 4,000 miles. Wheat, apples, corn, soya, alfalfa, sunflowers and now oranges, all boxed into straight lines, allowing the country to not only feed itself but to become an America that proudly 'feeds the world'.

But perhaps no plant spoke of American success quite like the humble blade of grass. When I eventually exited the orange groves, I entered field upon field of lush, cultivated green, meticulously trimmed, clipped and weeded by mostly Hispanic workers in sombreros. It was being shaved from the earth in three-inch-deep slabs and dropped on flatbed trailers, destined for golf courses, schools and newbuilds.

According to the Florida Turfgrass Association, the state's 3.94 million managed acres are worth almost $8 billion a year to the economy, supporting roughly 175,000 jobs. Plane and pristine, the enormous expanse resembled a city-sized snooker table. From a distance, farmers looked like cricketers inspecting a pitch on the first day of a test match.

Up there with the blue Ford pickup or yellow Dollar General, my memories of America will be stained a bright shade of green.

I barely spoke to anyone all day. Or, more accurately, hardly anyone spoke to me. Instead, I sat in the saddle for ten sweltering hours, sticking to mostly blacktop country roads. Eddying with heat mirage, the lemony, grassy verge smelled like citronella.

By the time I reached Clewiston – 'Florida's sweetest town' thanks to its abundant sugarcane – I had 130 miles on the clock and the hunger of a bear. So I checked into the cheapest motel, took a quick shower and went out in search of dinner.

When I returned an hour or so later, I walked straight into a hubbub. Two motorcyclists – a husband and wife dressed in leathers – paced around the lobby in a state of mild hysteria.

'Dude, how's your room?' asked the man.

'Yeah, fine,' I said, lacking the energy to describe just how filthy it really was.

At which point, he took out his phone and showed me two, seemingly identical images depicting their motorcycle helmets sat on a chest of draws.

'Dude, do you notice anything different?' he asked, wide-eyed.

'No.'

'Dude, the helmet on the right. It's turned around!'

'OK.'

'I'm freaking out, man. We didn't do that. This place is giving me weird energy. Are you getting it?'

'No.'

The motel I'd picked at random was – apparently – 'one of the most haunted hotels in America'. The couple were now totally losing their shit, uploading videos to Instagram accompanied by the Halloween movie theme.

'Did you know this place was "haunted"?' I asked, fighting back an innate cynicism and the temptation to make quotation marks with my fingers.

'Yeah, dude. Everybody knows it's haunted.'

'So, you came here knowing it's haunted and now you're freaking out that it's haunted?'

'Dude, check out these reports!'

In their hands, the couple held reams of 'paranormal' sightings. Stories of orbs, floating apparitions and voices in the night. Some had been compiled by 'investigators' that had prowled the hotel's rooms and hallways with electronic voice phenomenon (EVP) machines.

One report described 'pots and pans banging in the kitchen'. Others told of phone calls lighting up the lobby switchboard and a little girl whispering the word 'mommy'. Which, for a pretty busy hotel, didn't strike me as paranormal but … normal. Other notes included 'felt a presence' and 'felt a chill'. Unnervingly, these temperatures seemed to be well within the boundaries of an air-conditioning unit. It all made for compelling reading and the couple were brilliant entertainment. It all felt so totally absurd that I wondered if I was part of a hidden-camera show.

Room 118 was where most of the action had taken place. 'Felt goosebumps.' 'Chills near the sink.' Reports of a 'lady in white' brushing her hair at the end of the bed. 'Some guests have reported her as climbing into bed with them.'

'Does that cost extra?' I asked, but my sarcasm washed over the lobby like ectoplasm.

'What room are you in?' I asked the couple.

'118!'

At which point, I couldn't help but let out a small, involuntary laugh.

'You don't believe it?' asked the woman, as I caught the receptionist rolling her eyes.

'No. People believe what they want to believe.' (Especially in America, I felt like saying.) And they really did. I couldn't imagine this scene playing out in any other country on earth.

However, just before floating off down the hallway to bed, I rifled through the papers for due diligence.

'Anything in Room 163?' I asked.

'No.'

'Alright, fuck this, I'm off.'

A few things did go bump in the night, but only because the hotel was frightfully bad. Mostly slamming doors, fizzing lightbulbs and the gurgling of a dozen broken toilets. Curiously, my antique bathtub had been painted with emulsion. There were also red stains on the ceiling above the bed. Some anomalies, however, are better left unanswered, and I departed as soon as daylight allowed, into a muggy morning, along a road now lined with palm trees.

I was less than a hundred miles from Miami and could almost feel a weight of concrete on the horizon. I had been worrying about this day for 4,000 miles. How would I get in, out and around a city of almost half a million people? I was reaching a bottleneck again, the necessary evil of choosing two specific, albeit arbitrary, points on a map.

By a stroke of luck, it was a Sunday and, rather than contend with commuter traffic, I shared the road with leisure cruisers: mostly big groups of men in studded leather waistcoats and bandanas on motorcycles. I stopped at a gas station to refuel on empanadas, expecting to attract some sort of two-wheeled banter. Not in Florida. After 20 minutes of snobbish glares, I left in the caustic backdraft of three men doing wheelies.

Highway 27 ran parallel with the Florida Everglades, a 4,300-square-mile expanse of marshland bursting with subtropical saw grass. It was known to the first Native American tribes as *Pa-Hay-Okee* – 'Grassy Water' – and they fished the waterways by dugout canoe. Later, the Seminole tribe fled here to avoid conflict and disease brought across the Atlantic by Europeans, building simple homes and cultivating crops on higher ground. They were eventually forced out by the US Army during the Seminole Wars (1817–18, 1835–42 and 1855–58).

In the past century, extensive urban and agricultural development has halved the Everglades' original size. Its waters have been polluted by fertiliser running off nearby farms and invasive species, such as Burmese pythons, have moved in, thanks to the irresponsible owners who released them there.

It took me all afternoon to tackle Miami's western fringes – another grey splodge, almost impossible to travel on a bicycle. But after a quick shower and a bite to eat, I found myself driving back out towards the Everglades, clinging to the back of a 4×4 belonging to professional python hunter Donna Kalil.

The 60-year-old started hunting in 2005 when she saw a photo in the *Miami Herald* depicting a 13-foot snake split in two after it had devoured an alligator. 'That's when I realised there was a huge problem,' she said, as we bumped down a limestone track, deep into the national park. 'This is an apex predator eating another apex predator.'

Burmese pythons are, as the name suggests, not native to North America, but Southeast Asia. They ended up in Florida's balmy waterways when their owners realised they were outgrowing their tanks. With a rapid reproduction cycle and a lack of predators, their numbers exploded.

'We're the only thing that can stop their movement and expanding their range,' Donna went on, as we used powerful spotlights to scour the dense vegetation for serpent eyes. 'Every single python we remove makes a difference to all the animals that python would have eaten.'

As a child, Donna enjoyed exploring an abundant south Florida ecosystem bursting with biodiversity. By the 2020s, though, populations of native species like racoons, bobcats, deer and rabbits had been decimated. Around 12,000 snakes had been killed to date, but Florida's Fish and Wildlife Conservation Commission estimated that between 100,000 and 300,000 pythons remained in the often-impenetrable Everglades. A conservationist at heart, as opposed to a blood-lusting huntress, Donna and her team of volunteers were providing an essential environmental service.

'They're fascinating creatures. I love all animals but they don't belong here. I consider myself an environmentalist; I'm just trying to restore the environment to the way it was.'

Climate change had made it even easier for the pythons to survive. A hard winter frost would be enough to kill off thousands. However, Donna had not seen temperatures that cold since she was a child. 'When I was at high school it snowed! That was rare, but when I was a kid, we would get three months in the forties [5–10 degrees centigrade].'

There was also the issue of rising sea levels. According to the Florida Climate Center, waters surrounding the state are eight inches higher than in 1950. 'I could take you to a road that's underwater now full-time,' said Donna. 'It didn't used to be. The sea level rise is real.'

On my journey across the country, I had met dozens of people who flatly denied any human responsibility for the degradation of our planet. What would Donna – a woman working on the frontline of conservation every day of her life – say to those people?

'How can we [humans] not be? I understand that people don't want to believe it because they don't want to make changes. But it is real. Beyond that, the key to our survival is our government taking the leading role. They need to tie our entire economy to the environment. We don't have a "Planet B", as they say.'

For six hours, we explored a vast network of tracks, while scanning the few feet of soggy vegetation either side of us. The task facing Donna, and hunters like her, was immense. Not even a needle in a haystack – we were looking for a perfectly camouflaged animal, while restricted to a single strand of navigable roadway. The mind boggled at just how many pythons lived in the waters beyond.

We spotted an alligator, a few birds, a tiny orange rat snake and thousands of nibbling mosquitoes. But having spent the whole night on high alert, expecting that at any moment I might need to jump from the vehicle and straddle an 18-foot-long, 90-kilogram python, the moment never actually materialised. Instead, I was dropped back at my hotel in the early hours feeling ever so slightly relieved.

It was tempting to spend the next day in bed, but with the biggest miles now firmly behind me, I set off midmorning into a world of spaghetti junctions and concrete flyovers as hot and as humid as a greenhouse in August.

This was, however, the start of a tapering-off I had been daydreaming about for almost ten weeks. After the 10-hour days and centurion rides, from here on in, I'd be cycling no more than 60 miles a day, on the flat.

The worst thing a long-distance cyclist can do is just stop dead. It can play havoc with the immune system. Instead, I've learned to wind down gradually, to appreciate the dying embers of an adventure and to tie up loose ends along the way.

The issue of gun ownership had followed me across America. In the hundreds of interviews I'd conducted, no topic seemed to divide opinion quite like it. The Second Amendment to the United States Constitution gives citizens the right to bear arms, and according to the Pew Research Center, around 40 per cent of Americans live in a household with a gun. I had seen firearms – mostly handguns – at a distance. Some that I assumed were legally owned and others that probably weren't. At least two dozen people had encouraged me to acquire one for my own safety. And briefly – at the height of my Midwest dog problem – I genuinely considered buying one.

In Homestead, a southern suburb of Miami, I called into a gun shop: Arsenal Arms, where the owner, Wayne Chung, was more than happy to chat.

'There's still a lot of misinformation out there,' said Wayne, who wore a Stars and Stripes baseball cap and drank iced tea from a large polystyrene cup. 'You still need to pass a background check before you can buy a gun. As long as you're not a felon or have committed crimes of domestic violence then you are OK to buy a gun.'

Florida was also one of eleven US states with a 'cooling off period' – a five-day hiatus between the buying and receiving of a weapon. The policy created a buffer of time for people in suicidal crisis or someone buying a gun in the heat of an argument. During our discussion, Wayne cited the Second Amendment.

'How relevant is the Second Amendment in the mid-2020s compared to over 200 years ago?' I asked.

'Still very relevant. It's about checks and balances. What's going to happen when someone who is not of sound mind decides to do something bad? There's no way of keeping them in check anymore. Most people in this world are good in nature, but there's a small percentage who are not. The gun is an equaliser for a lot of people.'

Only once had Wayne needed to draw his gun, to hold someone at gunpoint who was trying to steal his car. Firing it would be an absolute last resort, but just having it in his possession gave him a sense of safety and freedom: 'There's always someone bigger and tougher than you are, but a gun lets you live more free.'

Having interviewed everyday citizens on the right, left and everywhere in between, I'd concluded that most seemed resigned to the idea that America's relationship with firearms was both inevitable and irreversible. The country was too far down a track it could never reverse back from: millions of legal and illegal guns in circulation.

'If you got rid of guns today, only the bad people would have guns,' said Wayne. 'And therefore, you'd be less free than ever.'

As we paused for a few seconds, and I looked back on my journey, thinking of some of the people I'd met and the potentially dodgy situations I'd narrowly avoided, I stunned myself with what I said next: 'I agree.'

In a hypothetical world in which I needed to live with my young family in America, then I too would buy a gun – not out of choice, but a perceived feeling of necessity. Hoping never to use it, but just in case. Because if someone came at me, Alana or my child, what would I do unarmed? That conclusion shocked me to the core. It made me question the alignment of my entire moral compass and sense of self. America, for all its joy and magnificence, had left me feeling more unsafe and on edge that any other country on earth.

22

WARM RAIN

I arrived at the Florida Keys via the Overseas Highway, a 113-mile extension of US Highway 1, the 2,370-mile route that follows America's eastern seaboard from Fort Kent, Maine, to Key West, Florida. Blue skies, fluffy clouds and a light tailwind. Close to perfection, this really was the beginning of Florida's – and my – tropical end.

Until the early twentieth century, the only way in and out of the keys was via boat, weather depending. But then the industrialist Henry Morrison Flagler took on a challenge that many of his contemporaries dismissed as impossible: the Over-Sea Railroad, the most ambitious engineering project ever undertaken by a private American citizen. So impressive that the secretary of state at the time, Elihu Root, described it as 'second only to the Panama Canal in its political and commercial importance to the United States'.

Built by 4,000 mostly African American, Bahamian and European immigrants at a cost of $50 million ($1.56 billion in today's money), it quickly became the talk not only of Miami but the nation, and transported freight and gentry to the southeastern-most point in the continental USA: Key West. Some passengers arrived via special sleeper trains from New York City.

Sadly, the original structure lasted just 23 years. A hurricane ripped through at the wrong time: the economic decline of the Depression era. Three years later, though, the first Overseas Highway was built in its place, incorporating many of the railway's original spans and foundations.

The latest incarnation of the road was upgraded in 1982. But as I crossed the first of the keys' 42 bridges, linking an archipelago of 1,700 coral islands, it felt as though I was cycling in historic footsteps. Trains had kept me company throughout my journey, and as it came to an end it seemed only fitting to ride in the shadow of a fallen giant.

My father-in-law's friend's friend's sister just so happened to live in Tavernier – a small seaside town beside Highway 1 – and despite being away on vacation, had kindly offered me their home for a couple of nights. So I let myself in, showered, then grabbed a few cold beers at the local bar overlooking a small marina filled with yachts. Fishermen had just gutted their catch into the water and a pair of eight-foot nurse sharks nibbled at the yucky entrails.

The Florida Keys are notoriously expensive and within the space of just a few miles everything had jumped up in price. The cost of real estate, for buyers and renters, is enormous. In 2023, the average Key West house cost $1.4 million; meanwhile, rentals stood at $6,800 per month – the highest in Florida.

'For the working people, it's expensive to live here,' said Monica Woll, a supply teacher and kayaking guide who joined me for a drink. Her husband used to own an adventure sports business but sold up when he suffered burnout.

'You could get a good apartment for $500, then suddenly that jumped to $750. These days, you can't get much for less than $2,000. Up in New York, stockbrokers can afford to pay that for tiny apartments, but down here it's mostly service workers. The "American divide" in the Keys is as simple as this: the people who have three jobs and the people who have three homes.'

Besides the spiralling cost of living, Monica – just like Donna the night before – told me that rising sea levels and climate change had impacted their way of life. In 2016, the couple bought two small islands to camp on in their semi-retirement, only for hurricanes Irma (2017) and Ian (2022) to destroy roughly a quarter of their landmass.

'Hurricane Irma split one of the islands in half. It used to be nice high ground that we could camp on but now that's gone. We lost land and it's not going to come back. Only people with millions of dollars can rebuild with hundreds of tonnes of sand. We can't afford that.'

In the aftermath, Monica and her husband planted mangrove saplings and coconuts, and attempted to reclaim the land with a retaining wall. But every time the high tide arrives, more sand gets washed away. 'We planted around 700 saplings and only 15 survived.'

The same problems facing Monica and her husband are being seen throughout the Florida Keys. When I went for a short ride to stretch my legs the next day, some sections of bike path were under several inches of seawater. I had to lift my feet to stay dry.

Ninety per cent of the archipelago lies just five feet or less above 'sea level'. Even by the most conservative estimates of a seven-inch sea-level rise by 2100, some 56,000 residents and 76,000 acres of land could be affected, putting $27 billion-worth of property at risk.

The following morning, I left Tavernier and continued – somewhat oddly – west. Having spent more than 4,000 miles cycling east, I was now doubling back, following the Florida Keys towards the Gulf of Mexico and the north coast of Cuba.

Warm rain clattered against the luscious fronds of buccaneer palm trees, then ran over the tin roofs of mostly single-storey homes. Thankfully, refuge and black coffee were close by. The previous night, I had received a bowl of freshly made chilli con carne and a handwritten note from a neighbour asking me to call in at the local middle school, where her daughter taught. 'What exciting travels you must have had!' it read. Saying yes felt like good karma.

I had spoken at hundreds of schools over the years but this was my first in the USA. It was also the least prepared I'd ever been, but I'd managed to bodge together a few maps and short films. Mostly dressed in shorts and T-shirts rather than uniforms, they were bright, inquisitive and engaged students, bursting with questions.

What's in the bags?
What do you eat?
Were you scared?
What's Nebraska like?

After 15 minutes spent fielding their questions, I asked permission from the teacher to ask them a few of mine. Aged between 10 and 14, these were the youngest Americans I'd spoken to. What made them feel proud?

An 11-year-old boy threw his hand up: 'Strong military. Being able to defend yourself. My dad's a pilot in the Air Force.'

Another boy raised his arm. 'People died for us to have freedom for this country. Throughout history, we've had to fight other countries and sometimes ourselves in order to have the freedom that we need to have a normal daily life.'

For the next few minutes, the words 'rights', 'free' and 'freedom' were repeated several times. One boy was thankful he didn't live in a 'terrorist country'. Several believed the United States Bill of Rights and Constitution reduced political corruption. Another loved America for its geographical and environmental diversity.

Before wrapping up, I was eager to find out what sort of country the boys and girls believed they were going to inherit. Conceivably, some of these young citizens would be alive in the next century. Most of the older students, sadly, believed America, and our planet, was a lost cause.

'I feel like we're messing up the earth so badly that in the next 50 years we might not even be here,' said a girl in eighth grade. 'It's bad. We really need to take care of our earth more than we are. It's all downhill from here. We've messed up so bad we're trying to move to a different planet.'

The younger students, thankfully, were more optimistic. One ten-year-old boy wanted to 'go into space to collect energy'. But most of the others were intent on changing their earthly behaviours.

Another boy said: 'We need to pick up trash, use more wind turbines and solar panels. We'll be able to solve problems without fossil fuels.'

A final one chipped in: 'Everything we do, from putting less plastic in the ocean, to turning on lights and taking a shower, everything in our daily life has an effect.'

This inspired a collective hum of agreement and seemed like a suitably uplifting note on which to leave. The rain had passed but the sky was dense with moisture, and beneath my tyres, deep puddles had formed. In many places, the ocean was just a few feet from the road. According to Monroe County officials, the Keys need to find $1.8 billion in the next 25 years to raise it up. It remains unclear as to where exactly this money will come from.

If Middle America's climate change sceptics could see this, I wondered, would their opinions change, if water was, quite literally, lapping at their porches?

Lined by cafes, condos, resorts and cannabis dispensaries, Highway 1 felt more like a through road rather than a route offering genuinely interesting places to stop along the way. I cycled across long and lofty oversea bridges, like Long Key Viaduct, constructed by Henry Flagler as part of his ambitious railroad. Amusingly, I passed a man in boardshorts and flipflops who was either so relaxed or stoned that he had gone fishing without his fishing rods. 'Shit, dude. I'm an idiot,' he said, as he marched back to his car.

There was, however, a distinct absence of public beaches. Almost every spare inch of viable seafront had been developed in some shape or form. And if I'm totally honest, I wasn't remotely surprised. From what I'd seen across the country, the right to buy and own private property was sacrosanct. But if there was any place where this proclivity looked its most incongruous, then it was here – either side of a tiny sliver of tarmac.

No wonder the Florida Keys cost so much to live and vacation in. It seemed almost impossible to go there and just hang out for free, in a public space, in the same way you could in Cornwall, Rio or Sydney, for example. Which struck me as an immense infrastructural and cultural mistake. For a country with such an overwhelming cradle-to-grave obsession with 'freedom', so much of it was off limits.

I spent the night in Marathon, in a 1960s-style motel set around a pear-shaped swimming pool. For the price, I could have probably rented a house in Oklahoma, but I was now just 50 miles from Key West and the cost of accommodation was climbing.

This was, however, my final night as a wandering Road Man. The last time I would need to stuff dirty shirts into my panniers and wash malodourous cycling shorts under a hot tap. But there was no longer any need to torture myself with route planning: there was only one road in and out.

Elated but fidgety, satisfied yet desperate for more, I struggled to sleep. The following day was just like any other, I told myself. But it wasn't really. The final stretch spelled the end of an epic moment in my life and the start of the next, significantly more sedentary, chapter.

I headed out the next day into a warm and muggy morning, my shoulders proud with a sense of accomplishment, my legs as toned and as tanned as they'll ever be. I was eager to ride, but first had one final, no less important, meeting to attend.

Along Highway 1, I had passed several marine animal centres aimed at tourists – many describing themselves, somewhat suspiciously, as sanctuaries. One, however, seemed different: the Turtle Hospital, which rescued and rehabilitated injured sea turtles before then releasing them back to the wild.

'All America's sea turtles are protected by the Endangered Species Act, which means they are in danger of becoming extinct in our lifetime,' said hospital manager Bette Zirkelbach, as she guided me past greens, leatherbacks, loggerheads and hawksbills bobbing around in oxygenated tanks.

'Sea turtles are the oldest species known to man; they were swimming in our oceans when dinosaurs roamed our lands. Sadly, most of the injuries we see are human impact. We see fishing gear ingestion, entanglement and boat strikes. Also, fibropapillomatosis – tumours caused by pollution.'

At the southern edge of the nation, the Florida Keys were a flashpoint, a place where many of America's troubles had come to a head. Inflation, climate change, rising sea levels and now (among some) an apathy towards nature.

Sea turtles, Bette explained, are keystone species, the canaries in the coalmine. 'What we see happening to them is eventually going to happen to all life. Hot summers breed mostly females, colder summers mostly male. The past four years have been the hottest on record and have resulted in no male sea turtle hatchlings, and we obviously need them to reproduce.'

Built in a repurposed 1950s motel, the Sea Turtle Hospital opened in 1986, a year before the first *Teenage Mutant Ninja Turtles* cartoon was broadcast around the world. 'Everything kind of hit at the right moment,' admitted Bette. The hospital now welcomed over 100,000 tourists a year.

On a chalkboard outside the operating theatre, we looked back at the names of some of the hospital's recent patients: Bashful, Dopey, Grumpy, etc. 'We let the rescuer name them,' said Bette. 'And things seem to be following a *Snow White* theme at the moment.'

The challenge, however, was never-ending. Beyond simply helping injured turtles, much of their work revolved around advocating for a species that couldn't speak. Working on the frontline of conservation, Bette was incensed at the idea of some Americans dismissing climate change as 'a hoax' or even 'God's will'.

'We are an invasive species. To say that we are not part of that is an ignorance and people need to be educated. In the 23 years I've lived here, our reefs have turned into graveyards.'

Before I set off on my final 50 miles, I asked Bette what gave her hope. What nugget of inspiration could I take with me to the finish line? What kept her going, day after day?

'I remain constantly inspired by the resilience of these animals. And for as long as they are fighting for their lives, then we are fighting with them.'

Ignorance and education. So much of what I'd seen and heard across the USA boiled down to these two words. On one hand, there were people willing to engage with confusing topics they didn't fully understand, to put their faith in the acumen of experts working in their respective fields. People who believed in lively debate and peer-reviewed studies. Notably, people who were prepared to be proven wrong.

On the other hand, great swathes of America seemed categorically unwilling to back down on 'truths' they considered gospel. I get it; no one likes to hold their hands up and say, 'I got it wrong; I made a mistake, I've changed my mind.' It's embarrassing.

But just because a person might not have seen climate change, racism, homelessness or rising sea levels – either with their own eyes or depicted on their chosen news channel – wasn't proof those things didn't exist.

There seems to be an almost congenital attitude in America of 'don't tell me what to do. Don't tell me what car to drive. Don't tell me what food to eat. Don't you dare tell me my "facts" are wrong.' That free-spirited bullishness seems so engrained – perhaps born out of the rebellious European stock that founded the modern nation – that the same boldness that made the country so successful might also now hold it back.

The man playing Rage Against the Machine's 'Fuck you, I won't do what you tell me' on my very first night in Seattle seemed to be on to something. As it rang through my mind for 4,000+ miles, it echoed like an alternative national anthem.

To some of the nice people I met along the way, with seemingly fixed and immovable opinions, I wish I could go back to each of them, turn off their TVs or laptops and just say: 'Get out there! Go and talk to a hundred people of all shapes, colours and sizes. Some you agree with, but mostly the ones you don't. Test yourself. See what happens.'

The power of conversation is unassailable. But as modern humans, sadly, many of us have lost the willingness or desire to simply pass air through our larynxes and wobble our cheeks. Dozens of people told me they 'didn't talk politics anymore' for fear of conflict with their friends and family. If this trend becomes further entrenched in American society, it risks rotting the foundations of one of the world's biggest and most successful democracies. Thankfully, they had no qualms talking to me, a grubby British bloke in shorts and a T-shirt.

Meanwhile, the breakneck pace at which we live our lives and consume our information has reduced massive subjects to just a few minutes of airtime. But the world we live in is not that simple. America is not that simple. How can anyone expect to understand the minutiae of subjects like the Civil Rights Movement, the opioid crisis or planet-scale species extinction in such a pithy and laconic fashion.

There are, therefore, no better actions we can take to improve our societies than to travel, to talk, to lift our heads up from our smartphones and be vulnerable. Because when you look someone in the eyes, rather than an avatar on a screen, even the people you strongly disagree with become more agreeable.

And that is exactly the way I intend to parent. Because within a few months of finishing this journey, I would be responsible for feeding, clothing and – even more importantly – educating someone new. As a journalist, a writer, a traveller and now as a father, I am determined to instil within my child the notion that there are extremely few 'right' or 'wrong' answers out there. Just different opinions to yours.

Don't get sucked into the belief that you must have a complete and finite view on everything. Platforms like Facebook and Twitter have duped us into thinking that way, and as a byproduct, it has made the world appear more polarised.

It is completely acceptable to throw your hands up and say: 'You know what? I just don't know. It's complicated.'

So, as we reach the end of my journey, and this book, where I might be expected to make grand sweeping statements about all the aforementioned social issues, I'm afraid that I can't. In doing so, I would risk denigrating the multitude of verbatim I scooped up along the way. Three hundred and thirty million people cannot be summed up that easily. And, hopefully, by reading a couple of hundred random interviews which took place on a journey through 11 states, you can begin to see it that way, too. Heck, you might even want to go and do your own ride across America.

What I would say, however – now that I've cycled more than 8,000 miles across it – is that America's size probably hasn't done it any favours. Bringing 50 disparate states together under one 'country' umbrella was a poisoned chalice, creating an artificial sense of harmony. The landmass feels far too big to be a cohesive entity. And until relatively recently, it wasn't.

With all the private property, and weapons and dogs to defend it, at times – especially when moving very slowly – America feels almost feudal, like little kingdoms. The barbed wire and 'KEEP OUT' signs speak of a slightly archaic, eighteenth-century instinct to fiercely defend one's own patch of land. And all while people, almost unanimously, talk of 'American patriotism' – the idea of feeling part of something much bigger.

And herein lies the paradox. Can Americans have their cake and eat it? Is it possible to retain that seemingly hardwired sense of hyper localism while simultaneously feeling together as a vast nation? Perhaps not. The very name, United States, was a misnomer from the get-go. And now, in the 2020s, mediums like social media, 24-hour rolling news channels and internet chatrooms have merely accelerated and accentuated the divisions that have always existed.

But there is hope. And while agreeing to disagree, Americans can unite behind the many things they do still have in common, almost to a man. Their generosity towards weary travellers. Their love of sport. Their adoration of wild places and national parks.

Rather than dwelling on a lack of macro cohesion – which seems like a fool's errand – they can come together in the fertile, albeit fragile, middle ground they are proud of beyond all else: their small towns. And the values they represent.

These communities bridge the gap between the private backyard and the people's Capitol. They are the building blocks that hold Americans together.

Even more than God, guns and country.

EPILOGUE

My arrival into Key West coincided with the busiest weekend of the year: Fantasy Fest – a scantily clad street party. The streets were packed with topless women wearing nipple tassels and men in sequinned thongs.

My last few grains of adrenaline had seeped out of me into those final few miles of palm-fringed asphalt. I had deflated like a balloon. In ten weeks, I had cycled 4,373 miles through: Washington, Idaho, Montana, Wyoming, Nebraska, Kansas, Oklahoma, Arkansas, Mississippi, Alabama and Florida. I had lost three kilograms in bodyweight and seven percent in body fat. I'd worn through four tyres and suffered eight punctures.

Saved on my phone – which, thank goodness, I didn't lose – I had hundreds of hours of conversations. Plus thousands of photos and videos. The foundations on which these pages were built. Not a single person refused to speak to me. In fact, it was often hard to get a word in edgeways.

The end of a journey is nearly always an anti-climax, and this one almost ended that way, too. When I arrived at the Southernmost Point Buoy, a six-foot-high concrete bell marking the southernmost point in the continental United States, I was met with a queue of about 150 people, all waiting to take a selfie. It seemed so brilliantly ridiculous. I had spent 70 days battling extreme heat, wind and rain, but now needed to wait a final 45 minutes just to take a photo with an inanimate object. While surrounded by dozens of exposed arse cheeks.

Nevertheless, it was over. Done. Completed it, mate.

But I was alone and had absolutely no idea what I might do to celebrate.

Then, a body-painted woman approached me, pulling her husband along on a dog lead.

'Hey, where have you come from?' she asked.

I told them and they totally lost their minds.

'We're having a massive party tonight. We've got food, music and booze. You're more than welcome.'

ACKNOWLEDGEMENTS

We made it. Thank you, dear reader, for coming along on my biggest ever bike ride. I hope you grinned, grimaced, laughed and cried. And now, as you (hopefully) place this book on the shelf and buy copies for all your friends and family, you're left understanding America, and me, in a slightly different way.

I'd like to start by thanking Jacqui Miller, my university film studies lecturer, who nurtured my love of American cinema. Without her, none of this would have happened. Via Lumet, Kubrick, Scorsese and Coppola, we travelled to the nation's diners, deserts and court rooms when I'd barely used my passport.

And to the travel writer Peter Jenkins. His brilliant 1979 book *A Walk Across America* inspired the title of this one.

Thank you to Hannah MacDonald at September Publishing for believing in this book. It was a crazy notion from start to finish: cycle across the USA, write and edit 110,000 words and publish, all within ten months. Four months short of the 2024 presidential election. Phew.

Thanks to Tabitha Pelly for all her hard work securing press coverage and Amie Jones for her assistance setting up my live theatre tour.

Special thanks must go to Van Nicholas and Ralph Moorman for supporting me with such a reliable titanium steed. And Yellow Jersey, for helping out with a bicycle, health and travel insurance policy. Thankfully, it was never needed. And also Hammerhead, for providing a Karoo 2 bike computer, which was faultless for 4,000+ miles.

An enormous thanks needs to go to Tim Fogarty, my father-in-law, who helped with all the routing and rerouting, often late at night (with a glass of red wine in hand).

And to my wife, Alana, who not only held the fort while feeling rough from morning sickness when I was on the ride, but then had to live with an often-preoccupied husband doing 12-hour writing days in the spare room as the months ticked down to D-day.

But thank you, most of all, to all the wonderful people I met along the way. This book would have never been possible without your kindness and candidness.

Until next time.

Simon

ABOUT THE AUTHOR

Simon Parker is a multi-award-winning travel writer and broadcaster who has reported from more than 120 countries for the BBC, *The Times* and the *Telegraph*. In 2016, he sailed and cycled from China to London. His adventures have taken him to Svalbard, Saint Helena, the Namib Desert and Ittoqqortoormiit, Greenland – one of the remotest human settlements on earth.

His *Earth Cycle* TV show has been broadcast all over the world. His first book, *Riding Out*, charted a 3,427-mile bike ride around Britain. In 2022, he became the British Guild of Travel Writers' Broadcaster of the Year.

When he's not off galivanting he lives in the Cotswolds, north Oxfordshire, with his wife and (very) young daughter.

Visit his website: www.simonwparker.co.uk. Or follow him on social media: @simonwiparker.

69.24